LS

# THE ATTACK
# ON WORLD POVERTY

# THE ATTACK ON WORLD POVERTY

Andrew Shonfield

1960

CHATTO & WINDUS

LONDON

PUBLISHED BY
CHATTO AND WINDUS LTD
40–42 WILLIAM IV STREET
LONDON WC2

\*

CLARKE, IRWIN AND COMPANY LTD
TORONTO

© ANDREW SHONFIELD AND COMPANY 1960
PRINTED IN GREAT BRITAIN BY
COX AND WYMAN LTD
LONDON, READING AND FAKENHAM

# CONTENTS

INTRODUCTION     ix

## PART I
### DEVELOPMENT PROBLEMS

1 LIMITATIONS OF ECONOMIC AID     3
    Political obstacles     4

2 UNFAIR SHARES     8
    Central area of struggle     9
    Latin American problems     12
    Communist advantages     14
    Political and practical choices     17
    Pre-investment     19
    U.N. Special Fund     21

3 APPROACH TO ECONOMIC INDEPENDENCE     25
    Commodity prices and foreign capital     27
    Indian exports     29
    Emphasis on quality     32
    Self-criticism     33
    Political choice     35

4 TRADE WITHIN THE UNDEVELOPED WORLD     37
    Latin American Common Market     39
    Doctrinal battle with Monetary Fund     42
    Personality of ECLA     45
    Lesson from Central America     48
    Rules for rich nations     51
    Imperial Preference model     53
    Trade bargains in Asia     55

# CONTENTS

5 COUNTING THE COST                                57
    Saving is not enough                          59
    Three main claimants                          61
    Brazilian investment                         64
    Taxing the rich—Mexico                       66
    A billion dollars plus                       70
    Africa's needs                               72

6 LOOKING FURTHER AHEAD                            77
    Doubling the rate of growth                  79
    Exploding populations                        81
    No early relief                              83

## PART II

### INVESTMENT

7 THE INTERNATIONAL IDEAL                          89
    Soft loans                                   91
    The mirage of SUNFED                         93
    United Nations' weakness                     96
    Forces of inertia                            99
    A new approach                              101
    Impotent or irresponsible management        103

8 LESSONS FROM THE WORLD BANK                     108
    Position of trust                           111
    Banker-Client relationship                  114
    "Impact loans"                              115
    Capital replaces labour                     117
    "Shadow prices"                             119
    Failure in agriculture                      121
    The peasant's mind                          123
    Guaranteeing farmers' prices                125

9 WHAT THE BANKER CANNOT DO                       128
    Lending becomes more difficult              131
    Mr. Black and private enterprise            133
    Zero by 1968                                137

# CONTENTS

10 GENEROSITY FRUSTRATED 140
    Banker's charity 142
    A miniature IDA 145
    U.S. balance of payments 147
    Ceiling on British aid 149
    The cost of empire 153
    Spreading the burden 155

11 HOW TO GET MORE AID 158
    More tied loans needed 160
    Good obsolescent machines 163
    The principle of mutual convenience 166
    Agrarian revolution 169
    An international clearinghouse 172
    Technological leavings? 174

## PART III

### THE ROLE OF THE UNITED NATIONS

*(Together with Zuzanna Shonfield)*

12 THE MISSING THRUST 179
    Technical assistance 180
    Investment in ideas 183
    Colombo Plan 181
    Fragmented effort 185
    Community development 188
    Reasons for failure 190
    American methods 192
    Reforming the system 194

13 UNRAVELLING THE TANGLE 199
    Education to some purpose 201
    Assault on traditional culture 203
    Role of FAO 205
    The new ambassadors 206
    An economic boss 208

# CONTENTS

14 STRENGTHENING THE CENTRE     211
    Pushing the industrial revolution     214
    ILO's toughness     215
    A new agency     218

15 AN OPPORTUNITY     222

APPENDICES

    I. The flow of economic aid and long-term capital     228
    II. United Nations and its agencies—organisational     230
        chart and Glossary
    III. U.N. expenditure on economic and social activities 232

BIBLIOGRAPHY     235

INDEX     236

# INTRODUCTION

The assumption from which this book starts is that there is now widespread agreement about the need for a bigger effort to raise living standards in the undeveloped countries. I do not argue the case for this: the following chapters are concerned solely with ways of making economic aid more effective and getting more of it.

Nor do they discuss whether some nations are capable of economic development and others not, only how long it is likely to take. Again, I assume, that given the right impetus, all peoples are capable of compassing the basic industrial and technical revolution which has, in the past hundred years, made possible the elimination of poverty in the Western world. Until there is strong evidence to the contrary, it seems a reasonable and cautious premise that peoples do not differ so drastically as to make the deliberate application of science to the massive production of wealth—which is after all a comparatively recent phenomenon in the West—possible for one and impossible for another.

My approach to the problems of development in Part I is impressionistic rather than systematic. I have tried to pick out a few of the important strands, and then to argue in Parts II and III how aid might be organized, particularly by the international agencies, to meet the needs of the undeveloped countries more successfully. The reader will notice that Indian experiences and problems are constantly cited by way of example in the course of the argument. This is partly the impressionistic approach—I happen to have taken a special interest in Indian problems—but also because I regard India as a special kind of test case for the West. If we can manage this one, we should be able to deal with the rest.

The Ford Foundation has been my patron in this project: it financed the extensive travel and research that have gone into the making of the book. Mr. Stanley Gordon of the Foundation looked after my other needs admirably.

The book itself is in part a shared effort with Zuzanna

# INTRODUCTION

Shonefield, my wife; she is joint author of Part III, "The Role of the United Nations". But her contributions extend to many other parts of the text, on which I have have had the benefit of her constant advice and suggestions.

I owe a special debt to Mr. Ian Little of Nuffield College, Oxford, whose ideas have helped to improve the text. I am also grateful to Mr. Leo Pliatzky and Mrs. Caroline Miles who read the typescript and took me up on some contentious matters with which I had dealt inadequately. Throughout I have had help from Mr. Paul Hoffman, Professor Arthur Lewis (now Principal of the University College of the West Indies), Mr. David Owen, Mr. C. V. Narasimhan, Mr. Richard Symonds, and from a large number of other people in the United Nations and it agencies, including expecially the World Bank. It hardly needs to be said that they would probably take issue with several of the specific conclusions that I have reached in these pages, though not, I fancy, with the general spirit of criticism running through them. I have been struck by the uncomplacent spirit of these international officials, who know that the work that they are doing needs to be improved and are ready to encourage an outsider to suggest ways of improving it.

Among those responsible for pushing the work through at a high tempo the most important was Miss Gritta Weil, who handled all the typing and manuscripts. Finally the enterprise would not have been possible without the generosity of my employers, *The Observer*—and the enthusiasm of the Editor, Mr. David Astor—who organized matters at some inconvenience to themselves so that I could go off for several months and look at what was happening in the undeveloped countries.

*Part I*

# DEVELOPMENT PROBLEMS

CHAPTER I

# LIMITATIONS OF ECONOMIC AID

THERE are fashions in economic development. In 1959/60, when I was doing a round of visits to the international organizations concerned with development, the "educate 'em first" school was in the ascendant. In New York, in Geneva, in Paris, and in the outposts of the United Nations in Bangkok and Santiago I kept hearing the same story: people in the undeveloped countries were just not ready to use large amounts of additional capital in an effective way. Of course they would, if you offered them a lot of foreign exchange, be able to spend it. The question was, after spending it, how substantial would be the permanent gain in their productive power? In only a few cases was there a clear prospect that the gain would be sufficient to create a new economic momentum in these societies with sufficient force of its own to continue even after the special aid from abroad had lapsed. That is the test of a successful economic aid programme; and the experts and international officials whom I encountered in 1959/60 were quite clear that very few of the undeveloped countries would be able to meet it.

My own experience of the development problem at closer range certainly conforms with their conclusions. But whether they were also right in seeing the lack of education as the chief bottleneck is another matter. It is worth remembering that the first industrial revolution, in Britain during the late 18th and early 19th centuries—the original example of the power of modern technology to achieve the rapid accumulation of productive assets, which then make it easy for a society to go on and become steadily richer—was managed on an extremely narrow educational base. It is certainly not plausible to suggest that universal education and literacy are necessary for successful economic growth. No doubt they help a country to absorb new technology rapidly. But the British managed without effective universal education until the early 20th century. The relationship between cultural standards and economic success is a

3

good deal more complex than the devotees of literacy usually imply. Indeed, concentration on the alphabet, above all else, as the key to the first stage of the economic revolution, may serve to divert attention and energy from more serious problems.

The usual experience is that the lack of trained people makes itself felt as a serious impediment to progress in the middle ranges of industrial activity—at the level of foreman and factory manager, rather than of the operative at the bench. It is the same story in the professions. Yet one is faced by the fact that a country like Chile, with a crying need for improved medical services, has lost several hundred trained nurses— they go to work in the United States mostly—because there are no decently paid jobs for them at home. This tale of no jobs for the trained people on whom the revolution in technology depends is repeated again and again in Latin America. In several of these countries there are numbers of intellectuals educated in modern techniques. The trouble begins at the point where someone—almost inevitably within the government—has to make a decision to pay these men and women and to give them some real authority.

The reason why it is difficult to squeeze an adequate salary for such purposes out of the government's budget is, in almost every case, that the budget is already overloaded with the cost of under-paying masses of under-employed officials who have obtained their jobs, in one way or another, through political patronage. When President Frondizi's government in the Argentine decided, with unique daring, to attack this problem of redundant civil servants in 1959, it started out with an order that all employees in government offices would have to be at their desks at nine o'clock one morning. The resultant chaos, when the two or three different people holding down the same job as clerk or typist met over the desks, tables and chairs, which they had previously been using in shifts, publicly revealed the dimensions of a problem that is common throughout the continent.

### Political Obstacles

In Peru, Chile and the other republics the politicians are quite open about the fact that they are not prepared to risk

4

their political futures by embarking on a policy of counting heads in the civil service. In this, as in so many other matters, the political set-up turns out to be the first and largest obstacle to rapid economic progress. Apart from the entrenched civil service, most of these Latin American countries have to cope with an extremely powerful military class. A government which defies the officers openly will probably have to be prepared to fight them or to mobilize sufficient military power of its own to cow them. Even the occasional brave and impatient reformer is forced to adopt the slow and oblique approach. And the obliqueness of the method leads to some pretty strange results —like the decision of the President of Chile, Senor Alessandri, on coming into office at the end of 1958, that none of the fellowships for training Chilean technicians abroad, offered by the United Nations and other bodies, was in future to be accepted. The only way to get around this prohibition was to obtain his personal consent for an individual applicant. The aim, it became clear after a time, was not to call a halt to the acquisition of useful knowledge in outlandish places, but to curb the lavish expenditure of foreign exchange by members of the Chilean armed forces, who liked nothing better than a period away from home on attachment to some foreign army. Evidently it was regarded as politically impossible to deal with the soldiers and sailors without also stopping the ordinary scholarship boys.

The general conclusion from all this, which must, I think, be the starting point for any discussion on the problem of economic development, is first that there are certain countries where an effective use of foreign economic aid on a large scale to further the process of economic development is not feasible at the moment; and secondly that the obstacle which has to be surmounted is often a political one. There may be educational or cultural or technological obstacles besides. It may also be true that by hammering away steadily at primary education or by successfully creating a new class of technicians, the necessary change of government will eventually be brought about and the political obstacle removed. But the important practical conclusion is that here and now there are several countries in which the input of a large additional amount of foreign capital is not justified, if the criterion is the return which it will produce in the form of extra output devoted to speeding up the pace of economic development.

Or to put the matter in a more positive way—there are only a few countries at the moment which are ready to absorb a lot more foreign exchange and to use the money to achieve a marked increase in their rate of economic growth in the short term and total economic independence in the longer term. Let me identify straightaway three countries which seem to be in this position—India, Mexico and Brazil. There are others; but these are the largest and most obvious candidates in the field at the moment. It may seem a harsh policy to back only the obvious winners. But if the total amount of economic aid and capital is limited, and furthermore the aim is to create as soon as possible a number of new economies in the under-developed world which will be capable of achieving rapid progress under their own steam, then there is no other choice. In economic development we must frankly accept the principle of unfair shares.

There is an alternative approach: it is one which is implicit in much of the thinking of the exponents of economic develop-ment in Latin America. This is that the undeveloped societies should be treated rather as if they were handicapped economies, incapable of making as much out of the tools of economic progress as a normal economy. For example it is argued that if the steel industry of a developed country needs on average about $300 of capital investment in a new plant for every ton of steel produced, then it should be expected that it will take $400 or more of capital to secure the same result in an un-developed country. There are complaints that the World Bank sets too high a standard for projects in which it is willing to invest in Latin America. In my view the World Bank is quite right to insist that investment in new industrial plant should yield a high return in terms of extra output—though it is not necessarily always right in insisting on the highest standards of *profitability*, which is another issue. There is no reason to believe that a country in the early stages of economic development, but which is already capable of rapid growth, will lack enter-prises that offer opportunities for capital investment which are just as productive as those in a developed country. Of course if there were enormous amounts of capital going begging at

# POLITICAL OBSTACLES

low rates of interest, it would be possible to take a more generous view of the kind of return on investment that should be demanded from an undeveloped country before it qualifies for large quantities of economic aid from abroad. But at the moment money is very tight.

# CHAPTER 2

## UNFAIR SHARES

THERE is, it is true, a lot more money going into the un-developed countries today than ever before. Since 1955 the total amount of public funds—direct grants and loans from governments and international organizations—devoted to this purpose has increased by 50 per cent. (The figures which I use here and in the argument which follows refer to the undeveloped countries outside Europe and outside the Sino-Soviet Bloc. What is included is the whole of non-communist Asia, except Japan; Africa, except the Union of South Africa; and Latin America in its entirety. These territories have a combined population of around 1,200 million.) The marked expansion in the flow of money to the undeveloped countries is partly the result of the shift in the focus of American economic aid towards Asia; altogether America's contribution in the form of grants, loans and shipments of surplus food comes to well over $2 billion. Meanwhile, the rising prosperity of the other industrial countries in Western Europe has helped to finance a larger outflow of public funds from this source, though the total is still less than half of the American contribution. Total private investment, American and European, in the undeveloped countries has increased meanwhile to close to $2 billion a year. Finally, the outflow of funds from the Soviet Bloc to the un-developed countries has been growing rapidly since the Russians first showed an interest in the problem in the mid-1950s, while the military component in Soviet aid, which bulked large to begin with, has diminished. The main Soviet emphasis by the end of the 1950s was on capital goods, rather than aeroplanes and submarines.

Adding together all forms of public and private aid, the total for 1958, according to the best available estimates, comes to some $5½ billion. The main sources of this aid are shown in Appendix I. On the face of it, this is a very substantial figure: its value is equal to the cost of one-fifth of all the imports into the undeveloped countries. If that really meant that the hundred or so poor nations of Asia, Africa and Latin America were now able to obtain 20 per cent of the goods that they need to import, without having to earn the foreign exchange to pay for them, it would be a considerable achievement.

The trouble is that these global figures conceal some extreme concentrations of capital and economic assistance at a few points in the underdeveloped world and some wide areas which are very bare and bleak. There are important differences between the rich and the poor within the mass of low income countries. Some of them, notably the oil-producing countries of the Middle East, are not underdeveloped in the sense that the national wealth, measured statistically, is failing to increase by quite substantial amounts from year to year. It is rather that the whole of this increase is concentrated in a narrow sector of the economy and entirely insulated from the rest. The extreme case is Saudi Arabia; but even where attempts are made to use the oil revenues to further the country's whole development, as in Iraq and Persia, the results are extremely meagre so far.

## Central Area of Struggle

To obtain a clearer picture of the flow of resources into the main body of the underdeveloped countries, that is into the area which contains the great bulk of the 1,200 million-odd people living in poverty outside the communist countries, it is necessary to separate off the five main oil-producing territories —Saudi Arabia, Iraq, Persia and Kuwait in the Middle East, plus Venezuela. The combined population of these countries is under 40 million and they are the beneficiaries of private foreign investment on a scale quite out of proportion to their numbers. On the same principle the few countries on the periphery of Asia who, because of their important stategic position, receive an exceptionally large share of American aid ought to be treated separately. South Korea, the rump of Chiang Kai-Shek's China in Formosa, and the three successor states of non-communist Indo-China—Viet Nam, Laos and Cambodia —with a combined population of some 50 million received in 1958 altogether some $700m. of American economic aid, mainly under the Defence Support Programme. This was nearly one-third of all American economic aid.

Next we should, in order to arrive at the net contribution made by foreign capital, take off the amounts that have to be paid back each year by the underdeveloped countries to the developed ones on the investments already made in their territories. This is a substantial sum. Profits and interest due to investors in various private enterprises in the underdeveloped countries come to around $800m. a year[1]—apart from the earnings of the oil companies. To this must be added the cost of servicing the portion of their public debt which is owed to foreigners: interest and principal repayments on these loans amount to another $800m. or so annually. After all these deductions—for the especially fortunate oil countries, for the especially favoured (and vulnerable) allies of the United States, and finally for the cost of interest and repayments on past loans and investments—we are left with a figure of just on $3 billion.

The greater part of this money, it is to be observed, is derived from public funds. The net contribution of private investment, after the deduction of the cost of servicing the capital invested in the past, is comparatively small. On the public side, the World Bank, lending around $350m. a year to the underdeveloped countries, still plays a relatively modest role, in spite of the marked expansion of its activities since the early fifties. It just about equals the rate of Soviet loan disbursements to the underdeveloped countries at the end of the 1950s; but the Bank charges something a good deal higher than the going Soviet rate of interest.

Soviet aid generally comes in the form of loans at $2\frac{1}{2}$ per cent. Starting in earnest round about 1955, Soviet offers of aid built up from year to year, until the total had reached some $2\frac{1}{2}$ billion by the end of 1959. In that year alone the amounts contracted in Soviet loan agreements came to more than $900m., and Mr. Kruschev has promised a further expansion of Russian lending as the Soviet economy expands in the 1960s. Probably a little over half of the loans are made by the Soviet Union itself; the rest by Czechoslovakia, Poland and other members of the Bloc. The actual amount of Soviet money disbursed so far lags well behind the rate at which new commitments are being undertaken. That is inevitable in the early stages of any such programme, when loans are earmarked for the construction of factories and other capital works, which take at least three years to complete, and sometimes four or five. The big burst of Soviet lending came right at the end of the 1950s. and the main benefit in the form of money disbursed should come in the sixties. Because of the lack of detailed information about the timing of Soviet deliveries, estimates of what has so far been received by the undeveloped countries can only be approximate. The indications are that the actual outflow of Soviet aid received by the undeveloped countries was around $200m. in 1958, and increased to $300–$400m. in the subsequent year; some portion of this, but not a major part, consisted of military supplies. Apart from its loans to small strategically placed countries like Afganistan, the Soviet Bloc has made a substantial contribution to India's economic development plan, starting with a million ton steel plant and continuing with several large projects in the heavy engineering industry. Soviet aid accounts for some 20 per cent of total Indian receipts of capital from abroad.

War reparations from Germany and Japan continue to provide a useful addition to the funds available for development. But again the $180m. coming from Germany is heavily concentrated on one single country with a small population— Israel. Similarly, the $500m. of French public funds flowing into overseas economic development—the second largest contribution of any government after the United States—includes a substantial sum of money for investment in Algerian oil. Its effect on the economy of Algeria as a whole is, to date, still fairly slight. It is characteristic of this type of oil exploration in remote places that the bulk of the money tends at first to be spent on foreign equipment and foreign technicians. The oil-men moving around with their helicopters and their drills are at this stage a self-contained, mobile enclave inside the economy. Only later, when the oil is actually being produced in quantity, does the stream of foreign investment begin to reach out farther, with the creation of townships, roads, trading networks and so on.

It is indeed extremely difficult to isolate and identify that portion of Western capital and economic aid to an undeveloped country which makes any significant contribution towards raising the material level of the mass of people living there. A few favoured places with white settler populations, like Algeria and Rhodesia, absorb an unduly large share of the capital moving out of Europe. These are not, in the nature of the case, the areas of mass poverty where upwards of one thousand million people are pressing with increasing urgency on the means of subsistence. Into this central area of the struggle, and especially into the countries with no military commitment to the West, the broad flow of international capital and aid, which looks so impressive at the outset, is reduced to a trickle. Professor Richard Gardner of Columbia University estimates that, excluding Latin America, there is "a total annual capital flow of a little over $1 billion to the uncommitted, non-oil producing, underdeveloped areas of Asia, the Middle East, and Africa." [2]

### Latin American Problems

It helps to get the problem into focus if Latin America is treated separately. First of all, income per head in this region, although low enough, is significantly higher than in Afro-Asia. Secondly, there is nothing like Asia's problem of overcrowding on the land; there are still great spaces waiting to be exploited. Although stretches of unexploited land capable of maintaining much larger populations can be found in Asia too, notably along the River Mekong in the South-East Asia peninsula, this is exceptional. Thirdly, by comparison with Africa, most of the Latin American countries have the advantage of a much more numerous educated class. Finally, the Latin Americans have, in recent years, been the favoured recipients of much American private capital investment.

Indeed the problem in important areas of Latin America, notably in the extreme south, is not how to get the process of economic development started, but rather how to regain the momentum of economic advance, which looked so promising many years ago and has since been frustrated. Argentina, Chile and Uruguay make strange studies in the theory of frustrated development. In terms of income per head they are much the most advanced countries in the whole of Latin

America, but during the 1950s, while they stayed still, Brazil and Mexico forged ahead. Even in these two countries, however, the pace has recently been slowing down, and it will require a lot more capital investment than seems to be immediately in prospect if the rate of progress achieved during the early and middle 1950s is to be resumed in the 1960s. For the rest, the problem of Latin America is essentially that of some extensive agricultural slum areas in places like Bolivia and Peru. Here there are some of the most miserable living conditions in the world. But this is a hard-core problem, affecting a population of perhaps 10–20 million people, which will be expensive to deal with and will almost certainly take a long time. In the scale of priorities it cannot be given the same precedence as India and the *extra* one hundred million mouths that will be waiting to be fed there within the next ten years.

However, even those who accept the more pressing claims of the Indians may find it harsh doctrine that Brazil and Mexico are to be preferred over Bolivia and Peru, simply because the first two are already on the high road of economic development, with all the benefits of rising incomes and increasing opportunities for employment, whereas the other pair are not only poorer but also still miserably wandering in the byways without a sense of direction. It seems inhuman and unfair. It is also rather irritating to think that one might, as a citizen of a Western developed country, be taxed in order to provide funds for economic aid to poor countries, and turn out to have made some already rich Mexican or Brazilian entrepreneur— paying his work-people too little and making quite excessive profits for himself—a good deal richer in the process. But there is no escaping the ugliness and injustice of the early stages of capitalist growth, simply because some of the seeds are being provided, as an act of humanity, by the citizens of more advanced countries. The method of total state control under a communist system purports to remove these extremes of wealth in the midst of poverty, which are a natural concommitant of the early stages of industrialization in the traditional societies. Certainly there is less obvious evidence of flaunting privilege in China than in India, for example; moreover the principle behind Soviet-type privilege is always some kind of public merit, real or imagined, never the bare fact of inherited wealth. But the extremes of privilege exist none the less; they can hardly fail to do so in a primitive society where the mass of people are still pretty close to starvation standards, and the rulers, through the mere fact of ruling, are felt by themselves and by others to be altogether another kind of mortal.

I would justify the proposal to give advantages in obtaining economic aid for development to whole peoples, like the Mexicans and the Brazilians, partly on political and partly on straight practical grounds. Consider the political factor first, because although the less important consideration of the two, it is essential to be honest about this particular motive. The desire to cooperate with Russia in the task of helping the undeveloped countries—and I believe that there may well be scope for such practical cooperation during the next few years—should not be allowed to obscure the fact that our intention in the West is to present these countries with a working alternative to the communist technique of achieving rapid development. The dramatic successes in recent years appear to have been the communist ones. Moreover it has to be recognized that the traditional mode of capitalist development, with its timetable of building up consumer goods industries first and then gradually following with the capital goods to support them, does not correspond to the desire for very rapid growth in the undeveloped societies of today. They want to repeat the trick which the Russians taught the world first of all—the construction during two or three decades of austerity of a powerful and advanced capital goods industry, followed at the appropriate stage by the promise of a sudden and glorious burst of consumer pleasures, when the industrial machine is ready to be given a new direction and turned over to this purpose. What we have still to demonstrate is that the undeveloped countries can follow the same basic timetable, and yet avoid the excesses of tyranny which seem inevitably to accompany the early stages of communist industrialization, whether in Stalin's Russia or in Mao Tse Tung's China.

### Communist Advantages

The communists have several important advantages in

managing the affairs of an undeveloped country. To begin with they impose total mobilization and total discipline on labour. This is a decisive factor in economic development—at any rate, in the overcrowded countries of Asia, which make up three-quarters of the population of the underdeveloped world, where labour is plentiful, much too plentiful, and almost everything else is scarce. The technique which the communists have perfected is to use labour, during the early stages of development, as a direct substitute for machine power. I was struck by the contrast when, in 1959, I visited the great dam being built at Bhakra in the north of India—the largest dam in the country and the highest in the world. There was an almost complete absence on the site of pick-and-shovel men or of people carrying earth, stones or anything else. The skyline was filled with cranes and hoisting equipment, while a great length of machine belting, electrically driven, climbed like an endless vibrating snake over the hills, across a bridge over the river, and then up the steep side of the bank up to the dam itself, bringing its continuous load of stone from a quarry several miles way. Why, I asked the engineers in charge, did they not draw on the huge reserve of unemployed Indian labour to replace some of the machinery? They could also have saved some electricity, which was so short that it was holding up the production of factories in the area. The official answer was that the dam site was too narrow for masses of people to work on it; also a high dam by its nature requires a lot of mechanical handling. No one could deny, however, that there was plenty of room for many more people than were actually there. The essential point which emerged in the course of further conversation was that these technicians *did not want* thousands of primitive and probably half-starved Indians crawling all over their site. They would be out of control, they would get in the way, and everything would be slowed down. The truth was that machines were infinitely easier to manage than human beings—and a lot cheaper, after allowing for the deliberate time-wasting of people trying to spin out the job, as well as the minimum social services that would have to be supplied under the Indian labour law.

It hardly needs to be said that these are not problems which worry the Chinese. There the régime sets out deliberately, and brutally, to substitute surplus labour for scarce machinery. Moreover, the communists, through their ability to fix wages by fiat, after having suppressed any independent trade union organization, can squeeze a much larger volume of savings out of the community. Meanwhile the government itself takes all the profits. Again, the contrast between India and China is most striking. The extra savings which the Chinese communists command are used to push up the level of capital investment generally, and of the heavy industries in particular. Consumer goods industries are not allowed to compete for scarce supplies of steel and other metals; capital goods are given absolute priority.

The method, if it is to be completely effective requires a political tyranny. People can only be controlled in this extreme way when there is the full apparatus of terror exercised at the centre and all possible sources of opposition to the government have been eliminated. A communist tyranny also has the advantage of being able to promise political stability within the same broad framework for some years ahead. This is most important for effective economic planning. Officials simply do not plan ahead—and businessmen even less so—if the government in an underdeveloped country is thought likely to topple. Finally, there are the social consequences of communist revolution. The old class of landowners, who instinctively resist the new technology and methods of doing business —because they know that this will mean the end of their social dominance—are rooted out from their positions of power in one violent wrench. They are no longer capable of using their wealth and social influence to slow down the pace of innovation. In a non-communist society a weak middle class, without social self-confidence, has to try and do the same job, in cooperation with the army or one of the other traditional carriers of power within the community.

Considering all the advantages of communism, it might be thought that the wisest and perhaps the most generous course would be to let the underdeveloped countries get on with it and go communist. Certainly it is true that if two poor nations, equally endowed by nature, were starting from scratch, the odds would be strongly in favour of the one which adopted a communist system. The real objection is that the moral and political damage done to a nation by being pushed through the communist mangle is of a lasting character. The habits of totalitarian tyranny both in the rulers and the ruled take a long time to correct. That is no justification for running to the opposite extreme and trying to use economic aid as a weapon in the cold war. Cold war tactics are a separate issue—although the semantic confusion between communism and Soviet diplomacy has been responsible for some of the sillier panic phases of Western policy in the 1950s. Letting a country go communist is a risk that we must feel able to afford to take; otherwise the West is likely to be the permanent object of blackmail by all the least worthwhile and most oppressive governments.

In any case, the adoption of a communist system does not, as the example of Yugoslavia shows, necessarily mean adding to Russian power. But without being a cold war-monger, one may reasonably wish to demonstrate by a series of successes in the undeveloped countries that an alternative to the communist path is open—indeed, be desperately anxious to make this point, in order to deter those societies which are now emerging into the modern world from doing themselves profound damage. There is also the more selfish apprehension, which has certainly been given colour by the experience of Chinese behaviour to date, that a communist revolution tends to make a poor country an extremely awkward and scratchy neighbour to live with.

## Political and Practical Choices

One of the special difficulties on our side in any attempt at peaceful competition with the communists is our equivocal attitude towards politics in the undeveloped countries. I suspect that the equivocation is in the nature of the case. Although we recognize that a given political set-up may well present an insurmountable barrier to rapid economic progress, we preclude ourselves from going seriously about the business of trying to overcome it by bringing a government down. The communists have no such inhibitions. Implicit in our whole approach is the decision to try and push economic development by

purely economic means. We permit ourselves to hope that certain kinds of economic change will have political consequences;
the ideology of the West is Marxist enough for that. We expect
that the new middle classes will, once they are large and rich
enough, eventually overthrow the corrupt government to
which we are giving economic assistance today. But we are
not going to do anything directly to bring that government
down.

Of course, all lenders discriminate against some governments
and in favour of others. To take a current example, there
would seem to be little point in voting a large sum of money
for economic aid to Indonesia in the conditions of 1960. That
is not because the Indonesian government has the wrong
political colour: it is simply that the government is without
the effective power necessary to offer a reasonable prospect of
success in the difficult task of economic development. There
has to be some fairly stable concentration of power in the hands
of an identifiable group of competent people before a country
is worth backing. If this condition is not fulfilled, the risk of
civil war or the stultification of development through lack of
sufficient political authority at the centre is too great.

But that is no more than to recognize that political conditions
can present an insurmountable obstacle to economic progress.
For the communists, on the other hand, politics are primary.
As Mr. Gomulka put it to the Poles, "It is not money which
decides technical progress. The decisive factor is to be found
in socialism." [3] What we are trying to demonstrate is that in
certain circumstances money *will* do the trick. But we have to
keep a sharp look-out for the chance combination which offers
the opportunity, and then promptly give the help that is needed
to bring it to fruition.

However, it is unnecessary to press this political argument
very hard, because the purely practical considerations in
favour of concentrating economic assistance, rather than
spreading it out among a lot of countries on some principle of
fair shares, are usually sufficiently compelling. There is only a
limited sum of public funds available for investment in the
underdeveloped countries, and so there is a strong case for
putting as much as possible into the places where it is likely to
make a significant impact on poverty. This is not a matter of

making precise measurements of efficiency and then giving the prize to the people who come first. It is rather that in a situation where capital is scarce we should take precautions to avoid serious waste. And some of the undeveloped countries are littered with monuments to the wastefulness of unplanned investments.

Only a few governments have so far thought out anything like a rational order of priorities for economic development. It is not just a case of failing to concentrate on the most urgent task; the more usual trouble is that investment is undertaken in some attractive looking project like building a hospital, while no one does anything about producing and paying the doctors required to man it. The city of Lima, Peru, contains a vast monumental hospital of this kind, which the Americans helped to equip with the very latest and most expensive equipment, including a landing stage for helicopters on the roof. The hospital is used to only a fraction of its capacity, and the problem is to keep the empty spaces clean and decently polished. Often the instinctive reaction to an offer of foreign aid is just to ask for the most expensive toy on the market. There is a feeling that nothing but the very best will do when a poor country is being taken out on a spree by the rich one.

*Pre-investment*

That is why the emphasis on pre-investment activity is one of the really useful developments of recent years. The idea is that people should be encouraged to spend more money in preparing the ground before they import a lot of capital for a project—for instance in measuring as precisely as possible the return that they are likely to get from this project, compared with other alternatives, in training local technicians and managers who will be capable of operating it, in studying the implications of the project in terms of the demand that it will make on other economic resources, and so on.[4] In 1958 the United Nations Special Fund was set up, under the direction of Mr. Paul Hoffman, to deal with this set of problems. Its experience to date has already revealed a large amount of work waiting to be done in bringing projects to the stage when an engineer can be called in to prepare a blueprint for investment. The cost is often more than an undeveloped country can readily afford, especially as a fair proportion of the projects that are worth investigating fail to make the grade. Then there is the time factor. For instance, it takes up to five years to establish the basic facts about the flow of a river which must be known before it is possible to begin to work out a comprehensive scheme for power and irrigation. On several of the rivers flowing through the undeveloped countries, including the vast River Mekong in South-East Asia, one of the biggest wasted assets in the world, this basic data is missing.

It is not just a question of blanks in knowledge: the deficiency is often in the supply of trained men who would be able to interpret and to use the facts, if the facts were available. The Indian government for instance found, at the stage when it was working against the clock to lay down the programme for the Third Five Year Plan (1961–6), that it was faced with a critical shortage of industrial project engineers—that is, people who could make a blueprint for a new plant incorporating the very latest technology and also taking account of the peculiarities of local conditions. This lack of a relatively small number of especially skilled persons would have become a more serious brake on Indian economic progress in the late 1950s, if it had not been that shortage of foreign exchange and administrative delays were in any case holding up the pace of advance.

The Indian example brings out one important aspect of the relationship between pre-investment and investment activity. The two are not to be regarded as distinct and mutually exclusive phases of a country's development. Pre-investment work may be required in one field while in some other field large amounts of investment capital are already being absorbed. Broadly, the difference between a country which is on the threshold of rapid development, needing only some extra capital in order to push it over, and a country whose absorptive capacity for capital is still limited is that in the former case a great deal of pre-investment work has already been done. This formulation of the problem is in some danger of becoming a tautology: a country which cannot usefully absorb a lot of investment capital is one which ought to be engaged in pre-investment activity. There is, however, the practical point which is worth stating—that it is not sensible trying to invest in a country on a large scale until it has done the preliminary work of measuring its resources and training its basic cadres of skilled manpower. Only then does it become possible to bring forward a number of sound investment projects fairly fast; and to go on bringing forward more and more of them thereafter.

This is the point that India has now reached. But Pakistan, for example, is not yet there, nor indeed are any of the other countries in South Asia. They are still in the phase when the main emphasis must be on pre-investment. That is not to say that these countries cannot usefully absorb quite substantial sums of capital for a number of investment projects, and show a good return on them. But it is interesting to find that the officials of the World Bank who are concerned with this area and are trying to put more money into it say that the main obstacle is the shortage of good investment projects. It is true that the Bank's difficulty in doing business in these countries is partly due to the narrow limits that it has imposed on the type of lending in which it will engage. This is a problem which will be discussed in later chapters.* But there is little doubt that the absence of good investment schemes, even within the limited area in which the Bank is prepared to operate, does reflect a profound deficiency, which will have to be overcome before the pace of economic progress in these countries can be speeded up. Indeed the Bank itself was proposing at the end of 1959 to put some of its own money into the job of pre-investment—sending out a group of people to Burma for a couple of years to look around and smell out any likely looking prospects.

## U.N. Special Fund

There are thus a number of countries which still have to be pushed quite some distance before they are ready to cross the threshold leading to rapid economic development. This preliminary pushing includes a certain amount of social investment in basic facilities, like roads, schools, health and sanitation— and that will not be cheap—but such countries are not yet capable of absorbing large sums of capital for productive

* See Chapters 8 and 9.

purposes. It is indeed fortunate that the problem of finding the money to equip the underdeveloped world does not all come in one swoop. that the capital needs of these countries sort themselves out into some kind of queue—not on some criterion of precise relative needs, which would be a most delicate matter to determine and one which the Western donors of capital ought to try to keep away from if they possibly can, but on the basis of what kind of outside assistance these countries are able to *use* at different stages of growth. For pre-investment work does not usually cost very much: the amounts required are measured in millions, rather than hundred millions of dollars. Occasionally there is a costly job to be done, for example, a complete pilot plant may have to be set up in order to determine whether a novel method of production is feasible or not. But more usually it is a matter of bringing in comparatively inexpensive pieces of equipment. The average project taken on by the United Nations Special Fund in its first year cost around $725,000. That represented a little under half of total project cost, the rest being covered by the recipient country itself; including the latter, the average cost was $1·8m. The most expensive single job was the scheme for desert locust control, a six-year regional project covering the Mediterranean area, the Middle East, Pakistan and India; this is going to cost the Fund nearly $2·5m.—and the eighteen participating governments another $1·3m. or so.

It is likely that this kind of work will grow more expensive, as it becomes more ambitious. At the start the Special Fund was most anxious to spread its resources as wide as possible, and also to favour the modest kind of project which seemed to have an obvious and solid prospect of success. Professor Lewis, who was the Deputy Managing Director of the Fund during its initial year, said at this stage that a project was not worth looking at unless he could feel the big money already "breathing down its neck". This rather demanding attitude was partly the result of the limited financial resources of the Special Fund—some $26m. in its first year. That figure has since been substantially increased; and the interim objective is to raise it to $60m. a year. My own guess is that as countries become more familiar with the systematic approach to pre-investment work, the demand will turn out to be considerably larger than the creators of the Fund originally expected. I gained the impression that there are quite a few responsible people in the undeveloped countries, many of them officials in governments, who have been nursing experimental ideas for increasing the national wealth, which are now waiting to be put through the severe practical tests that the U.N. Special Fund has been designed to undertake.

Mr. Paul Hoffman has set a target figure of $150m. for the combined requirements of the Special Fund and United Nations Technical Assistance for 1963, which is two and a half times as much as the amount made available for these two programmes in 1959. This may be compared for size with the foreign capital needs of India alone in its current investment plan—$1 billion a year. It is only when the job of pre-investment has been successfully done that economic aid to the underdeveloped countries becomes really expensive. With luck and good management, this is the stage which should be reached in a number of Asian and Latin American countries by the middle and late 1960s. Africa may take longer.

What we have to envisage is that the need for large draughts of capital and economic aid will grow substantially in the next four or five years. At the moment it is only a very few countries, with India at the head of the line, which urgently require big sums for immediate use in productive investment. It would be reasonable to hope that some of the other immediate claimants, notably Mexico, would be in a position to go to the ordinary private capital market for most of their needs, after another five years or so of successful development. But the Indians do not have this prospect of a rapid transition to commercial forms of borrowing. The odds are that India will continue to be acutely short of foreign exchange over the next decade, for although its productive capacity at home should expand rapidly (assuming that the investment programme goes forward) there is not likely to be the same quick growth of Indian earning power abroad.

*Notes*

1. On capital assets whose value it is impossible to assess precisely, but which was almost certainly over $8 billion. (See "The International Flow of Private Capital", United Nations, and "Capital

Imports into Sterling Countries", by A. R. Conan.) Profits and interest are of course a normal charge, just like wages, against the earnings of a business investment; the only reason why they are singled out for special treatment here is that because they pass into the ownership of foreigners, they form a debit item in the balance of payments of undeveloped countries.

2. "International Measures for the Promotion and Protection of Foreign Investment". Proceedings of the American Society of International Law, 1959.

3. Quoted in the *Guardian*, 3rd February, 1960.

4. The concept of pre-investment and the way in which it can be distinguished—not always precisely—from investment proper is discussed in detail in Chapter 12, pp. 181–3.

# CHAPTER 3

# APPROACH TO ECONOMIC INDEPENDENCE

IT is the weakness of the undeveloped countries as exporters during the stage of accelerated growth, the crucial stage of what W. W. Rostow calls "the take-off",[1] which makes the attempt to force the pace during the 1960s exceptionally difficult. Our desire to force the pace is motivated in part by ordinary humanitarian considerations—the countries of the West are now rich enough and technology is advanced enough to make rapid progress possible in the rest of the world—but the overriding practical reason why the need to accelerate has become so urgent in the 1960s is the population explosion.

Of course the rapid increase in population is characteristic of all the industrial revolutions of the past; but the suddenness of the advance, the way in which it is being accelerated by the autonomous forces of medical progress, rather than as a result of economic change, and finally the universality of the phenomenon over populations numbering many hundreds of millions —all this is new. There are two complications which follow: first, the low-income countries cannot afford to be modest in their investment programmes, their import bill for capital equipment will be exceptionally heavy in the next few years, because they have to make haste in increasing their productive capacity before the next generation catches up on them; secondly, many of them will almost certainly go through a period in which they are dependent on large imports of food. The latter is simply the result of the fact that newly implanted industry naturally takes advantage of modern technology, whereas traditional agriculture is extremely resistant to it. Industry forces its own disciplines even on recalcitrant people; indeed the acceptance of technical innovation, which is imposed by the industrial process itself, is perhaps the most important spiritual discipline that has to be acquired by a traditional society.

However, it is argued by some economists that the fact that

food production is likely to lag means merely that the developing countries of today will have to concentrate more energy on the export of goods that will earn them foreign exchange with which to buy imported food. They will be compelled to follow the British pattern of growth in the 19th century, rather than the American one. It is also pointed out that the export trades have often acted as a powerful stimulus to economic progress in the early stages of development.[2] This is a substantial point. Quite apart from anything else, an export industry imposes standards of quality and general efficiency on a commercial community, which are usually absent in the traditional societies. The nucleus of exporters may then become, if they are successful and influential people, pace-setters for the rest of the economy. This is what happened in Japan during the period after the First World War. On the other hand, there are enough cases where the beneficent influence of the exporters has failed to work its way through a society. Latin America is full of them.

But even if it could be shown that being forced to export was necessarily good for the soul of a country in the early stages of development, the question remains whether a very large increase of exports is feasible over a short period of time. Here we come up against the fact that the export markets for the traditional primary products of the undeveloped countries have been growing much more slowly than the rest of world export trade. This is largely the result of the new technology which helps the industrial countries to get along with rather less raw material for any given volume of output. The total quantity of raw materials required with each year of advancing industrial output continues to go up, but the proportion of raw input to finished output diminishes, as synthetic fibres and plastics make further progress and as industrial research discovers new methods of making a given amount of material go a longer way—with a better quality article produced at the end of it. That means simply that the rate at which the demand for raw materials increases is less than the rate of industrial expansion achieved in the developed countries; and this is one reason why the gap between the living standards of the developed and the undeveloped countries keeps on increasing. The markets for the goods that we produce are on the whole much more buoyant than the markets for what they produce.

As the same time we have learned to apply technology more successfully to the production of food. Sheltering behind tariff walls, farmers in North America and Western Europe have increased their efficiency tremendously, and are now producing a great deal more food with far fewer people than before the war.

## Commodity Prices and Foreign Capital

The result is not just that the quantity of food and materials which the undeveloped countries can sell is reduced. There are indirect influences on prices too. For example, the price that Burma is able to command for its rice exports today would almost certainly be higher if U.S. production of rice had not been so enormously increased. In this instance, it happens that the chief beneficiaries from lower Burmese prices are the other undeveloped countries in Asia. But taking all the commodities together, there is no doubt where the balance of advantage lies. The drop in commodity prices during the 1957/8 recession alone, combined with the simultaneous rise in the cost of the industrial goods which the undeveloped countries import, is estimated to have cost them over $1½ billion in twelve months.[3] This, as we have seen, is not far short of the total sum of private capital received by the undeveloped countries. There has been some recovery since, but commodity prices are still below the level of 1952, *after* the Korean War boom.

To some extent the weakness of commodity prices during the late 1950s was a reaction from the extremely high level which these prices reached during the decade after the war. A study by the Economic Commission for Latin America has shown just how much the countries in this region gained from ten years of extremely favourable terms of trade.[4] The large investments which many of the Latin American countries made during this period were sustained chiefly by the steady rise in export earnings, which went up by 5·4 per cent a year. But the actual volume of exports rose from year to year by under half of that amount; it was the uninterrupted rise in prices which was the main source of Latin American prosperity. And this leads on to the stark conclusion that if the Latin Americans achieve the same rate of advance in exports during the next decade as during the first postwar decade, but with a stable world price level, the rise in their foreign earnings will not keep pace with the annual 3 per cent growth of population. ECLA comments that "Latin America is entering upon a phase in which the repercussions of international trade on economic development will resemble the influence it exerted between the depression of the thirties and the Second World War . . ." [5]

However, before the analogy between the 1930s and the 1960s gets pressed too far, one very important difference between the two periods should be noticed. In the thirties, because of the depression, the supply of foreign capital for investment in the undeveloped countries dried up at the same time as commodity prices collapsed. In recent years weak commodity markets have been accompanied by a sharp increase in the flow of public and private funds into the undeveloped countries; and it is now greater than ever before. That too raises problems. It is a pity in some ways that the undeveloped countries have started to worry seriously about their ability to repay loans, just when the developed countries have worked themselves up to the point where they are willing to lend them a lot more money. But the dangers of borrowing too much are real enough.

Consider, for example, the arithmetic of India's Third Year Plan, beginning in 1961. Taking the most conservative estimate of what the Indians will need to carry out a substantial pro-gramme for the development of heavy industry and fertilizer factories, the foreign trade deficit during this period will average an amount equal to roughly two-thirds of India's export earnings today. Next, assume that the Indians manage to increase their export sales during the coming five years— or alternatively to reduce their imports—so that the figure of the annual deficit (i.e. the amount that has to be borrowed) is reduced to one-half of the value of their export earnings. This would mean that by 1966 the debt accumulated over the Five Year Plan would amount to two and a half times the value of the country's enlarged export trade. Finally, let us assume that the Indians are lucky and manage to get these loans on something better than current market terms—say at 5 per cent interest, repayable over twenty years. Thus the Indians would have to find each year a sum in foreign exchange, for interest and principal repayments together, equal to 10 per cent of the total amount borrowed during the five-year period. Since the five years' borrowings added up to two and a half times the value of the country's annual exports, the annual cost of servicing the post-1961 debt would absorb 25 per cent of exports. But by 1961 India's load of debt-servicing obligations on the money borrowed for the Second Five Year Plan will already be absorbing over 10 per cent of export earnings. This has to be added on, so that the total figure by the end of the Third Five Year Plan would be nearer to 35 per cent. The upshot is that successful borrowing, at something better than market terms, would require a rise of one-third in India's export sales—if the country had to become solvent quickly— over and above the big increase in exports that is already being postulated in order to reduce its dependence on further foreign capital to finance its investment programme.

## Indian Exports

My conclusion is that since India is, after all, an undeveloped country and not some kind of commercial Hercules, the task of pushing up exports—or alternatively of cutting back imports of essentials by making these things at home—at this speed during the crucial stage of an investment programme is just not a practical proposition. It is not merely that it would be difficult to force the Indian people to forgo the benefits of their increased production altogether, so that enough resources were set aside to sustain both the high investment programme and the massive increase in exports. That is another moot point —but it is not the point at issue here. Even if the Indians did go without consumer goods and services, it is very questionable whether the resources so released could, within the next five years, be converted into a mass of articles of equivalent value which they could sell in export markets. No doubt, by denying people at home bicycles, sewing machines and refrigerators, steel could be released for making more of these and other products for export. The Indians have already made an entry into foreign markets with such products as electric fans and sewing machines, as well as a few simple machine tools. But this type of export still produces only a tiny fraction of India's foreign exchange earnings today, and no one on the spot seriously believes that the amount sold abroad can be quickly multiplied very many times. India's staple exports like jute, tea and cotton textiles seem unlikely to expand very much; so that the whole weight of the new export drive will have to be borne by the newer industries, mainly in the engineering field.

There is in addition a useful Indian trade with the Soviet Bloc countries in cheap consumer goods, notably shoes. This could conceivably develop into something much bigger, if the Russians decided one day to use international trade purposefully to raise their own standard of living. The Soviets and the undeveloped countries are in many ways ideally complementary as trading partners. All the evidence suggests that Soviet industry can make capital goods cheaply and efficiently, while it is much less competent at making simple consumer goods, which have been neglected during long years of austerity. Now the Russians have the opportunity to take advantage of the products of cheap labour in the undeveloped countries, and in return they would be able to sell the surplus output of the more highly paid Soviet workers in heavy industry.

This would require a willingness on the part of India to undertake a profound reorientation of its trade, which would make it dependent on the Soviet Union for a large part of its capital goods and spare parts. Even assuming that the Indians were ready to take the risks inherent in such a decision, they would still be left with a serious practical problem about fulfilling their undertaking to supply consumer goods of a standard quality to their Soviet customers. Quality is bound to be a major problem when an attempt is made to mobilize the primitive handicrafts sector of an undeveloped economy for an export drive. The Japanese were able to do it, as a result of a triumph of organization and discipline; but it took even them a long time. The Indians do not start off with the peculiar cultural background which gave Japan unusual advantages for an export drive of this kind. One does come across heroic attempts in India to impose industrial discipline and standards on the handicrafts. An outstanding example is the shoemaking industry at Agra, the old city of the Mogul emperors, which contains the Taj Mahal. But even after the most strenuous attempt to check on materials and workmanship, with a horde of official supervisors watching each phase of the operation, the customers from the Soviet Bloc—the Russians, Poles and East Germans —were still, at the end of 1959 when I visited the place, rejecting 15 per cent of the finished products after they had been boxed, on grounds of poor quality. No one suggested that the Soviet inspectors, who went round the warehouse before the consignments of shoes were shipped, were being excessively stringent in their standards.

No doubt the rejection rate will be reduced; it was already lower in 1959 than it had been when this trade started three years before. Perhaps, too, the Indian craftsmen will in time overcome their greatest handicap—the use of hides from animals which have died a natural death, because the killing of cattle is forbidden to Hindus. They may either modify their religious practices or discover improved techniques for dealing with the hide of a cow that has died. But either solution seems likely to take some time to work itself out. And the hand-made shoe industry of Agra, which employs some 40,000 people in the courtyards about the narrow streets and the big crumbling houses where the old magnates used to live in the city, is among the most highly developed handicrafts in the country. It is conveniently concentrated in a confined urban area and strenuously organized. The Indians would probably, in time, be able to create a dozen other Agras if the Soviet markets for a variety of hand-made consumer goods were offered to them firmly as a long-range proposition. But it is most unlikely that the method would achieve results large enough and, even more important, quickly enough to cover any substantial part of the foreign exchange gap during the critical years of development.

The great advantage of the Agra method is that it produces foreign exchange with the minimum amount of equipment— no more than a wooden last and a hammer. Cheap and abundant labour is the complete substitute for capital—the ideal arrangement for a poor over-populated country in the early stages of development. The reason why this advantage is of more limited value in selling to the export markets of the capitalist countries of the West is that they, unlike the Soviets, developed full-scale consumer goods industries first and then built up their capital goods industries to serve them. Competition in consumer goods produced by very cheap labour abroad therefore comes up against the resistance of some of the oldest and politically most powerful industries in the developed countries. Even so, it is sometimes possible to overcome them, at any rate up to a point, and win a useful market —as the Indian textile producers did in Britain during the 1950s, before their further inroads were restricted by a "voluntary export quota". But the British Government's readiness to let the Lancashire cotton industry decline in the face of competition from Asia, ignoring the anguished cries for protection from the trade unions as well as the employers, was highly untypical of the behaviour of developed countries in this kind of situation.

Certainly, India and other undeveloped countries would be foolish to rely on a similar lack of resistance, when they move on from textiles to large-scale exports of other consumer goods. Even if the Western countries grow wiser than they have shown themselves to date, and come to recognize the logic of contracting certain of their industries quite deliberately in order to make way for a more fruitful exchange of goods in international trade with the undeveloped countries, the process of contraction is likely to prove a slow and long drawn-out business. The political pressures from workers threatened with displacement will ensure that it is. In the end, the West will have to adapt itself to a much larger inflow of manufactured goods from the low-income, low-wage countries—or it will have to resign itself to trading with them less and less. But the propensity to protect traditional industries when they are in trouble through no fault of their own will not be easily overcome.

### Emphasis on Quality

Apart from textiles and the handicrafts, for which there is no great unsatisfied demand in Western markets, what else could India export in increased quantities? A few manufactures made by a few firms are up to the quality required for export trade; but these are still exceptional. Perhaps the most hopeful sign is that the Indian authorities are increasingly preoccupied with this problem of quality. They deliberately go out to cultivate a mood of self-criticism among manufacturers; and this is not easy when people are profitably making goods that the country has not produced before.

Manubai Shah, the lively Minister for Industry, goes around preaching the doctrine that quality is the key to India's economic independence, the answer to the balance of payments problem. "If the only trouble is that you are uncompetitive", he explained to me, "you can always cut your export prices or subsidize them for a while. But there is nothing that a government can do if the quality of the goods that exporters are trying to sell is wrong." It was a characteristic all-or-nothing point made with characteristic emphasis by this engaging Gujerati, with the mobile yet unlined face of a very intelligent youth. He went on to describe the strategy of India's future export drive, which he saw as the only way to long-term economic independence. But the emphasis was on the long term. It was an illusion he said, to imagine that India could do now what Japan did in her day, and achieve a rapid breakthrough into world markets. For one thing there are no longer the worldwide opportunities to sell textiles; everybody in Asia has a textile industry now. But more important still is the fact that the Japanese have already done the trick and are firmly established in the field. Indian wages are lower than the Japanese, but this is more than offset by India's handicap in quality. To catch up will require a steady effort over a number of years. Manubai Shah's own metaphor was—"Exporting is like preparing a girl for marriage. She has to find her fiancé, then study what he is like and what he wants, and then look very carefully at herself, gradually making those small and subtle changes that finally make all the difference."

## Self-criticism

It is, of course, easy to allege that something is impossible because it is acknowledged to be difficult. After a little experience of the undeveloped countries one becomes accustomed to, and suspicious of, the gambit. In this instance, however, there

33

was no mistaking the genuineness of the effort being made to overcome India's export handicap and the honest judgment about short-range possibilities. Taking a longer view, Manubai Shah has a kind of rumbustious optimism about India, which he takes so much for granted that he is ready to criticize with equal frankness the faults of Indians as entrepreneurs and his own Ministry's frequent lack of imagination in dealing with the needs of business enterprise. This capacity for self-criticism, with the emphasis on irony rather than passion, strikes me as one of the most attractive characterisitics of the upper ranks of the Indian administration today, both in the civil service and in the government itself. It is also a major source of strength. Some foreign observers in New Delhi, remarking the absence of ballyhoo—at this top level, though not lower down— conclude that the rulers have now grown tired and cynical, with no drive left in them. But one only has to go a little way beyond the ironic conversational posture to discover the long hours which the members of this *élite* spend at work—they must be among the longest of any civil service in the world—the intense seriousness with which they approach the business of making practical decisions, and their profound sense of responsibility. The danger of the situation is that there are too few of these men. The next level down registers a steep drop in quality. But at the very top it is rare to find so many people of unusual ability in positions of power.

The irony, perhaps a little self-conscious, the almost deprecatory approach to problems, which foreigners sometimes find so irritating—so un-American and equally so un-Russian in spirit—has some important practical uses, too. I remember the following comment, still on the subject of exports, thrown out with characteristic wry humour in the course of an interview with the head of a government department, a very patriotic Indian, in his office in New Delhi. "It is much more difficult to export now that we have no imperial masters", he said, looking out of the window at the cobbled courtyard and pink stone of the immensely imperial architecture of Government House, which the British bequeathed to the Indians. "In the old days the efforts made by the London business houses to find cheap sources of supply over here and marry them at a good fat profit with the customers that they

had at their command over there—all this was called exploitation. But times have changed and nowadays we are looking
around for energetic people in Western Europe and saying
to them: 'Please come and exploit us.' "

This was not just a phrase: the important fact that it is
easier to develop a strong export trade quickly in collaboration
with foreign businessmen who understand the markets abroad
has been grasped. Admittedly there is also a strong party within
the Indian government which continues to press for a policy of
hostility towards foreign enterprise; but the dominant group
has turned right round in the short period since the achievement of Indian independence. It is even prepared to see virtue
in the foreign middleman, the most unpopular figure of all in
the folklore of undeveloped countries. I could not help wondering as I parted from this civil servant in New Delhi, how many
people in authority in Mexico, for example, would have been
ready to take such a clear unworried view of their national
deficiencies and of their dependence on foreigners.

I do not want to suggest that a blinkered, enthusiastic and
violently nationalist approach does not have its uses in economic
development. There is plenty of that in India too. But a civilized
leadership with a highly developed spirit of self-criticism is a
help when a nation faces ten years of intermittent balance of
payments crisis and dependence on foreign goodwill, as the
price of development.

*Political Choice*

The foregoing argument about the earning capacity of undeveloped countries does not ignore the importance of the
"will to export".[6] The fact is, however, that the will by itself is
not enough to produce results quickly, if a country which is not
subject to totalitarian controls is also trying to build up new
capital goods industries to meet home requirements and raise
agricultural output at the same time. In theory, it can restrict
consumption to the point where both the needs of the domestic
programme and of the export drive are met. This is what
China appears to be able to do. But in India and other low-
income countries which are not communist it is impossible to

operate a full-scale control over all aspects of consumer behaviour without at the same time stultifying private enterprise. Here is indeed one of the disabilities of the private enterprise system in the earliest stage of economic development. The communists have the definite advantage at this stage, when the industrial objectives are simple and clearcut and the flexibility associated with the multiple initiatives of private enterprise is less important than it later becomes.

The political choice means that the achievement of economic independence in a country like India is bound to take a longer time than in China. Specifically, it seems unlikely that even if India gets all the capital that it requires from abroad to carry through its Third and Fourth Five Year Plans, the deficit on its balance of payments will be eliminated before 1970. We must be prepared to subsidize India pretty heavily with foreign exchange for the next decade—though it is reasonable to hope, with smaller amounts towards the end of the decade than at the beginning.

*Notes*

1. "The Stages of Economic Growth", by W. W. Rostow (Cambridge).

2. See particularly W. Arthur Lewis's "The Theory of Economic Growth".

3. The "World Economic Survey, 1958", United Nations, estimates the total loss suffered by the primary producing countries at $2 billion; of this $1·6 billion was attributable to the undeveloped countries, according to calculations of the U.N. statisticians.

4. "The Influence of the Common Market on the Economic Development of Latin America", ECLA, May 1959.

5. Op. cit.

6. See W. A. Lewis, "The Theory of Economic Growth", comparing the export performance of Italy and India in the first part of this century with the success of Japan.

CHAPTER 4

# TRADE WITHIN THE UNDEVELOPED WORLD

ONE way in which the undeveloped countries could surely help to relieve the pressure on their balance of payments is by trading more among themselves. It is not just a matter of taking in each other's washing. Surplus production of a commodity runs to waste in one country, while in another people go short of it, because the mechanism of exchange fails to function efficiently. A lot more food could and would be grown in the great surplus agricultural area of Asia which runs from Burma across the South-East Asian peninsula, if there were an assured market for it. But it only needs one good rice harvest for Burma to be faced with the nightmare of surplus stocks. That is what has happened recently. There are no adequate storage facilities, the rice rots, the price falls—and next time the peasant does not bother to grow so much or to bring it to market.

The reason given for the Burmese failure to sell the rice to the Indians is simply that the Indians cannot afford it. That is true in the sense that the Indian government is not prepared to allocate anything out of its very inadequate reserves of foreign exchange to pay for additional imports of rice. It is clear, in fact, that if there is to be any substantial increase in this or in any other trade among the undeveloped countries—who are almost certain to be short of foreign exchange as soon as they try seriously to speed up their economic development—it will be necessary to by-pass the normal machinery for making payments. If Burma demands to be paid, like everyone else, in sterling or some other convertible currency, it will be left holding its surplus rice, and everybody will be that much poorer.

Indeed, one would have thought it elementary that these nations should be encouraged to engage in barter trade, wherever this helps them to put their actual or potential surpluses of production to some useful purpose. It came as a shock, therefore, when I was in India at the end of 1959, to run into a mission from the International Monetary Fund engaged in a vigorous effort to break up an Indo-Burmese barter agreement. The IMF started by hurling anathemas. What the Indians were doing was a sin against the principle of untrammelled multilateral trade, with equal freedom for all exporters to enter a market. Only by holding to this principle could a nation be assured that it was buying its goods in the cheapest market and so keeping its own costs competitive. Moreover, the IMF was able to back up its doctrine by brandishing a big deterrent. It commands a large sum of money for short-term loans. The Indians happened to owe it a lot, and the debt was going to fall due for repayment in 1961/2; they also knew that they were likely to need to borrow some more.

The particular object of the Fund's wrath was a clause in the Indo-Burmese trade agreement which committed the Indians to take an extra 150,000 tons of Burmese rice, paying for this out of the proceeds of any margin of *additional* Indian exports to Burma above the average level of the previous five years. In other words, the Burmese were promised a market for their rice if they agreed to import more Indian goods than they had done up till then. A barefaced piece of bilateralism, certainly: the IMF no doubt congratulated itself on having stamped on it in time. But people who are not devout worshippers of an economic doctrine, which was after all designed primarily to provide a set of decent rules to govern the commercial contests between developed capitalist countries, may wonder why such violent objection should be taken to a sensible scheme for raising the level of consumption and output in some undeveloped ones.

The IMF under the leadership of Mr. Per Jacobsson, the conservative Swedish economist who became its managing director in the middle 1950s, has been most active in smelling out heresies in trade policies in the underdeveloped world. His men move in with determination to snuff out the trouble before it has time to spread. It is a strange experience to see them at work, because they bring to it some of the spirit of a crusading order defending the true faith. They have a kind of moral self-confidence, which seems to belong to another century—certain that however painful the decisions which they force on poor nations, they are truly defending them, for their own sakes, against their evil natures. Usually, the issues on which the IMF asserts the primacy of its doctrines are so obscure to the ordinary person that he has not the intellectual patience to understand, and resent, its interventions in national policy. But every now and then there is an eruption, as for instance when the students in Rio de Janeiro came out on to the streets to demonstrate against the Monetary Fund. It so happened that in this case the issue had by then become involved in local politics, and justice was by no means all on the Brazilian government's side.

### Latin American Common Market

The problem that poor countries have when they try to push through these purely doctrinal obstacles erected by this "rich man's club" (as many of them call it) is seen most clearly in the attempt of the Latin American countries to create a regional trading bloc, within which they would exchange their products free of import restrictions and tariffs. As part of this scheme it was proposed in 1959 that Latin America should set up a "Payments Union" on the lines of the European Payments Union, which, until its demise at the end of 1958, played such a big part in keeping trade moving in Western Europe during a period of the 1950s when many of the national currencies were intermittently in trouble. The European Payments Union, with its system of credits for countries in payments difficulties, created a basis of financial security which made the nations of Europe ready to trade more freely with one another. They knew that if they ran into trouble because they were importing too much from their trading partners, they would be able to draw automatically on the pool of credits to which all the partners contributed. Governments were therefore willing to take some risks which they would otherwise have avoided, and this helped to bring about the tremendous expansion of intra-European trade during the 1950s. The essential point was the existence of a kind of insurance cover. It was not 100 per cent cover, but the presence of the European pool of credits did make governments feel that they were not going to be completely overwhelmed by sudden crises, if something went wrong in their calculations. They would have time to make the necessary adjustments in their policies without panic.

The European example has made a deep impression on Dr. Raul Prebisch, the head of the Economic Commission for Latin America (ECLA), and the originator of the whole idea of a Latin American Common Market. This remarkable man has somehow managed to build up a continent-wide political pressure group behind the idea. It has been most skilfully done. The Latin American states are by nature and tradition among the most particularist, parochial and devoted to the principle of *sacro egoismo*. To persuade them even to think along the lines of sacrificing some small portion of a national commercial interest for the sake of a greater good is a considerable achievement. It could not have happened without the emergence of a new *élite* of younger men to positions of power during recent years. And that has been made possible through a series of revolutions which in the 1950s toppled one government after another in South America. Prebisch's men, many of them ex-officials or trainees of ECLA in Santiago, have moved in. More important, they and their friends among the new generation of intellectuals have succeeded in creating an atmosphere in which it is now accepted that something radical must be done to stop the waste of the continent's resources, caused by the barriers to trade within Latin America. There is indeed a certain similarity between the work of Raul Prebisch and his coadjutors in America and that of Jean Monnet and his Committee for Action on European Unity in Europe. Both set out to create a high level pressure group, starting at the level of prime ministers, which was designed to induce the people who legislate and make big business decisions to take seriously a number of new ideas about the relationship between national and international interests. The appeal was not of a popular kind. In Europe its success initially was due to the carefully worked intellectual content of the schemes put forward. Only at a later stage did the idea of the Common Market begin to generate real popular interest. That stage has still to come in Latin America.

The initiative of Dr. Prebisch and his small group, working through the Economic Commission for Latin America, has gradually brought the governments of the region to a point where they have accepted, as a cardinal principle of policy, that they must trade more with one another, and cease to regard their short-term national interests in commerce as always absolutely paramount. This may not seem to be very much; but it is vastly more than has ever been achieved before. Hitherto the channels of trade of the Latin American countries have seemed to be almost deliberately designed to bypass one another. The value of the goods which they buy and sell amongst themselves represents less than 10 per cent of the total trade of Latin America. There are of course historical reasons here, as well as in Asia and Africa, why goods flow outwards from the coasts to Europe and North America, rather than inland. The export trade was originally developed by foreigners, Europeans and North Americans, with their own markets in mind. The specialized production of crops, like cocoa and coffee, or minerals, like copper and tin, was in any case unsuitable for any large-scale development of trade on a regional basis. The markets were in the rich countries outside. And because the trading relationship with the developed countries was well-established and worked smoothly—sea transport being in any case cheaper than opening up new roads into the hinterland—imports into the undeveloped countries, even of goods which they could have supplied to one another, tended to move along the same trade routes.

Now, however, with the new effort in these regions to establish a much more diversified output, including the whole range of advanced industrial products, in which the undeveloped countries are bound initially—and probably for some time—to be at a competitive disadvantage, there is urgent need to start trade moving in fresh directions. The argument for strong regional trading groups ought to appeal to the donors of aid in the Western countries on grounds of economy alone. Plainly it is going to be a lot cheaper to finance industrialization if the new industries in the undeveloped countries can be planned from the start to reach the most efficient size—and this means in most instances that they must be able to look beyond their national markets. Apart from the waste of resources which goes on now, because these nations do not exchange their surpluses with one another, there is the vast potential waste that comes of setting up new high-cost industries in markets that are too small to allow them to pay their way. This is not just a vague menace for the future: it is already happening on a considerable scale. It is tragic to find Burma, for example, spending its substance on setting up a steel plant, which cannot at this stage or for some time be large enough to be economic. The Burmese could concentrate their investment on more urgent needs, if they were only prepared to see that the wisest course over the next few years would be to make a deal with India or someone else to supply them with steel, in exchange for rice or some other commodity which Burma produces cheaply. The time will come when Burma will need a big steel plant of its own, but it is absurd to give it any priority at all for some years yet.

### Doctrinal Battle with Monetary Fund

It is strange that the leading Western countries, nurtured in the traditions of the international division of labour, gave no encouragement whatsoever to Dr. Prebisch's scheme when it was first proposed. And as it took practical shape the coldness turned to active hostility. Once again it was the International Monetary Fund which took to the field, clothed in the familiar shining armour of unblemished economic principle. The proposal for a regional payments scheme which would induce the nations taking part in it to allow each other more freedom to trade with one another—on the European model of the early 1950s—provoked its sharpest hostility, and the IMF set to work to mobilize opposition to it among the Latin American countries. It soon developed into a personal struggle between two men—Prebisch of ECLA and Jacobsson of the Fund. Both are university professors of economics, characteristically passionate and intransigent in the manner of such people; Prebisch, an Argentinian teaching at the University of Buenos Aires, was the man who brought Keynes's message to Latin America in the 1930s—the message that the economic misery of slumps can be avoided by intelligent management—while Jacobsson's economics were largely shaped by the pre-1914 world. This world, in which there was no escape from the rigours of the gold standard, in which sinners (those who ran a deficit on their balance of payments) were automatically punished, and the virtuous (the ones with a surplus) were able to indulge in expansion on a full stomach, is really the Fund's ideal. Jacobsson's watchword is "discipline"; the impression that he leaves on one is a little reminiscent of a certain kind of schoolmaster arguing in favour of corporal punishment—"*We* had to take it and it did us good, so don't let us be soft and ruin the new generation." One of his main fears seems to be that economic aid too generously given to the undeveloped countries will simply entrench them in a number of nasty habits.

Although the World Bank and the IMF occupy two sides of the same corner building in Washington, crossing from one to the other feels like moving into an entirely different world. It so happens that the building is poorly insulated, and if one makes the transition through the sole connecting door on the top storey, at the end of a lonely corridor, one is liable to get a warning electric shock of quite some strength on turning the handle. The symbolic significance only strikes one afterwards, inside the office of the managing director of the Monetary Fund. There is a kind of bear-like Scandinavian bonhommie about Per Jacobsson which tends to mislead at first. His ferocious attachment to certain esoteric principles, most of them of an *a priori* character, soon emerges. The whole new aspect of the undeveloped countries of today—the new humanitarian approach which will not let the problem of too many poor people solve itself by starvation and disease, the new technology which makes it possible for everyone to live decently, and so on—all this is just elbowed aside into the old shaky categories of traditional economic theory. Rarely have I had the feeling that economics had quite so much in common with an old-fashioned version of Calvinism. Jacobsson has considerable talents as a journalist and an orator, and presents his case with *panache*. There is also a faint professorial bumble in his manner —and a certain squareness. Square glasses set on a square head, sitting squarely between two broad shoulders. The rigidity vies (successfully for me) with a certain conversational charm. "What would you suggest, Mr. Jacobsson, to help the undeveloped countries to move forward faster?" "Well, the main thing is to stabilize their currencies."

After this meeting in Washington I was less surprised to

43

encounter the eccentric objections advanced in Latin America by the IMF's representatives against the proposed regional payments scheme—that this was a move which would jeopardize world currency freedom. Having at last achieved a system of convertible currencies on a world-wide scale, it must be a retrograde step, so it was argued, to introduce a new arrangement in which some credits and debits would be payable only in a restricted number of currencies, and not convertible into dollars. And was it really worth while setting up this elaborate scheme just to deal with a tiny segment of Latin American trade, amounting to barely one-tenth of the total? It was this argument which seemed to bring Dr. Prebisch closest to a feeling of indignation during the struggle over his scheme for a Latin American payments union in 1959/60. He is a person of great aplomb, knowing too much about political realities to get easily worked up by opposition to his plans. But he is also sufficient of a university professor to be annoyed by what he regards as intellectually hollow criticism of a serious project. "Surely it is clear", he said when I discussed the point with him in Santiago, "that we do not need the new arrangements to finance the trade that *already* exists, but to support the much larger increase that we are trying to bring about." Characteristically, Jacobsson had omitted the dynamic element from his economic thinking. The aim that has been set out by the Economic Commission for Latin America, is a rather more than tenfold increase in intra-Latin American trade by 1975. This is almost certainly too sanguine—though it has to be observed that even if it were achieved, the proportion of intra-regional trade by that date would, according to the projections made by the economists of ECLA, still be only a little over 40 per cent of the total trade of Latin America. In continental Western Europe today it is nearer 50 per cent. On the face of it, it would seem that Latin America with its variety of climates and natural resources would offer, in the long run, much more scope for the exchange of goods than the compact industrial area of Western Europe.

But the Western Europeans have one overwhelming advantage: they are used to trading with one another. It is this kind of habit that Prebisch is hoping, with the aid of all kinds of artificial inducements, to build up in Latin America. Without these special inducements, nothing much is likely to happen in a short enough time to make any real difference to the problem of economic development in the 1960s and '70s. The political decision is primary; that was the experience of the European Common Market. After the political base has been firmly established, the movement towards economic integration develops a momentum of its own. Businessmen begin to act as if the projected trading system were already in existence, shaping their investment plans to take the maximum advantage of it.

## *Personality of ECLA*

In Latin America the cultural affinity of the member countries should make it easier to work towards a commercial union —much easier than in Asia for example. They can all understand each other in Spanish or Portuguese and many of their ideas have been shaped by the same traditions. They even have the experience of their liberation from Spanish imperialism in common. This sense of belonging together in some historic experience, combined with the ability to communicate readily, without the intervention of an opaque cultural barrier, can be a powerful aid—as we have seen in Europe since the war— in advancing through the complicated and delicate negotiations that must precede the formation of a common market. Unfortunately, the Latin-American nations are, rather like the West Europeans again, an enormously quarrelsome lot. There are injuries done by Chile to Bolivia and Peru three-quarters of a century ago, or by Brazil to Paraguay, whose memory is richly preserved, so that they can be resented with all the freshness of newly spilled blood as soon as the appropriate circumstances arise. Western Europe does seem to have got past this stage of primitive and unforgiving national resentments, at any rate since the last war. Perhaps the holocaust was too great to make such emotions appear tenable any longer. Whatever it is that causes the change, the Latin Americans have not managed it yet. It is only necessary for Peru to buy a second-hand cruiser from Britain, as it did in 1959, for relations with its neighbours to grow thick and explosive with mutual vituperation. There is a kind of permanent undercover arms race. Only rarely does a government have the strength of character to stand up against it: the honourable exceptions are Mexico and Costa Rica, both of whom boast about the meagreness of their military budgets and of the money that they have been able to divert to more useful purposes.

This atmosphere of national strife and international affinity helps to explain the rather rhetorical mood in which ECLA approaches the task of spreading the gospel of the Latin American Common Market—a mood which is, it seems, particularly obnoxious to the empirical Anglo-Saxons. The British, usually in concert with the United States, have been consistently the bitterest critics within the United Nations of the doings of the Economic Commission for Latin America. It is, in fact, easy to pick holes in some of ECLA's more grandiose plans and projections. This is particularly true of the Latin American Common Market. But what the northern critics fail to recognize is that in the Latin American context a regional commission of the United Nations plays a quite different role from anywhere else. It has some of the character of a political opposition —albeit a responsible opposition, in the Anglo-Saxon sense, which is an unknown phenomenon in this part of the world.

Aside from the Church, there is in these societies no independent centre of influence and authority outside the government of the day or, in certain circumstances where this government is severely weakened, outside the group of conspirators who are banding together to form the government of tomorrow. There are none of the independent and highly organized citizens' groups, exercising power through sustained moral pressure, which make the very stuff of West European and North American democracy. Even the universities in Latin America have been debauched by state power. To some extent Dr. Prebisch and his organization are consciously trying to fill this gap; certainly, their suggestions would have no practical impact at all if they did not present them as *grandes idées*, indeed occasionally ideas that are slightly over life-size. It is no use some British civil servant telling them that they ought to be content to start with small craft and give more attention to navigating them; their business, they make it clear, is to launch an intellectual battleship.

This can be rather irritating. Practical men from the temperate regions of the north feel that these Latin Americans would be more likely to get something useful done if they stated their aims a little more modestly. In spite of the Treaty of Montevideo, signed in February 1960, the chances of establishing a fully-fledged free trade area in a matter of twelve years, which would leave only the strongest and most efficient industrial enterprises to survive the continent-wide competitive struggle, are not to be rated very high. Indeed, Dr. Prebisch, who is nothing if not a realist, has unobtrusively introduced a small but significant device which will do a great deal to mitigate the rigours of the system. The agreed objective for the present is not the total elimination of tariffs between the countries of the Latin American region, but only the tariffs on those goods in which there is already a substantial amount of intra-regional trade.* To begin with, therefore, a small proportion of all imports and exports will be affected, since regional trade is under 10 per cent of the total. Even as the proportion increases, it will be possible for a country with a few vital industries, which it is determined to protect completely, to maintain very high tariffs against competitive products from other members of the free trade area, while cutting the rest of its tariffs down to zero. There is an understanding that over the twelve years *average* tariffs in intra-Latin American trade will be reduced to 5 per cent; but that will still allow plenty of scope for major national interests to be defended against commercial infiltration from any too enterprising Latin American neighbours.

The important practical point, however, is that the Latin American countries commit themselves to act together in a positive way over a period of time to increase their trade by the grant of commercial favours to one another. Plainly, the Brazilian government is not going to let its large but not very efficient textile industry be destroyed by competition from other Latin American industries, nor will Argentina be allowed to export cheap beef in quantities which would make difficulties for cattle farmers in their home markets elsewhere in Latin America. The kind of result which the Latin American Free Trade Area may achieve is to help the relatively efficient

* Montevideo Treaty, Article 7

Chilean steel industry to grow rather faster than it otherwise would or to give a further fillip to Mexico's light engineering and durable consumer goods industries by providing them with a lot of new customers in markets to the south. It is, however, too much to expect that Latin American governments will become quite suddenly so infused with the notion of the common good that they will quietly let all of the plums of the development programme—the steel mills, the chemical plants, the motor factories, and perhaps the atomic reactors—go to some country which happens to be able to show higher standards of efficiency and lower production costs than the others. There is bound to be a demand for "fair shares"; and fairness is usually the enemy of effective investment. For industry, specially in the early phases of development, tends to operate on the principle of concentration: by putting up a new factory in an area where a number of other factories already exist, the businessman tries to assure himself of the essential industrial services that may not be available elsewhere, and also of a supply of labour which is not quite raw.

## Lesson from Central America

The difficulties of making any kind of equitable distribution of national benefits in the development of a region containing several countries appears in an acute form in a subsidiary scheme of the Latin American Common Market—the Central American Integration Project. This, again at the inspiration of ECLA, aims to bring together the five republics inhabiting the area between Mexico and Panama—Guatemala, El Salvador, Honduras, Nicaragua and Costa Rica—in a joint programme of development. The combined population of the five countries is around ten million, and there would be little scope for the establishment of modern large-scale industries if they had to rely on an outlet in any single national market. It has been agreed in principle, therefore, that investors in new industries shall be guaranteed freedom of trade for their products throughout the whole region. In this way, it is hoped, foreign capital may be attracted into Central America and, perhaps even more important, some of the rich Central Americans themselves may be induced to invest more money in productive enterprises within the region.

However, trouble has arisen almost at once because one country, El Salvador, is sufficiently in advance of the others—in terms of business sophistication, labour discipline and sheer talent—to attract far more than its due share of the money that is going. Travelling along the new stretch of the Pan American Highway from San Salvador airport into the capital, one passes a dozen plants of substantial size, all very recently built. Their neighbours, in Guatemala and Honduras, refer to the Salvadorans as "the Scotsmen of Central America"—and sometimes by rather more derogatory names. They are afraid that El Salvador will sweep the board, and in order to safeguard their own interests they have insisted that if one country obtains the right to construct an "integration project" (i.e. an industrial venture whose products will be given the privilege of free entry into the whole of the Central American market) then no further integrated enterprise may be allotted to it, until each of the other four countries have been allotted an integration project of their own—and so on in a series of rounds of five projects at a time. The bustling industrialists of El Salvador say with some justice that this attempt to deal out a lot of new industrial enterprises between countries as if they were cards out of a pack makes nonsense of the whole idea of integration as a means of attaining higher efficiency and more rapid industrial progress. Very few investors, they point out, would be eager to invest their money in setting up new industries in countries quite so undeveloped as Nicaragua or Honduras.

There is no easy way out of the conflict between fair shares and the realities of investment—except by way of a political decision on the part of the national governments to put the interests of the whole region first. But the modest attempts that have been made so far to achieve some measure of political collaboration between the five countries, even in dealing with such everyday administrative matters as passports, are not encouraging. The five agreed at one stage, as part of the effort to stimulate tourist travel among themselves, to reduce passport formalities and make do with a simple tourist card for any citizen of Central America. But pretty soon Costa Rica was being accused by Nicaragua of abusing the tourist facility in order to collect a small expeditionary corps of "invaders" and send them into Nicaragua. The Somoza dictatorship in backward Nicaragua is particularly unpopular with the more advanced Costa Ricans, who pride themselves on their high standards of education and their political freedom. The matter developed into an angry dispute in which all five countries soon became involved; and in the end not only were the passports reintroduced, but also an improved system of checks, so that the unfortunate Central American had to obtain a visa as well, before he could move from one petty republic to another.

There is indeed a certain unreality about the way in which the enthusiasts talk about the progress of the Central American Integration Project. Enormous trouble is being taken over the preparation of a common external tariff against imports coming into any of the five countries from the rest of the world; but hardly anything has been done to reduce the barriers to trade between the countries themselves. They preach integration but they practise isolation; and all but a few *illuminati* are entrenched in an extreme provincial variety of nationalism. The best hope lies in the fact that a few of these intellectuals of the younger generation, usually economists, have managed to acquire some political influence and even a little power, while the businessmen of the region are now beginning for the first time to meet each other in conferences organized under the Integration Project and to recognize that they have a number of problems in common. But the political will which is required to give momentum to a revolutionary scheme of this kind is weak. It seems to be especially difficult to persuade an undeveloped small nation to take a long view of the advantages to be obtained through a modest sacrifice of its immediate national interests. It is rather like asking people who have not got beyond the perspective of a village to approach the problems of some large-scale communal endeavour in the spirit of big city folk. Perhaps the most serious weakness is that there is no metropolitan experience at all anywhere in Central America —only a series of overblown provincial cities, each afraid of being deflated by the loss of this or that small privilege.

Yet even here something will undoubtedly be gained by persuading nations to bargain over the exchange of commercial advantages in the course of industrial development. Central America is particularly interesting because the weaknesses appear as if they had been put under a showcase made of magnifying-glass. They suggest that the answer to the problem of trade between backward countries does not lie in a fully-fledged system of integration and a common market. It requires a high degree of sophistication to keep hammering away patiently at the modest and unspectacular, but politically sensitive, tasks which have made the European Common Market a reality. There is no evidence that the experiment of voluntary association in a tight economic unit, without forming a political association first, has much prospect of success at this stage in the underdeveloped world.

## Rules for Rich Nations

The trouble is that the only respectable way in which nations are allowed to give commercial favours to one another nowadays is by going through the form of creating a common market or a free trade area. These are the methods laid down in the post-war international treaty on the rules of commerce—the General Agreement on Tariffs and Trade (GATT). The GATT's chief aim is to achieve equality of treatment for the exports of all nations: it sets out to prevent anyone from applying different tariffs on the same goods because they come from different countries. The rule is: one article—one tariff, regardless of the supplier. The only exceptions recognized, after a sharp dispute with Americans at the time when the GATT was being negotiated just after the war, are the old colonial preference systems, of which the most important is British Imperial Preference. This gives free entry without import duty to most Commonwealth products imported into Britain and a lower rate of duty than the normal on British exports to a number of Commonwealth countries. It was indeed just this kind of exclusive arrangement, typical of the much resented discrimination practised during the 1930s, that the GATT was dedicated to root out. Although the British Commonwealth was reluctantly permitted to maintain the trading agreements already established among its members, it was laid down that no *additional* tariff preferences of any kind were to be introduced from the date of the signing of the treaty onwards.

However, since one of the GATT's aims is also to push down the general level of tariffs in the postwar world, it could not set its face entirely against customs' unions between nations uniting to eliminate their tariffs against one another altogether. This of course involved discrimination too—since it meant that nations outside the ring had to export over a tariff barrier while those inside did not—but it was regarded as virtuous discrimination. That was because it led to complete freedom of trade, though within a limited geographical area.

On the whole this line of approach seems a sensible way of dealing with the trade of the developed countries. These countries account for much the greater part of the world trade, and so it was reasonable for the GATT to concentrate its attention first on them. The commercial bullying and discrimination of the 1930s led to great bitterness between the nations and helped to exacerbate the already explosive situation in prewar Europe; the GATT had good cause to be anxious to establish a recognized code of good conduct which would prevent a repetition of such international strains. As originally conceived, the organization itself was to be an agency of the United Nations, to be called the International Trade Organization (ITO). But owing to various difficulties, mainly with the United States, the agreement on the ITO was never ratified and the GATT was established in its place—with an *ad hoc* status and a somewhat more independent role.

It is nevertheless housed with a decided air of permanence in a charming 18th century country mansion tucked away in its own grounds on the edge of the Palais des Nations in Geneva. People sometimes have difficulty in finding their way to it. For all its modesty, it does manage to exercise considerable moral authority. That is mainly because the powerful trading nations have come to recognize that life would be much more awkward if the GATT did not exist. Of course it is no fun for any government to have its commercial doings criticized in public, and then be forced to defend itself before an international forum against a charge that its actions have been guided by the too selfish pursuit of national advantage at the expense of others. All this is extremely healthy, and the world certainly benefits from the long and tedious sessions which are held annually by the GATT, usually at Geneva—for it is only by being ready to be tedious over long periods that the enormously complicated factual material, which often underlies one of these familiar trade wrangles, can be sorted out.

But all this has nothing to do with the question of how the undeveloped countries ought to organize their trade among themselves in order to force the pace of economic development. That was never even considered when the rules of the GATT were being drawn up. The problem was barely identified in the intellectual landscape of the 1940s. At that time the industrial nations of Europe, propped up like so many giant corpses, filled the horizon while the primary producing countries, commanding high scarcity values for the commodities which they sold in world markets, had never had it so good. It was only in the 1950s that the profound economic weakness of the primary producing countries in an age of rapid technological advance became clear. But by then the rules of the GATT had become firmly fixed.

## Imperial Preference Model

The case is like that of the International Monetary Fund— another powerful organization whose shape and prejudices were fixed too early, and whose rules were tailor-made to meet the problems of the developed countries. GATT, however, is rather less of a busybody than the IMF when it actually comes to dealing with the practical problems of the undeveloped countries. It is more ready to turn a merciful blind eye on minor deviations from the rules, and even to feel that the poor must, after all, be allowed some latitude in looking after themselves. But it cannot tolerate a major disobedience. And it happens that what is probably the most promising instrument of all for stimulating trade among the undeveloped countries at the moment has been outlawed by the GATT international code. This is the technique, discussed above in connection with the British Commonwealth system of Imperial Preference, of exchanging special trading favours, particularly lower tariffs,

E                                  53

among a group of countries with the aim of creating new markets for one another at the expense of outsiders.

Although the whole basis of the Imperial Preference system has become archaic today, with the profound changes in the economic structure of the most important nations of the Commonwealth, it did in its time serve one profoundly important purpose. By assuring countries of a favoured outlet for their exports, at a time when export markets were terribly uncertain, it induced them to buy more from their partners in trade than they would otherwise have risked doing. There is the same virtue in a bilateral trade agreement: it limits the risk of foreign exchange losses, and so permits goods to move between countries which would otherwise be paralysed by their foreign exchange shortage. I do not suggest that this is a satisfactory permanent way of trading. But like the Imperial Preference system in the 1930s or the postwar system of liberalizing trade among the countries of Western Europe (at the expense of the United States), the technique can, if it is used intelligently over a limited period of time, act as a powerful stimulus to the production and exchange of goods.

Indeed, if the matter is examined more closely, this preferential trading system is the hard core of the scheme for the Latin American Common Market. As was shown earlier, the Latin Americans are not committed in practice to a fully-fledged free trade system among themselves. What they are doing is to offer each other duty-free entry for a certain number of products, on which they charge tariffs to outsiders. There are also specific arrangements for negotiating the exchange of "preferences" within the group during the first twelve years of the life of the treaty; these are tariff concessions which countries are able to revoke if the bargain does not suit. However, the important point is that the Latin Americans treat what they are doing, and are able to present it convincingly to the rest of the world, as part of a great regional free trade plan; there is enough political and cultural cohesion among the countries concerned to make this treatment acceptable.

Unfortunately, in Asia there is nothing comparable. This is one of the first things which strikes a visitor to the Economic Commission for Asia and the Far East (ECAFE) in Bangkok —the organization which fills the same role as ECLA in Latin

America. It is not just the difference between the bracing hill climate of Santiago, ECLA's headquarters, and the hazy heat of the tropical rice plain which encompasses Bangkok. One soon becomes aware that the Asians are at some disadvantage compared with the Latin Americans, because they have no common language of their own: their *lingua franca* nowadays is English. And that fact is only a reflection of deeper divisions. The Indians and the Japanese, who provide most of the sophistication and technical expertise in the Bangkok organization, are deeply distrusted by the other nations. These active go-getters seem to evoke a kind of wondering disdain in the relaxed Thais, which is shared by many of their neighbours in the South-East Asia peninsula. They are profoundly different peoples.

There are great areas of mutual incomprehension, formed over many centuries of hostility and cultural separation. Still today, the strife between India and Pakistan, the fight between the two Chinas, the violent bickering among the successor states of Indo-China, and so on, make it impossible to achieve a sense of community of the kind that would allow ECAFE to contemplate a scheme on the lines of the Latin American Free Trade Area. What has happened since the war is that instead of breaking down trade barriers, more of them have been erected as new national frontiers have been carved out of the old colonial empires of the Western powers in South Asia.

## *Trade Bargains in Asia*

It is no use trying to solve the problem of trade in Asia by some grand comprehensive formula. Progress can only be made by piecemeal bargaining among countries which have been convinced that there is a prospect of making solid gains by trusting one another—to a limited extent. The aim should be an arrangement which will encourage the Burmese, for example, to take more Indian manufactures, even though they may be of poorer quality than the equivalent Japanese or Western products, in return for an assured market in India for more Burmese exports of rice. Perhaps the worst waste at present is caused by the fears of the food surplus countries, which could produce a lot more for export, but are deterred by the efforts of their neighbours in Asia to achieve self-sufficiency in agriculture. The simplest way of dealing with the matter is by means of bilateral trade agreements—and these happen to be the object of intense disapproval nowadays in the West. It is only when one sups with the devil or the Soviets that one is allowed to use this particular long spoon.

Leaving aside the doctrinal objections, there is the real danger that a series of competitive trade agreements, arrived at between pairs of underdeveloped countries in Asia, would produce more commercial strife and political quarrels than useful business. That is why the United Nations regional bodies like ECLA and ECAFE are so important. What is required is an organization which is expert enough and sufficiently well informed to make a job of coordinating a series of bilateral deals. It also needs to provide a permanent forum where the inevitable trade wrangles that occur even between friendly countries can be sorted out with the maximum amount of factual information. The issues are often tediously technical. This kind of forum where nations have to justify their actions before a jury of their peers can, as the GATT has demonstrated in its long and little publicized annual conferences, be quite effectual. At the least, it puts a curb on too frequent cheating in international trade.

But the first step is to get a new set of trade rules endorsed by the GATT to meet the needs of the undeveloped countries. The Western nations must be prepared to encourage new forms of preferential trading arrangements among the Asian and African countries instead of standing aside in an attitude of stern disapproval—or worse still, sending out their emissaries in the international organizations, like itinerant Grand Inquisitors, to put a stop to all this wickedness.[1]

*Note*

1. Gunnar Myrdal, "Economic Theory and Under-developed Regions", points out the complacent assumption of the orthodox theory of international trade that "trade starts a movement towards income equalization, while instead a quite normal result of unhampered trade between two countries, of which one is industrialized and the other under-developed, is the initiation of a cumulative process towards the impoverishment and stagnation of the latter."

# CHAPTER 5

# COUNTING THE COST

EVEN if the undeveloped countries make a successful effort to stimulate trade among themselves, by means of preferential arrangements and other discriminatory devices, at present outlawed, they are still going to need more capital from outside. How much more? There are two problems that have to be distinguished before an attempt can be made to answer the question. There is first of all the need for foreign capital which arises because a country is too poor to save enough to meet its own investment needs. In this case the role of economic aid from abroad is simply to conduct a holding operation, while the national income of the country rises to the point where its own savings will support an investment effort on a scale sufficient to ensure a steady rise in the standard of living. According to the evidence available, which is very sketchy, societies at a primitive economic level save something of the order of 5 per cent of their national income. If the population of such a society begins to grow, because the usual holocaust of new-born children is reduced with the help of a few imported drugs or because, with a modicum of medical care, people begin to stretch their lives out a bit longer than the wretchedly short existence to which they have been accustomed, the 5 per cent saving will not suffice to create the new productive assets that are needed to support the extra people at the same standard of living. Primitive agriculture using a limited stock of land tends to show a steeply diminishing return for additional man-hours of work. Income per head falls.

What is required then is a rise in the level of investment from around 5 per cent to 10–12 per cent of the national income.[1] This is a very rough sort of calculation, and it is based on the following rule of thumb. The conventional reckoning of economists nowadays is that on average productive capital assets, if they are properly worked, will yield extra output roughly equal in value to one-third of the original cost of the assets each year.

Or to put it another way, there is a normal three-year cycle of reproduction: if people could, by some miracle, devote the whole of their output to the creation of new capital assets—meanwhile relying for manna from heaven for their daily food—they could double their productive capacity every three years. However, as we have seen, primitive societies consume as much as 95 per cent of their output merely in the process of maintaining their low living standards, before the population explosion hits them. The 5 per cent left over has no sort of hoisting power. The reason why economists think in terms of a target of 10–12 per cent for investment is that they are looking for an output increase of 4 per cent a year. Of this about 2 per cent would be absorbed by the annual increase in population—rather more in some regions of the underdeveloped world—and the remaining 2 per cent would go partly to raise the level of investment each year and partly to improve the standard of living.

Plainly if the whole or the greater part of the residual 2 per cent could be devoted to investment, the share of investment in the national income would continue to rise fast: if living standards were absolutely static, it could be pushed up from 10 per cent of the national income to 20 per cent in less than five years, with production rising at an accelerating pace all the time. That is what the communists do when they go in for a policy of compulsory saving designed to hold down consumption and push investment. The method requires a watertight system of controls over the behaviour of consumers, and this means, first of all, the dispossession of the property-owning classes and, second, the destruction of any independent workers' organization which might succeed in forcing up wages against the wishes of the planners. Without total control, it is inevitable that a portion of any increase in the output of a poor society will go into clothing and feeding people better and in providing some extra amenities for the new classes with money—notably the businessmen and the skilled workers. The shift of population from the country to the towns in the course of industrialization will, in any case, result in some increase in the demand for food and consumer goods, unless this is actively prevented by rationing and controls over all supplies.

This is one reason why it is hard to push up the rate of saving rapidly in an undeveloped country which is not subject to a totalitarian system. India has during the 1950s achieved a savings ratio of 7–8 per cent of the national income, and the aim is to step it up steadily year by year from now on. In the meanwhile, the Indians have been able to maintain their rate of investment at a higher level than their domestic savings, because the equivalent of another 3 per cent of the national income has been supplied in the form of loans and grants from abroad. Before the foreign aid arrived, they maintained themselves by running down the country's foreign exchange reserves; but these funds saved up in the past, before anyone had begun to think seriously about development, were soon exhausted. By such expedients India brought the level of investment to 10–11 per cent of national income by the late 1950s, while enjoying some slight rise in the standard of living at the same time. If the whole of the additional investment had depended on increased domestic savings, there would have been no room for even the small increase in consumer incomes which has occurred.

## Saving is Not Enough

However, providing a supplement to domestic saving is not the sole function of foreign aid. If it were, then it would be a matter of indifference in what form the foreign aid arrived. Donations of food and consumer goods would be just as effective a way of speeding development as providing capital equipment from abroad to go into new factories. This introduces the second aspect of the problem of the capital requirements of the undeveloped countries—the gap which has to be filled is not simply a lack of domestic resources caused by inadequate savings, it is a specific need for certain types of capital goods and materials, which cannot physically be produced at home. A nation may pinch and scrape and save heroically, and yet be unable to acquire the things that it needs to carry through a programme of industrial investment. Theoretically it should be possible to solve this problem by a sufficient measure of austerity: food, clothing or anything else denied to the domestic consumer is sold at knockdown prices abroad,

59

and the proceeds used to buy capital goods—always assuming that the price cuts do not involve an even bigger loss of earnings on existing export trade. But in practice a new export business of any substance cannot be acquired quite so easily just by suddenly slashing prices. And even if it could, the political and human obstacles to such a policy, carried to the extremes of sacrifice that would be required to make the necessary impact on world export markets, would remain. One school of economists has attempted to equate self-sustaining growth with the achievement of a given level of domestic saving. In the long run, when there are no technological obstacles to converting resources saved at home into an equivalent export-earning or import-saving capacity, the equation works; but in the all-important short run, covering the critical years of growth, savings by themselves do not suffice.

This is one of the difficulties of the Indian development plan. The planners are hoping to increase the proportion of savings by close to 1 per cent of the national income each year during the Third Five Year Plan; so that starting at 8 per cent, it will have got well past the 72 per cent minimum by 1965. This means in practice more than doubling the absolute amount of money saved, because the Indian national income itself will have increased substantially over the five year period. The Indians are, it is true, thinking in more ambitious terms than the 2 per cent minimum rate of increase in *per capita* national income, which I mentioned earlier; they are aiming at an increase of 3 per cent per head, starting from a level which is one of the lowest in the world.[2] (That means a 5 per cent annual rise in the national income, allowing for the 2 per cent addition to the population each year.) But even if the target were more modest, while the effort to increase savings were just as heroic, that would not ensure that by the end of the Third Five Year Plan the Indians would be in a position to pay out of their export earnings for the considerable imports of capital equipment that would still be required, as well as meet the debt service charges on the large sums borrowed in the preceding years.*

It is therefore impossible to put a definite term to the period during which developing countries will continue to need foreign economic aid to meet the deficit in their balance of

* See Chapter 3, pp. 28 *et seq.*

payments, even after their rate of saving has reached a respectable level. It was shown in Chapter 3 that the need for such economic assistance to India is unlikely to be eliminated before the 1970s. In the two most promising Latin American countries, Mexico and Brazil, the gap in the balance of payments—or more precisely, that part of it which cannot be met by foreign investment on ordinary commercial terms—ought with luck to be closed earlier, say by the second half of the 1960s. The chances of doing this will be greatly improved if the Latin American plan for a free trade area goes ahead and offers the Mexicans and Brazilians a growing outlet for their exports of manufactured goods.

This timetable is closely relevant to any calculation of the amount of economic aid that will be required in the 1960s for the undeveloped countries as a whole. If, say, by the mid-1960s Mexico has made sufficient progress to be able to sustain a high rate of growth, without a balance of payments deficit no larger than can be supported by normal private investment, then there should be that much more aid available for the new countries which will be joining the queue on the threshold of rapid economic development. The hope is that Mexico will by then be in the position that Japan, for example, is today, and that Brazil will not be far behind. But it seems inevitable, however successful the Mexicans and Brazilians may be, that the queue of special cases, needing generous help to be brought over the threshold, will increase much faster than the number of those passing through, to move forward under their own momentum on the other side.

### Three Main Claimants

Perhaps we can obtain an idea of the order of magnitude of the financial problem by looking at some of the outstanding needs for additional development capital that lie immediately ahead. The three largest and most obvious claimants are the countries mentioned earlier,* India, Brazil and Mexico. What makes them such strong claimants is, first, that they have a class of entrepreneurs and modern industrial managers, who are

* See Chapter 1, page 6

capable of using capital efficiently in productive enterprise, and secondly, that they have governments which are putting large resources into the creation of the expensive infrastructure of a modern industrial society. The mixture of public and private enterprise differs from country to country, and so does the relative efficiency of the public and private sectors; but there is sufficient of each in all three of them to offer the promise of dynamic development, once capital is made available. Moreover, these countries account for a significant part of the population of the underdeveloped world: India is almost half of non-communist Asia, and Mexico and Brazil together contain half of the people in Latin America.

There is nothing of either comparable size or comparable promise to be found in Africa. The settler-dominated communities, like Algeria and Rhodesia—both underdeveloped and both capable of very rapid economic growth—might be thought to be exceptions. But the primary consideration here is how to recreate European living conditions for European settlers: the effect on the native people is secondary. It is to be observed, too, that the natives will be able to count on the considerable benefits, which rub off on to them from the active, confident and expanding European community in their midst, generously sustained by investment funds from its mother-country, only so long as they are prepared to accept a certain kind of political bargain. If the non-European majority were to take full political control, foreign capital would almost certainly move out along with a lot of white people. For these reasons I regard Rhodesia and Algeria as highly uncertain, as well as highly untypical portions of the underdeveloped world.

India's need for assistance from abroad to meet the foreign exchange deficit during the Third Five Year Plan, 1961/5, is estimated at about $1,100m. a year, exclusive of aid in the form of large consignments of American surplus food supplies. During the 1950s the Indians were able to cover part of the sudden big increase in their import bill, which occurred when the Second Five Year Plan got under way, partly by using up their foreign exchange reserves and partly by obtaining short-term credits from their foreign suppliers. They will not be able to depend on either of these expedients to any extent in the future: the foreign exchange reserve is now very low, and India's capacity to take on any new short-term credits will be limited by its ability to pay back this expensive type of loan. At best, a fresh lot of short-term credits will be made available by India's creditors to help pay off the instalments on the old ones as they fall due. In this way the Indians, like a man who keeps on paying back an overdraft to his bank and then overdrawing again, will be able to convert money which was originally supplied as temporary accommodation into the equivalent of a long-term loan.

But none of this will help to finance the buying of any new goods and services for the Third Five Year Plan—only to stretch out payments for things already supplied under the Second Five Year Plan. All told, the funds received by India in long-term credits and grants, other than American surplus food, during the late 1950s came to around $600m. a year. The extra amount which is required to sustain the higher rate of investment in the development of Indian industry during the next phase is, therefore, some $500m. a year, for five years.

The problem of estimating capital needs is not so readily definable for either Brazil or Mexico. There is no comprehensive plan of development, in the Indian sense, and so we must fall back on guesses about the amount of external capital that would be required to achieve the rapid accumulation of productive capital which would lead after a few years to economic independence, with the promise of a steadily rising standard of living. It may seem at first sight that both of these countries are already doing pretty well, without being buttressed by any special measures of foreign aid. Their national incomes have been rising at a rate of between 4 and 5 per cent a year during most of the 1950s. This is, however, less impressive than it looks at first, for the population is growing at a rate of some $2\frac{1}{2}$ per cent per annum in Brazil and 3 per cent in Mexico. Income per head in recent years has been increasing at barely 2 per cent a year.

This compares with the Indian target of a 3 per cent annual increase in *per capita* income. Admittedly, both Brazil and Mexico start from a level of *per capita* income today which is three to four times as high as the Indian. But if, alternatively, comparison is made with the performance of communist countries, like Yugoslavia, whose income per head is nearer to the Latin

American standard, the rate of progress in Brazil and Mexico does not look very fast. And the reason is not far to seek: the level of investment is lower than in Yugoslavia and in the Soviet Bloc countries as a whole.

## Brazilian Investment

In Brazil the proportion of the national income devoted to investment fell during the 1950s, and the rate at which the national income itself was growing fell off at the same time. In the period from 1949 to 1953 *per capita* income rose by an average of 4 per cent each year—more than double the rate of growth in the late 1950s. Admittedly, this rapid accumulation of wealth in the earlier period owed something to the accident of high world coffee prices; that made the Brazilians get rich quicker then they would otherwise have done, and equally, the drop in the world coffee market from the mid-1950s onwards made them poorer, through no fault of their own. But it was less the direct effect of the loss of foreign earnings than its indirect influence on the distribution of income within the country which has the decisive effect on the Brazilian rate of growth. So long as Brazil was raking in the windfall export income from high coffee prices, it managed to keep up a high rate of investment at home without strain; but otherwise not.

In the early 1950s, during the coffee boom, *net* investment* amounted to 11–12 per cent of national income; and the immediate aim for the 1960s should be to regain at least that level. To do so will mean increasing the funds devoted to investment by about 3 per cent of the national income, starting from the level of 1958/9. Barring some quite unexpected upsurge in coffee prices—which seems a most improbable eventuality with the world surplus of coffee at the beginning of the 1960s larger then ever—the Brazilians will either have to find some way of taxing themselves far more effectively, in order to produce the extra funds, or they will have to try to borrow them from abroad. Even if they manage to force up the level of domestic saving, they will need to supplement this by drawing

* See Note 1 to this chapter

on outside sources of capital on a much larger scale than they have been able to do of late. During the last years of the 1950s Brazil, in fact, was obtaining no net contribution to its capital needs from abroad. A tangle of short-term foreign debts, the result of desperate borrowing to stave off recurrent balance of payments crises, has tied up the country's foreign exchange earnings. Its borrowing power abroad has also been damaged as a result of quarrels with the World Bank, the International Monetary Fund, and the American Treasury. Meanwhile the inflation at home, which has been used as an engine for robbing wage-earners, and anyone else with a fixed money income lagging behind the rise in prices, of part of their earnings, in order to provide resources for the investment programme, has got out of hand.

Constant inflation when it is on this scale—a 20–30 per cent price rise per annum—becomes less and less efficient as an instrument for forcing people to save (by cutting down the volume of consumer goods that they can afford) and diverting resources to investment. More and more people come to anticipate the next price rise and, where possible, act to avoid the loss of purchasing power; anyone lending money allows for it in the interest that he charges and anyone taking on a job tries to insure himself against rising prices in advance. Even so the inflation has served to maintain investment at a higher level than it would otherwise have reached if the government had been compelled to depend on the vagaries of the tax system, plus anything that it could borrow in the open market on state loans, to meet its need for capital. There is no doubt, however, that it would pay to stop the process now and make a new effort to build up public confidence in the currency and the credit-worthiness of the government; to that extent the International Monetary Fund is in the right in its dispute with the Brazilian government—though not in its doctrinaire condemnation of any form of inflation as an aid to investment.[3] The problem is to make the transition from the present hyper-inflationary method of financing development to a normal budget and a stable currency, without causing a drastic drop in investment. That will require initially a large amount of capital from abroad. Subsequently, if the stabilization programme worked, the government would be able to tap new sources of domestic saving, and in particular draw back some of the money that the Brazilian rich are carefully hiding away abroad as an insurance against the depreciation of the currency.

How much foreign capital would be needed to provide the equivalent of an extra 3 per cent of national income to add to investment? According to estimates of Brazilian requirements made in the mid-1950s,[4] an increase in investment equivalent to 1 per cent of the national income would at that time have been met by an extra $100m. of foreign capital. This was on the assumption that the whole of any additional output which the country obtained from such foreign capital would be reinvested; in other words, that the inflow of additional foreign investment would itself help to raise the level of domestic saving and that this would offset the extra purchasing power of workers drawing wages from the new enterprises financed by foreign money. If this result really did follow, what would be required today (allowing for the expansion in the Brazilian national income that has occurred in the interval) would be something of the order of $350m. of foreign capital, in order to add to investment the equivalent of another 3 per cent of national income. It should be observed that, even at this higher level, the rate of investment in Brazil would still be well below Soviet standards. But there is much that the Brazilian government itself could still do to mobilize internal resources for investment more effectively.

### Taxing the Rich—Mexico

A thorough overhaul of the tax system would undoubtedly yield big returns, both in Brazil and in Mexico. The problem is to find men sufficiently expert and incorruptible to do it, and politicians with enough power and courage to back a thoroughgoing project of tax reform all the way through. After all, any serious attempt at reform would be interpreted at once as a frontal assault on the new property-owning classes, very rich men with strong political backing, who have assumed hitherto that it is their privilege not to pay taxes. To bring them under control, and to make some sort of a beginning towards meeting the crying need for a less brutally unequal distribution of wealth, are steps which these two leading Latin American countries must undertake sooner or later.

Hitherto it has been possible to argue persuasively that the process of rapid accumulation of wealth in the hands of entrepreneurs, who were forcing the pace of capitalist growth, ought not to be disturbed by tax collectors acting too energetically on behalf of the state. Some of the more sophisticated people in the Mexican government are quite conscious of this bias in the system. As one senior official said to me: "It has not mattered very much that these men have got rich at the expense of the tax collector. The important thing is that they have ploughed back most of their extra wealth into fresh investments, which have built up Mexican industry. They have enriched the country, too." But by now (early 1960), he suggested, conditions had changed. Enough new manufacturing capacity had been created to sustain a rise in the living standards of the ordinary wage-earner; real wages of unskilled labour were no higher by 1960 than in the late 1940s, in spite of the big rise in the national income during the interval. Indeed it might well be a positive stimulus to the growth of investment in ordinary manufacturing industry, if mass incomes were allowed to rise, so that all the gains ceased to be concentrated in a still comparatively small middle and upper class. In other words, part of the economy had already reached the more advanced stage of capitalism—of which the United States provided the first clear example—when the requirement for growth is not just a high level of savings, but also a mass market for the products of consumer industries.

The second reason for taxing the new class of capitalists in Mexico is that by now their enterprise is neither of the type nor on the scale necessary to carry through the next phase of industrialization. The kind of enterprise that is required now is the big integrated steel works, costing $200–$300m. to erect, the chemical works manufacturing synthetic materials, and the other large and expensive plants for making the intermediate products on which modern industry increasingly depends. The capitalists of Mexico—and this is true of Brazil also—are used to extraordinarily high profits made very quickly. The Mexicans are accustomed to paying rates of interest of 15–18 per cent on borrowed money, which indicates just how high the common expectation of profit is. This has nothing to do with inflation: it is a reflection of a number of economic factors making for an extremely large return on capital, among which the very low level of wages is probably the most important. The upshot is that the local capitalist is not enthusiastic about investment in the large-scale enterprises of modern industry, where there is a long waiting period before production begins and a still longer period of years of steady production before the investor gets his money back with a profit. Foreign capital, which means in this context United States capital, would probably be prepared to fill the gap in investment; but here the intense nationalism of Mexican business legislation, a relic of the xenophobia which inspired the revolution and has continued for another quarter of a century after it, is an obstacle.

There is besides the practical business argument on the Mexican government's side that anyone who sets up a steelworks, for example, at this stage of the country's growth is not in fact taking a risk—his market is fully assured for a long time to come—so why should the country saddle itself with the burden of future remittances of big equity profits to a foreign investor? Since the investment in this large segment of industry which is now in its infancy in Mexico is, it is claimed, largely riskless, the way to deal with it is by means of government enterprise—if local private enterprise will not tackle it. But in order to provide the capital to finance it some of the profits of the private sector of industry have to be extracted and transferred to the public sector.

The Mexican government also needs more foreign exchange than the country's exports are likely to earn, to cover the big purchases of capital equipment that will have to be made abroad to carry through the next phase of industrialization. A steady and substantial flow of American capital has come into the country since the war, and this has been a potent factor in the rapid development of Mexican manufacturing industry, especially of consumer durable goods. It has not only been the American capital, but also the American technical expertise and high standards of management which have come over the border. Now, however, the task of pushing through the process of industrialization to a fully successful conclusion requires a concentrated input of capital on a larger scale into certain key sectors of the economy. There are no official estimates of what this might cost. Applying the same criteria as those used in the estimate of Brazil's needs, two differences emerge. First, the Mexican population is growing rather faster, at 3 per cent against Brazil's 2½ per cent a year, and second the level of investment is higher than it is in Brazil. Helped by a more far-sighted administration and by the rising output of a more efficient agriculture, Mexico has been able to keep up the rate of investment, while it was falling off in Brazil and elsewhere in Latin America, as a result of the decline in commodity prices during the late 1950s. The available data suggest that Mexican *gross* investment was maintained at about 17 per cent of the gross national product, up to 1958 at any rate, while in Brazil the proportion of gross investment, starting at about the Mexican level in the early 1950s, fell to under 13 per cent.[5]

Nevertheless the rate of growth of *per capita* national income has not been markedly higher in Mexico. It may be that it will take a little time before the decline in the Brazilian rate of investment has its effect on production. Alternatively the Mexicans may be entering the difficult phase of development, which Argentina and Chile experienced in the 1950s, when industrial capacity is not fully used, because of insufficient demand, so that the country's capital stock taken as a whole becomes less productive and growth slows down. What is clear is that the Mexicans, after a period of successful development following the war, based on a combination of new agricultural crops and the development of a number of secondary industries, have still to make a major effort, if they are to turn themselves within the next few years into a modern industrial society. Because the effort probably requires, at one and the same time, a wider spread of consumer benefits and an increase in the volume of investment in new forms of state enterprise, the country's resources will be stretched and the external balance of payments is likely to come under strain. Any rise in real wages, which is now overdue, will also reduce the extremely high rates of profit, which have helped hitherto to finance industrial investment. There will therefore be less from this source of savings. For these reasons the Mexican authorities need

F

some extra room for manoeuvre if they are to carry out the radical economic and social changes that are necessary; and that is essentially what foreign economic aid should provide.

## A Billion Dollars Plus

It was estimated in an official survey made during the late 1950s that an increase in Mexican investment above the level of 1957/8 by the equivalent of 1–2 per cent of the national product was required at that time to enable the country to realize its considerable potentialities. Allowing for the possibility that domestic saving might be temporarily reduced, as a result of any redistribution of income in favour of the poor, and that there might also be some initial flight of capital abroad, if the property-owning classes felt that some of their present privileges and immunities were being whittled away, a larger supplement to domestic capital resources would probably be required—perhaps 2–3 per cent of the national product. This would mean an extra $200m. or so a year to be obtained from abroad, over a brief but possibly explosive period of intense economic development.

It may seem on the face of it unfair that although Mexico's population is smaller and its income per head higher than Brazil's, it should qualify for so much foreign assistance: $200m. would give it about the same amount *per capita* as Brazil. This is of course a matter for dispute, in which all sorts of criteria, apart from the strictly economic, can be legitimately introduced. My reason for suggesting this favourable treatment for Mexico is that the present Mexican lead is in large part the result of the more effective distribution of available resources. In this the government has played a big part. An outstanding example is the advance made by Mexican agriculture, helped by a steady and expensive effort from year to year, to bring more land under irrigation and to feed it with fertilizers. Alone among the undeveloped countries, Mexico has managed to keep its agricultural output rising in line with its industrial production. All this suggests that there is sufficient administrative capacity here, as well as long-range vision, to use any additional investment funds that are made available to considerable effect. If after a few years of special help from abroad, the Mexicans are able to float off on their own entirely unaided, the policy of open favouritism will have turned out to be economical, as well as inequitable. That is likely, if anything, to increase its unpopularity. It is impossible to offer the undeveloped countries an alternative which will have the same popular appeal as the traditional demand: "Fair shares for all —and sovereign freedom to waste the lot!"

The three major claimants, then, seem to require sums which added together amount to rather more than $1 billion a year. Fortunately, there are no other demands of this size immediately in prospect. Probably the next claimant in order of magnitude is Pakistan. But this country has not yet advanced to the point where it is able to absorb very large sums of capital for productive purposes; there is still some massive work of preparation to be done. Even that will not be cheap: the Pakistan government estimates that it will need something over $300m. a year of foreign capital and aid for its Five Year Plan, 1960/5— that is about $100m. per annum more than it was receiving in the late 1950s. There is some doubt whether enough projects are likely to be set on foot to use as much additional foreign exchange as this.

No doubt there will be other valid and substantial claims from one or two smaller countries. In addition, there are those countries teetering near the threshold, like Argentina—the Argentinians have in fact been teetering there for rather a long time[6] —who might conceivably, if political conditions were right, be brought rapidly over to the other side with a comparatively small amount of special external assistance. I must emphasize that the figure of $1 billion or plus is intended only as a starting point for arriving at an order of magnitude of cost. Besides, staking out these individual claims for the largest countries which are standing ready to go right ahead does not mean that the backward and less promising areas are to be denied the benefit of capital investment altogether. Concentration of the massive sums in the areas which seem likely to produce the quickest returns still leaves us with the problem of finding money for important, slowly maturing projects in other regions which are far behind. This is particularly true of Africa.

71

# COUNTING THE COST

## Africa's Needs

So far African development programmes have concentrated overwhelmingly on the creation of the first layer of the substructure which is required to support a modern society. Fourfifths of the expenditure under the various development plans is going into roads and other basic facilities and into the social services.[7] So long as this situation lasts, the need for foreign exchange to finance the import of industrial equipment and supplies from abroad will not be large. It is to be expected that the proportion of African development expenditure devoted to industry and agriculture will increase gradually; but there is little evidence that a shortage of foreign exchange is at present seriously impeding the progress of development.

Fortunately the continent is endowed with the kind of natural resources which nowadays attract foreign capital in large amounts. If an underdeveloped country, not too thickly populated, were allowed to choose three things which would give it the best start in life with foreign capital in the second half of the 20th century, it would surely plump for oil, aluminium and iron ore. The chief advantages of these commodities are that the companies interested in them are very large and very rich and also tend to take a generously long view about the return on their investments. Oil, aluminium and steel concerns are used to thinking ten years ahead—and also tend to expect that if they are going to be faced with a problem at the end of ten years, it will be a problem of supply, rather than of insufficient demand.

This is the background to the interest of American and European steel companies in the development of the iron ore deposits of Gabon and Mauritania in French Africa, and of Guinea and Liberia. In Guinea, too, an international consortium of aluminium companies is engaged on a project which has begun to exploit the large local deposits of bauxite. Farther down the coast, in Ghana, the Volta River scheme, again linked with aluminium, is likely to require a total of some $500m. of capital over the next five years or so; the greater part of this should be obtainable from American private enterprise, though there will still probably be a substantial sum to be found from other sources. In the Belgian Congo there is

72

another of these combinations of bauxite deposits in the neigh-
bourhood of water that is capable of providing cheap and
plentiful electricity; American investors and the World Bank
have shown an interest in this too, though in a rather more
tentative spirit than in Ghana, where an effective government
has made the post-colonial transition and where both the standard of education and the material wellbeing of the people are
considerably higher. Ghana is probably the most advanced of
the Black African countries.

The uncertain factor in all these schemes is political, rather
than economic. That is true also of the development of oil in
the north, in Algeria and Libya. So far the big foreign companies have been willing to take their chance on the establishment of stable and fairly effective governments in the ex-
colonial territories of Africa. The smaller businessmen may
easily panic and cause problems for a while through the flight
of capital, as they did in the Belgian Congo with the approach
of independence and also in French Colonial Africa. But so
long as the basis for the long-term political calculation is not
destroyed, private business capital from the large enterprises
should be available in sufficient amounts to supply a considerable part of Africa's needs during the early stages of
development. In addition, some of the African countries
belonging to the British Commonwealth, notably Ghana and
Nigeria, have substantial reserves of foreign exchange of their
own, in the form of sterling balances, on which they will draw
as soon as their need for imports of capital goods begins to rise
faster than their export earnings—as it inevitably will, if their
development proceeds.

Elsewhere in the African continent, however, there are
important long-range projects, which cannot be financed out
of sterling balances or by bringing in private capital. The outstanding examples are Egypt's Aswan Dam and the Sudanese
irrigation plans farther up the Nile. Aswan by itself is estimated
to cost an average of $50m. a year for some years. There is a
promise of a low interest loan from the Russians to cover the
greater part of the expense. A start ought also to be made on
the programme of agricultural rehabilitation round the shores
of the Mediterranean, both in North Africa and the Near East,
where the land used to yield generous crops, but has been

73

progressively ruined over several hundred years of soil erosion. The Food and Agriculture Organization of the United Nations has put forward a proposal for afforestation and other measures to restore the fertility of this land by the 1970s. The programme of tree planting alone in this region is estimated to cost around $200m. spread over fifteen years.

Put all these needs together and they add up to a substantial, but not impossible sum. The Volta River and the Aswan Dam, which are the two biggest items in the list, may easily between them absorb $150m. of capital a year. But there seems to be a fair chance that American private enterprise will take care of a large chunk of the first and Soviet state enterprise of a considerable part of the second. With luck—and that means chiefly political luck, which will allow the new African states to establish themselves as stable societies—African demands for capital during the 1960s will not require special economic aid on a large scale from the West.

There is also less urgency, on ordinary grounds of humanity, about the African economic problem, for the reason that the population has not begun to expand at the frightening pace, which is now common in the rest of the undeveloped world. No attempt has yet been made to grapple seriously with the problem of malaria, which it is estimated kills off about 12 per cent of all Africans before they become adults. The experts say that it is going to be much more difficult to eradicate the mosquito here than in Latin America, where the job is now almost done. It is also likely to take a long time, even starting with the experience and the improved equipment now available. All of which suggests that the full blast of the population explosion may be delayed for a while yet on the African continent. It is a stroke of fortune that these explosions in the three continents of the undeveloped world seem to be occurring in series and not in parallel. It would be much more difficult to cope if the extra babies and the extra lifespan took effect everywhere at the same time.

*Notes*

1. See Arthur Lewis, "The Theory of Economic Growth", and W. W. Rostow, "Stages of Economic Growth". Several of the undeveloped countries, e.g. India and Brazil, envisage a much more favourable capital/output ratio—closer to 2 units of capital to

produce 1 additional unit of output—than the 3:1 ratio. In the earliest stages of development a lot of money has to go into the creation of the basic sub-structure of a modern economy—e.g. roads, a government administrative machine, schools and technical colleges—which results in very little increase in output in the short term. At this stage investment has an unfavourable capital/output ratio. But at the next stage, the stage that has been reached by India and Brazil, any new capital introduced becomes much more productive.

The investment referred to here is *net* investment, i.e. the value of new assets created, after allowing for the cost of renovating and replacing the capital assets which are being used up in the course of production. Because a primitive society is poorly endowed with equipment and achieves most of its output by manual labour with the aid of simple and inexpensive tools, the amount required each year to cover the depreciation of its capital assets is comparatively small. Arthur Lewis (ibid.) estimates that depreciation absorbs 2–3 per cent of the national income of poor countries, compared with 7–10 per cent in the most advanced industrial countries. In Britain close to half of all investment has in recent years been devoted to the replacement of capital assets: net investment has been less than 12 per cent of the national income. This point should be borne in mind when making the conventional comparisons of gross investment between developed and underdeveloped countries. Here is one way in which the undeveloped country does have an advantage: the same amount of *gross* saving and investment will produce a larger *net* addition to the stock of capital assets than in a developed country.

Another, slightly more subtle, point is that when calculating net investment, one is not always referring to the actual volume of resources devoted to *new* investment. Net investment is a national figure reached by deducting each year the amount that would be necessary to replace, e.g. a steel mill at the end of twenty-five years. The deduction represents the amount of money that a prudent man *would* put aside in any one year, not the actual amount of resources that have to be set aside for replacement in that particular year. Of course when a country has reached maturity and is endowed with a great stock of capital assets of varying ages, this distinction between new and net capital investment makes little practical difference; about the same proportion of output has to be devoted to the actual replacement of assets from year to year. But in a country in the early stages of development the amount that has to be spent each year on the actual replacement of assets, most of which are new, is much smaller. So in this respect too the undeveloped country has an advantage.

2. Indian plans depend on the realization of more favourable capital/output ratios than 3: 1 (see note 1). They hope ultimately to be able to sustain an annual rate of growth of 6 per cent in total national output, without foreign aid, when the rate of saving goes up to 16–17 per cent, possibly by the early 1970s.

3. In Chile and in Argentina too the IMF's effort in the late 1950s to halt the extraordinary excesses of inflation, with currencies losing as much as a third of their purchasing power in a year, was plainly sensible. Indeed, South America provided the ideal opportunity for the operation of the IMF's currency stabilization schemes, since there inflation had become self-stultifying. It is the particular tactics employed on occasion by the Fund as well as a certain rigidity of attitude which are open to criticism.

4. "Analyses and Projections of Economic Development: II. The Economic Development of Brazil", United Nations, 1956. The calculation assumed a capital/output ratio for Brazil of around 2 : 1. $100m. of foreign capital was at that time equivalent to 0·7 per cent of national income; but with the addition of the domestic output produced by this capital the total amount of extra resources available for investment came to 1 per cent of national income.

5. To bring this estimate of *gross* investment on to the same basis as the earlier calculation of Brazilian *net* investment as a proportion of national income (or net national product) it is necessary to subtract the cost of depreciation of capital. Brazilian calculations put the annual depreciation cost at about 5 per cent of gross national product (see "Analyses and Projections of Economic Development: II. The Economic Development of Brazil", United Nations, 1956). If the same proportion is applied to Mexico, net investment there works out at something over 12 per cent of national income, compared with the Brazilian net figure of around 8 per cent. However, this estimate of the amount required for depreciation seems on the face of it rather high (see Note 1 above). If that is overestimated, the actual increase in new capital assets is greater than the figures suggest.

6. W. W. Rostow suggests that Argentina reached the stage of "take-off" in 1935 or even possibly several years earlier—much before any of the other Latin American countries. See "The Stages of Economic Growth".

7. See "Economic Survey of Africa Since 1950", United Nations.

# CHAPTER 6

## LOOKING FURTHER AHEAD

THE examination of some of the main areas of immediate need suggests that something well over $1 billion, but probably less than $2 billion, a year is the kind of amount of additional capital that could be fruitfully used by the undeveloped world almost at once. The trouble with figures of this kind is that they very quickly become separated from their original purposes—and from the provisos that surrounded them at the start. This particular figure, it must be repeated, is intended to illustrate the size of what is required immediately to deal with the biggest and most obvious cases only. And even some of the obvious have been deliberately omitted. For instance, I have not attempted to assess the needs of other smaller countries in Latin America and Asia, and I have ignored altogether the demands of the underdeveloped countries in Europe—partly on the principle that any big increase in the amount of capital going into these places, over and above the substantial sums already being expended there, would be unlikely to produce the high rate of return that we are looking for in India, Brazil and Mexico. There is the further point that the capital requirements of countries like Spain or Portugal will probably be met with little difficulty from nearby European sources, once the governments of these countries begin to be actively concerned to create the opportunities for constructive investment, instead of showing a large measure of indifference to them and an occasional small measure of hostility. Official indifference to economic growth, it is to be observed, is quite enough to result in effective sabotage in societies where the traditional ruling classes do not want change anyhow.

There is a further proviso that must be made about almost any figure that one dares to mention in relation to the needs of the undeveloped countries. The amount is not intended as a measure of the human requirements of upwards of a thousand

77

million people, who are living well below what most of us in the West would regard as the extreme limit of imaginable poverty. If one were considering the matter in terms of simple charity, there would be no practical limit to the billions that could be usefully donated to provide them with food, clothing and shelter. But the problem to which I am addressing myself is not the cost of alleviating misery here and now, but of creating with the maximum speed the conditions for spontaneous and rapid economic growth in as many countries as possible. While there is a shortage of funds for this purpose, it is essential that the operation shall be conducted with the minimum of waste, and the criterion to be applied in choosing countries worth investing in is that the "yield" on the capital put into them is not markedly below the standards set in countries which are already developed—the yield being measured in terms of the extra output which the investment produces, not the profit from it. All the same, while the main stream of economic aid must be guided by these businesslike criteria, it is to be hoped that we do not become so exclusively obsessed with the problem of economic growth that we forget about the ordinary demands of charity altogether. Poor people have to be helped, even if they refuse to grow.

Finally there is the question of the speed with which the more backward nations can be pushed to the point where they are able to undertake normally productive investment on a large scale. The sooner this can be done the higher the cost of economic aid during the 1960s and 1970s is going to be. Assuming that the business of pre-investment is now taken more seriously than it has been in the past, and that there is a much more active search for ways in which the ground can be prepared to absorb more productive capital,* then it might reasonably be expected that the amount required for economic aid to the undeveloped countries would go up steeply by the second half of the 1960s. It might happen before then. Countries which look extremely unpromising today may suddenly push forward fast, as a result of a change of government or because of some other completely unplanned incident—like a lot of people coming in from outside and applying fresh enterprise at some point which happens to be crucial for the whole economy.

* See Chapter 2, p. 19

A recent example of what may happen is the way in which refugees from Pakistan have helped to give an impetus to the new small-scale engineering workshops which are now thriving in the north of India. In Pakistan itself the revolution by the army leaders in the late 1950s opened up the possibility of doing things, not considered practical before, which are necessary to prepare the country for the stage of high investment; above all, there are now the makings of an effective administrative machine, which will not be prevented either by corruption or by incompetence from carrying through a centrally directed plan of development. Political change could make a decisive difference to the economic prospects of other countries in South Asia, for example Indonesia. Equally, some countries which look stable and promising today, notably in Africa, might well slip back. In view of all this, it would be foolish to try and calculate even an approximate figure of the eventual needs of the underdeveloped countries for outside aid. But it is not difficult to conceive of circumstances in which the additional amount of some \$1–\$2 billion that seems to be required today would rise to \$3–\$4 billion by the mid-1960s. That would mean doubling the net amount of economic aid and capital that was flowing into the main body of the underdeveloped world* in the late 1950s.

The purpose of the argument set out here is however not to fix on some particular figure. The practical conclusion which it suggests is that to make a noticeable impact on the problem of development will require the expenditure of considerable and increasing sums of money during the 1960s, but sums which are, after all, well within the means of the rich industrial countries, without imposing any serious sacrifice of their material well-being.

### Doubling the Rate of Growth

The same broad conclusion about the order of magnitude of the required sum of economic aid has emerged from other, more comprehensive studies of the investment needs of the undeveloped countries taken together. Mr. Paul Hoffman,

* See Chapter 2, p. 10 and Appendix I.

the Managing Director of the U.N. Special Fund, has made a calculation[1] which starts from an estimate of approximately $100 billion for the aggregate of the national incomes of the undeveloped countries in 1960. Their total income is estimated to have increased at a rate of some 3 per cent a year during the 1950s, but since the population has been going up at an annual rate of 2 per cent at the same time, the improvement in income per head has been no more than 1 per cent per annum. The objective which Mr. Hoffman sets is to double the rate of growth of *per capita* income, requiring an additional $3 billion of investment a year. That is on the basis of the formula discussed earlier* that to produce $1 billion worth of additional wealth—the equivalent of the desired increase of 1 per cent in the income of the undeveloped world—will require the investment of about three times as much capital.

Mr. Hoffman goes on to suggest that it will take "two or three or possibly four years" to increase the annual flow of capital by $3 billion. He also makes it clear that he does not expect either the investment or the material progress resulting from it to be evenly spread among the one hundred countries included in his survey. Many of the countries will, he anticipates, achieve something less than the average increase of 2 per cent *per capita* national income per year; in some countries there may be even a decline. The essential aim is to concentrate resources heavily on a minority of promising nations which will be able to go forward at a much faster pace than 2 per cent. Thus the practical significance of Mr. Hoffman's global figures is to illustrate the size of the financial problem, if aid is effectively applied to a few countries—he suggests 10 or 15 countries may make the grade in the decade of the 1960s—rather than to calculate the cost of a truly global programme of economic aid.

All these estimates are full of uncertainties. The figures given for the national incomes of the undeveloped countries are usually the result of a more or less inspired bout of guesswork by a visiting statistician from a Western country. Occasionally a government is ready to go to the trouble of sending out some trained observers to watch what is actually produced and consumed in a typical village community, in between visits from the tax collector. But it is not often that the guesses are backed

* See Chapter 5, page 57 and 58

up by this kind of factual evidence. Few countries have reliable data even about the size of their population; in some places the authorities will admit privately that they may be several million out in their estimates of the number of people that they think they are looking after. It is no surprise, therefore, that when economists try to work out a figure of future capital requirements on the basis of national income and population estimates, there should be some variations in the results. For example an analysis prepared for the European Economic Community in 1959,[2] using the same targets for economic development as Mr. Hoffman—a 2 per cent annual rate of growth of income *per capita*—arrived at a figure of $4 billion a year (instead of Mr. Hoffman's $3 billion) for a slightly larger group of countries, including notably the poor European nations of the Mediterranean area. It would be idle at this stage to try and adjudicate on the merits of these different estimates. They merely strengthen the impression that roundabout an extra $3–$4 billion is likely to be required in the long run.

## Exploding Populations

More important than the question of precisely how much is the question—how soon? The problem of mounting an effective investment programme in the poor countries will grow more difficult with each year's delay. The reason is simply that their population is growing far more rapidly than has ever happened before in recorded history. Moreover, it is growing without the economic and social changes, which have accompanied, and sustained, such increases in population in the past. This time the agent of the demographic revolution is medicine alone.

Of course there is nothing new about the effect of improved medical care on the size of population. What makes the new situation unique is first of all its scale. During the first industrial revolution in the 19th and early 20th century in Europe a few tens of millions were involved; moreover the Europeans had a ready and comfortable outlet for the surplus manpower by emigration to America. Secondly, the rate of increase was largely determined by the pace of industrialization: so long as people remained fixed in the traditional agrarian pattern there was no large increase in numbers.

Fortunately the full blast of this eruption of population has not yet been felt in Asia where three-quarters of the population of the underdeveloped world resides. Only a few of the smaller countries like Ceylon, Malaya and the Philippines, have so far had to face the kind of pressure that is now common in most of Latin America. But it is predictable that the rest of Asia will follow suit after only a few years' delay. It is just a matter of how long it will take to bring into general use the small improvements in medical practice, which make such a dramatic difference to a country's death-rate. Perhaps the most powerful instrument for fostering population growth is the modern anti-malarial campaign. It is cheap; it is quick; and where it is successful it not only lengthens the average lifespan enormously, but actually increases fertility by making people more capable of sexual intercourse. Ceylon has shown just how rapidly fatal diseases can be fought back by a vigorous national health programme, in which measures against malaria played a large part: the death-rate per thousand people dropped by almost half in the six years from 1946 to 1952. The population of Ceylon is now expanding at a rate of some 3 per cent per year.

The critical question is what is going to happen in India and the other major centres of population in non-communist Asia. The Indian case is the best documented, as well as being the most important; so, it is worth looking at the figures more closely.[3] During the first twenty years of this century the Indian population was static. From 1920 onwards it began to rise at a cumulative rate of about 1 per cent until the middle of the century. Then in the 1950s the rate of increase shot up as a result of more positive health measures; the lifespan of the average Indian lengthened by several years. It is still lengthening. The speed with which this change took place caught the Indian planners off balance. When the broad objectives for the new series of Five Year Plans were being formulated back in 1955, the official view grossly underestimated the likely fall in the death-rate and overestimated the effect of a slight rise of income in reducing fertility. In consequence the prospective increase in the population during the decade of the 1960s was estimated at 50 million. On the basis of more recent information, the Indian Planning Commission has had to revise this figure to over 100 million. The average life expectation, which was only 32 years in 1946, will if present trends continue rise to 50 years by 1966.

## No Early Relief

It is hard to see anything that will prevent the rate of growth of the Indian population from increasing to 20 per cent by the 1970s—other than a war or a series of natural disasters. In absolute terms this means that there will be some 14 million added to the population each year, instead of 8 million a year in the late 1950s. That provides some measure of the urgency of the problem of development. If the Indians were to wait for another ten years before embarking on the sustained capital investment programme which is needed to create a modern industrial system supported by a productive agriculture, the sacrifice that would then have to be imposed on the people would be enormously greater, for the economy would contain a hundred million more consumers, without a corresponding gain in the number of producers.[4] Unless massive investment is undertaken before the event, the extra labour power will not be absorbed into productive work.

There is usually several years' delay before a major investment in agriculture yields its full return. For example, the first stage of building a dam, designed to provide an area with irrigation all the year round, takes a few years. But that is only the beginning. The peasants have to be induced to build a whole network of feeder canals from the main stream, across each other's fragmented holdings. And when they have got the water, they still have to be induced to accept the revolutionary change in their traditional pattern of life, which is implied by moving from a one-crop-a-year system to a two, three or four crop method of cultivation. It is only when the extra crops are being efficiently produced right through the irrigated area that the agricultural investment yields its full return—and that may be as much as ten years later. It frequently does take as long as this to bring a piece of major agricultural capital to full capacity operation. Similar considerations apply to a fertilizer programme, such as the Indians have now undertaken. The scheme for building a series of vast new factories at top speed is ambitious enough; but even if this comes off, the problem of distributing the stuff to the right places at the right time and securing its proper and efficient use will take several years longer to solve. Once it has been solved, of course, the use of fertilizers by the peasants goes up very rapidly indeed, and so does agricultural output.

Some of the Asian planners allow themselves to be too readily encouraged to foresee an early solution to the population problem by the experience of Japan. There the birth-rate reached a peak in the 1920s, which was as high as anything in Asia today. By the middle 1950s it had been halved; and as a result of the encouragement of abortions[5] it has fallen a great deal further since then. The Japanese experience—apart from the drastic final phase of the attack on the population problem —conforms fairly well to the pattern established earlier by European industrial countries. There is no reason to believe that the rest of Asia will behave differently, when people reach a certain level of sophistication and material welfare. But there is in fact little hope that any of the other Asian countries will arrive at this level for another quarter of a century. After all, by comparison with India today the standards of the Japanese in the 1920s, both in terms of education and material welfare, were pretty high.

It is necessary to argue by historical analogy, because so little is known about the use of birth control and why the attitudes of people towards its practice seem, at a certain moment, quite suddenly to change. What is clear from the experiments undertaken in India is that it is extraordinarily difficult to induce women living in fairly primitive conditions to cope with a calendar count designed to indicate the "safe period" for intercourse, or with any other common method of contraception. No doubt the invention of a cheap oral contraceptive would make it possible to anticipate by several years the normal downturn in fertility, which occurs with rising living standards. But at most this may ease the problems of the 1970s; it is extremely unlikely to solve them. After all, the rate of population growth that is in prospect by then is more than double that reached at the peak of the industrial revolution in Europe. Even if the Asian rate were halved, the situation would still be difficult. Europe had a lot of advantages during its period of high population pressure, including a monopoly position in the world export market for manufactures, which are not possessed by these poor overpopulated countries today.

*Notes*

1. "One Hundred Countries—One and One Quarter Billion People", by Paul G. Hoffman.

2. By Professor Tinbergen on behalf of M. Monnet's "Action Committee for a United States of Europe".

3. Most of the data in the following section is derived from "Population Growth and Economic Development in Low Income Countries", by H. A. Coale and E. M. Hoover (Oxford).

4. The essential point is that the marginal product of a primitive agriculture will decline as more labour is applied to a limited stock of land.

5. Abortions were legalized in Japan in 1948, though officially only for certain restricted purposes. The restrictions were gradually lifted, until by now any woman can demand an abortion from her doctor or hospital. Estimates of the average cost of the operation vary from under $2 to about $6; but in extreme cases of poverty the price is as low as 50 yen ($0·14) and in some places the operation is free for destitute women. The result of these measures, combined with the rapid growth of contraceptive practices, is that the Japanese live birth-rate is now one of the lowest in the world.

*Part II*

INVESTMENT

# CHAPTER 7

# THE INTERNATIONAL IDEAL

T HE next stage of this argument takes a leap into the frankly improbable. Say that the rich nations decide to meet the immediate requirements of the undeveloped countries and put up an additional $1–$2 billion a year, with no strings attached and no political purpose, other than to help those societies which seem already capable of rapid development to a higher standard of living—what would be the best way of organizing the use of this money? The point of posing this question is not the fear that we may be caught unprepared when a plan for joint disarmament bursts on an astonished world, and the big powers offer to make the savings on weapons and soldiers freely available to the poor countries. The intention is rather that by taking a preliminary look at what are thought to be the ideal solutions, we may be better able to make a critical choice among the more modest alternatives with which we are likely to be faced in practice.

But first of all it is necessary to clear up one matter about the nature of the money that is required for this purpose. In the course of the discussion in Part I, I have described the additional funds needed for the undeveloped countries as "special aid", meaning that the money was not going to be forthcoming from ordinary commercial sources. That is true as the situation stands at the moment. If, however, a new dynamic element of public aid is introduced at those points in the undeveloped world where it is likely to produce the maximum turbulent effect, then the basis on which private calculations of profit are made is likely to change too.

One has only to look at what happened in India during the Second Five Year Plan to see how the firm commitment of large-scale public investment in productive enterprise has the effect of stimulating private investment, which would not otherwise have occurred. For all the grumbling among Indian businessmen that the public authorities are trying to capture too large a slice of an exceptionally rich cake, the fact is—and some of them even realize it—that the cake would not be nearly so rich without the contribution of public enterprise towards the making of it. It is after all a commonplace of experience in the developed countries that when a state corporation commits itself to a long-term programme of expansion, e.g. on the railways or on electric power, this has a revolutionary effect on the profit expectations and the investment of capital in the privately owned concerns supplying the state industries. And that in turn helps to stimulate more private investment elsewhere. A clear and generous policy towards the undeveloped world, publicly undertaken, would itself reduce the demands that have to be made on the public purse for carrying it out.

On the other hand, some subtraction from the flow of private investment funds now available to certain countries must also be allowed for. As we saw earlier, the mountain of indebtedness to foreign investors piles up at a frightening pace, once a country gets seriously involved in the business of rapid industrialization.* Beyond a certain point—and this is a point that lies immediately ahead for several of the Latin American countries, and only a short distance farther on for India—it becomes extremely difficult for a poor country to go to the stock market or even to an institution like the World Bank, which applies commercial criteria, and obtain a public loan. When the burden of debt service payments absorbs more than a certain conventional proportion of a country's prospective export earnings —some bankers put it as low as 10 per cent, others more generously at 20 per cent—the word goes out that its "creditworthiness" has been exhausted. What this really means is that the bankers judge such a country might in a crisis find the temptation to default on its foreign debt overwhelming, if its annual debt service payments were absorbing so high a proportion of its earnings. It is indeed, a piece of elementary prudence on the part of the bankers, and they try to vary the calculation on the basis of a rough and ready estimate of the propensity of various nations to default in a crisis—e.g. Japan rather low; Latin Americans rather high—but the net effect of the desire not to lead people into temptation is that countries

* See Chapter 3, pp. 28 *et seq.*

which have been able to borrow easily in the 1950s will be able to borrow less, or not at all, in the 1960s. Unfortunately two of the most promising of the undeveloped countries, Brazil and India, are particularly menaced by a decline in their "creditworthiness", as their debt service payments on past loans rise, without a corresponding increase in their export earnings. Certainly, from now on many of the undeveloped countries will be looking much more closely at the future bill for debt service that they are undertaking, when they are offered the convenience of an immediate loan to meet some urgent project in their development programme. Even some of the easy-seeming Soviet loans, at $2\frac{1}{2}$ per cent interest with twelve years to repay the lot, can add up to a sizeable burden on a poor nation's balance of payments.

It is, therefore, going to be difficult to obtain any substantial part of the additional capital requirements of the undeveloped countries from private investors. Of course, if one could foresee an early increase in the export earnings of the undeveloped countries, the prospects of attracting foreign capital would be that much improved. But for the reasons explained in Chapter 4, it is unlikely that a successful export drive can be mounted on the required scale within the critical period of the next ten years or so.

*Soft Loans*

That is not to say that the only acceptable form in which the bulk of the economic aid to the underdeveloped countries can be provided is in outright grants. It is, in my view, desirable that a large part of it should be in the form of grants, on the model of the Marshall Plan; but there is no inherent reason why other devices, which will soften and delay the impact of foreign borrowing on a poor country's balance of payments, should not be used. Alternative methods which are contemplated by the new International Development Association (the affiliate of the World Bank) include the arrangement of long-term loans at exceptionaly low rates of interest and loans with an extended period of grace before any repayments at all have to be made. The World Bank itself often allows a period of a few years of grace before the first annual instalment of the principal of a loan has to be paid. Indeed, one of the ways in which the Bank could most directly and immediately help countries like India, whose further borrowing capacity is in jeopardy because of the great weight of annual service payments on debts already undertaken, would be by extending this period of grace by several years more. Now that the World Bank has accumulated, out of its own profits, a reserve which is exceptionally large by normal banking standards, it should be able to make this concession without difficulty.

The conventional banker's objection to such a course would be that that he had a limited amount of money at his disposal and wanted to turn it over reasonably fast in order to make a profit. Under Mr. Eugene Black's presidency, the World Bank has been extremely successful in using this technique—selling off its obligations to insurance companies and other investors on Wall Street, and so putting itself in funds for further lending. But it has no real need to press the poorest of its debtors to pay up quickly, for the Bank—especially since the doubling of its capital to over $19 billion in 1959[1]—commands vastly more resources than it has shown any signs of using so far. It is sometimes alleged that the Bank has only managed to maintain its position in the capital markets of Western countries because it has pursued ultra-conservative banking policies. This is the standard argument used against any proposal for loosening or lowering its fairly stiff terms when it is dealing with an especially indigent class of borrower.

Granted that the institution must keep up a tough appearance and give a fair imitation of a hard-faced banker, if it is to keep its relations sweet with Wall Street and other money centres. But lengthening the term of a loan, by offering a country, say, an extra five years before it has to begin repaying the principal in annual instalments, surely need not be interpreted as a dangerously soft and unbusinesslike act, when interest and other charges amounting to a total of over 6 per cent per annum (the current level in 1960) are to be paid by the borrower right through the extra five years during which the loan will be outstanding. Some people might regard this as rather a good investment. Indeed, it would be remarkable if the World Bank, backed now by a reserve fund of its own of about half a billion dollars, as well as by several billion

dollars of guarantees from the United States and other governments of irreproachable credit, could not please itself in this
respect without ruining its standing on Wall Street. No doubt
some of the brokers and investment bankers would shake their
heads a little at first, as they invariably do whenever some object
on the fixed horizon of banking conventions shifts its position
ever so slightly; but they would soon recognize that the security
of this highly profitable investment in World Bank bonds had
not been reduced just because some of the loans were going to
be left to earn interest for a few years longer.

### The Mirage of SUNFED

Such an arrangement for enlarging the scope of international
lending would however meet only part of the problem. The
future role of the World Bank and of the International Development Association will be discussed in detail later on.* But first
we ought to look at the other extreme—the proposal for a pure
grant aid institution, to be run by the eighty or so members of
the United Nations on the principle of equal votes. This is
plainly regarded as the ideal solution by the undeveloped
countries themselves. It is not unkind to suggest that they may
be partly influenced by the thought that they would generally
be able to command a majority of the votes in such an organization. They seem to envisage a complete specialization of
functions, the donor nations solely concerned with the giving
and the receiving nations with the disposal of the funds.

This would have been the effect of SUNFED (Special United
Nations Fund for Economic Development), which was first
mooted in 1952, and has since become a sturdy perennial of the
United Nations General Assembly. The idea was that the Fund
should start off with $250m. to give away, and that it should be
replenished with about this amount each year. There is no doubt
that the scheme has strong attractions: it is generous and accepts
the principle of equality—one nation, one vote—avoiding the
World Bank's system of weighted voting, which gives the rich
contributors an automatic and overwhelming majority.

It was partly for this last reason that the Americans and

* See Chapters 8–10

the British together opposed the SUNFED proposal vigorously right from the beginning. (The other reason was fear of Russia's presence in an international aid programme.) U.S and Britain control over 40 per cent of the votes in the World Bank—and also incidentally in the International Monetary Fund. In both institutions voting power is related to the size of the contributions of individual nations. What this means is that the United States and Britain in combination with two or three of the richer European countries, e.g. France and Benelux, hold an effective veto over any proposal. Indeed the whole SUNFED controversy, with its implied accusations of niggardliness and attachment to privilege aimed at the rich Western countries, came to develop strong emotional overtones—on both sides. And when the United Nations set up the Special Fund to deal with pre-investment problems,* with Mr. Paul Hoffman as its Managing Director, great care was taken to keep the emotionally charged initials out of its title; getting rid of the "S" (for "Special") altogether was one idea, but then someone noticed that this left an ominous sounding combination. The happy solution was eventually hit upon of simply displacing the letter away from the beginning, so that it became not the Special U.N. Fund, but the U.N. Special Fund.

There is, however, a more basic objection to the SUNFED scheme than the fact that the Americans and the British, as well as the Germans, Swedes and Swiss, among the potential donor countries, are opposed to it. It is that the United Nations could not in practice administer such a scheme. No doubt it would be able to dole out money to the poor countries each year on some simple criterion—e.g. equal shares for all or some system of weighting according to size of population, or even according to national income. But the United Nations as it now stands is not an executive organ which is capable of exercising discriminating and purposeful control over a development programme of this magnitude. And if it were able to do so, the undeveloped countries which have been pressing for SUNFED would almost certainly like it no better than they like the World Bank or the International Development Association.

One of the diseases of the United Nations is an excess of formal parliamentarism, with too little of its substance. The

* See Chapter 2, p. 19 *et seq.*

international officials are compelled to report in inordinate detail on matters which the permanent delegates who have to listen to them are rarely expert enough to understand and debate in a useful fashion. This applies especially to the field of economic development. There is no discussion on matters of substance that could, by moving the opinions of the participants, influence the votes of the governments whom they are supposed to represent. They are puppets and their deliberations are a simulacrum of parliamentary debate. The delegates are supplied with extensive notes for set speeches by their governments; and when it is a subject on which all nations feel that they ought to be recorded as having an opinion, the ceremony of discussion is reminiscent of nothing more than of two parallel lines taking an extraordinarily long time about not meeting.

But the speech-making, which appears so intolerably time-consuming and tedious to an outsider, can apparently be borne by the men who run the organization in the great skyscraper on the edge of the East River in New York. Some of them do show signs of severe strain as the long weeks of the annual session of the General Assembly approach their conclusion; but most of them seem to have accepted the fact that the price of power in an international society is the ability to appear to listen. The more serious difficulty arises when officials try to exercise initiative, in conjunction with the appointed representatives of member nations, involving any transfer of funds from one country to another or even from one component body of the United Nations to another. The competition between the specialized agencies, like the Food and Agriculture Organization (FAO), the Educational, Scientific and Cultural Organization (UNESCO), and so on, is just as fierce as it is between the sovereign states which are represented in New York. The fact is that the whole United Nations structure has been built up as a loose federation. In relation to the heads of the specialized agencies, the Secretary General of the United Nations is only *primus inter pares*. A characteristic comment from an official of one of these agencies, when I suggested that there might be an adverse reaction from the United Nations to a certain proposal, was: "You know, my chief is under no compulsion to be polite to Dag Hammarskjöld."

*United Nations' Weakness*

The U.N. General Assembly and the other organs of majority rule in the United Nations were set up as deliberative rather than decision-making bodies. It is true that the General Assembly has managed, through a tactical sleight of hand, to acquire some initiative in certain political emergencies. But the original intention was to concentrate the effective political power in the Security Council; if that has not worked out in practice, it is because of the cold war and the unrestrained use of the veto. On the economic side, however, there was not even formal provision for a type of Security Council procedure. The truth is that no one at the start conceived of the need for a United Nations economic policy which would, to however limited an extent, transcend national sovereignties. The Economic and Social Council (ECOSOC), which is supposed to look after these matters, has one advantage only—smaller numbers: eighteen members, instead of over eighty in the General Assembly. But ECOSOC is not only smaller than the General Assembly, it is also wholly subordinate to it and duplicates rather than supplements its functions.*

When the first serious effort was made by the United Nations to help the economic development of poor countries, with the establishment of the Technical Assistance Board (TAB) in 1950, the U.N. created an administrative machine with an incredible number of independent levers—almost a patent device to cause the maximum amount of trouble in spending small sums of money. The machine has been modified and somewhat improved since then, but the essential internal structure of elaborate checks and balances, ensuring the dissipation of large amounts of administrative energy, remains intact; together with the ingenious multiplicity of external controls, this makes it possible to guarantee the frustration of any attempt at purposeful direction. The Technical Assistance Programme continues to move forward largely because the momentum of its own operations in the field prevents it from standing still; and that momentum will continue, if only because of the excellence of many of the United Nations experts in the undeveloped countries. But it would be foolish to pretend

* See Chapter 15, pp. 223–4

that the United Nations as a collective entity is able through its Technical Assistance Programme to express a coherent view or to exercise any discriminating choice in the use of the funds at its disposal. Occasionally, in an emergency, Mr. Hammarskjöld has been able to gather up a limited amount of technical aid funds and to use them for some specific purpose. The emergency in Laos in 1959, when increased communist activity and the sharp American reaction to it had created an explosive situation, was an example. But the essential questions of policy in this case, as in others in which the Secretary-General has acted, have always been political ones; no one has ever singled out a country for special treatment in this way on grounds of purely economic policy.

Indeed, one has only to state the proposal to feel that there is something unreal and awkward about the whole idea—with the United Nations constituted as it is at present. Its political policy-making to date has been concerned with emergencies. A certain amount of initiative is surrendered by the sovereign states to the U.N. Secretariat, when they recognize the threat of war in a given situation. But economic policy-making in relation to the undeveloped countries is essentially of a long-term character; it means for example taking a view of the underlying trends in different countries and meting out quite different treatment to different governments on the basis of this assessment. There is rarely the "either-or" quality in economic situations, which would provide a good public reason for making these invidious distinctions. Yet the whole SUNFED proposal presupposes that they would fit neatly into the ethos of the United Nations.

The example of the Technical Assistance Board is worth looking at in detail, because it shows in an extreme form the kind of difficulty that the United Nations is liable to encounter even in the most limited kind of operation in the field of economic development. The proud legend of TAB is that it was the first United Nations body to be given complete freedom by the member states to allocate funds. In a sense this is true. When the Chairman of the Technical Assistance Board has announced his decision about how the annual sum of $25m.–$30m. is to be distributed among the under-developed countries, his ruling is not questioned in the General Assembly or elsewhere. But since the division of the spoils each year is made on almost the same basis as the year before, that is hardly a reflection of executive power. It simply points to the fact that the member nations, however reluctant they may be to accept the *status quo*, know that there is no alternative to it on which they could possibly reach agreement. They will occasionally allow adjustments in their conventional quota of funds in order to make room for special cases—like the newly independent state of Africa entering the United Nations in the late 1950s and early '60s, and claiming their share of technical assistance. But no one is ordinarily prepared to surrender any tittle of advantage acquired, however accidentally, in the conventional share-out in the past.

When the United Nations programme started in the early '50s, only a few of the nations were wise enough to see the benefits that were to be obtained from a supply of foreign technicians recruited by the United Nations and from the free training offered to their own people in some of the best industrial plants and technical institutes in the world. Among the majority there were still the suspicions of imperialism, as well as the barrier of pride making some of them unwilling to admit that they needed a foreigner to teach them anything. However, there were others—Yugoslavia and Israel were outstanding examples—who went straight in and made the most of the opportunity offered to them. They had no inhibitions about locating the gaps in their own technical abilities or about getting foreigners to teach them to overcome them. The result was that these two countries obtained a rather larger share of the funds available than they would have been given in a share-out based on population or need—at a time when the United Nations were still trying to sell the idea of technical assistance to a number of reluctant customers—and they have continued to benefit since from the favoured position in the queue which they managed to establish for themselves. It is true that Yugoslavia and Israel have both made extremely good use of the resources put at their disposal, probably better use than anyone else so far. But it is arguable that by now others with larger populations or more urgent requirements should be given precedence over them.

*Forces of Inertia*

There are moreover other built-in factors adding powerfully to the forces of inertia. The share-out of the technical aid funds is not made on the authority of the Chairman of TAB alone, but in conjunction with the heads of the specialized agencies[2] and the Technical Assistance Office of the United Nations (UNTAO). Each of these men comes forward with a complete dossier of what the officials of his organization are doing in each country; he then proceeds to put a strong case for continuing what is being done, and if any one of his programmes happens to be coming to an end, to present proposals for replacing it quickly with a new one. It is indeed only by adding up what the World Health Organization (WHO), the Food and Agriculture Organization (FAO), the International Labour Organization (ILO), and so on, are doing in each country that the final figure for the technical aid grants to be made to each of the nations is arrived at.

It is an enormously roundabout way of arriving at something which is never very different from the *status quo*. It is especially tiresome since three-quarters of the technical aid projects vetted each year (every second year when the reform of bi-annual programming for technical assistance is introduced in 1961) form part of continuing programmes anyhow. No agency is likely to propose that one of its own going programmes should be given up, because in that event another agency might come in quickly and mop up the money saved. However, the complicated bureaucratic rigmarole does serve one purpose. It helps to make the point to the recipient countries that they are ultimately dependent on the specialized agencies of the United Nations for the calculation of their share of the technical assistance fund. Once the money has been allocated, each country is at liberty to spend it with any U.N. agency that it likes. So it is at this stage that the agencies become anxious; and they try, each in turn, to impress upon the national governments the need to continue with their particular programmes, and not to switch any of the money over to something else. Abundant energy is devoted to this competitive task; no one would suspect, observing their behaviour, that these people were all part of the single family of the

99

United Nations. Special missions of high pressure technical aid salesmen are usually sent out from each of the main agencies to make a round of several countries in a region and ensure that the governments are convinced. They usually are.

So on top of the fixed conventions of the annual country share-out, there are the strong pressures tending to make the actual use of the funds within a country in this year as much like last year as makes no odds. Of course there is the occasional difficult government which likes to go its own way. But the ideal that almost everyone recognizes is that everything everywhere stays put.

That is not because the men who run the programme want it this way. The United Nations and its agencies contain people of energy and talent, who know that periodic changes in direction and content are both necessary if it is to be effective. Mr. David Owen, the head of the U.N. Technical Assistance Board, once privately described his role as being to keep a sort of village shop providing technical aid in penny packets: the one virtue that he could claim for the system was that the shop was always open and nobody went away entirely empty-handed. Such initiative as the head of TAB can exercise is confined to the control of a contingency fund of up to 5 per cent of each year's financial resources and a planning reserve which takes 3 per cent of the money provided for field programmes. This gives him a maximum of some $2m. a year to use on his own authority.[3] He used it for example when the republic of Guinea in West Africa, which was deserted overnight by its French technicians, after the country had voted in the referendum organized by General de Gaulle in 1958, shortly after his accession to power, against membership of the French Community. Technical aid in a hurry was in this instance a matter of life and death. Here, indeed, is the kind of emergency task which the United Nations can, even with its limited resources, perform much better than anyone else. The whole delicate operation is politically sterilized, in a way that would be impossible if any single nation, however generous, were to take up the burden of providing technical aid. But success in an emergency operation—again, it is to be noticed, of a political character—is no substitute for an economic policy.

## A New Approach

It was partly because of the failure of the United Nations to develop any independent initiative of its own in the field of technical aid to undeveloped countries—indeed finding that its role chiefly consisted in acting as a kind of baby-minder for a fortuitous *status quo*—that when the U.N. Special Fund was established in 1958, a deliberate attempt was made to break away from the existing conventions and routines. To begin with the Special Fund, whose work on pre-investment could readily have been taken into the United Nations Technical Assistance Programme, was set up as a separate entity. Then Mr. Paul Hoffman, the first Managing Director, refused to countenance any system of sharing out the available funds among the undeveloped nations. The use of funds was to be decided by the experts from above, not democratically from below. Next he ran into a dispute with the United Nation agencies, like ILO and UNESCO, who, being the experts, wanted—as under the TAB system—to direct this money into pet programmes of their own. The agencies, which are mainly located in Europe, tend to regard their work as having only a tenuous connection with anything that goes on in New York. It took some sharp argument to establish the principle that control over the use of the money to be devoted to pre-investment was to rest entirely in the Special Fund's hands, with the independent agencies of the U.N. acting truly as its agents, on a fee basis, for any project that they were employed to undertake. All this was, in fact, part of a deliberate effort to put power and authority back into the centre of the United Nations in New York. Naturally it was resisted: the feuding princes of a loose federation, who have been vigorously pursuing demarcation disputes among themselves, have always resented the centralizer.

But there was a further problem for the U.N. Special Fund within the New York headquarters itself. Perhaps its most difficult task was to resist being caught up in the political aims of the United Nations, and to assert firmly that it was concerned with the objective of economic development alone—concentrating on those countries which seemed capable of using the resources offered to them to pursue an effective economic policy. The matter is by no means settled yet. It raises extremely delicate questions about the relationship between an economic organization of this type and the main body of the hierarchy of the United Nations.

The Secretary-General, Mr. Dag Hammarskjöld, has managed gradually to enlarge the area of political initiative allowed to the Secretariat. These are important gains. By comparison the scale of the U.N. economic effort has so far been of almost negligible significance. It is therefore not surprising that the upper levels of the Secretariat, led by the Secretary-General himself, instinctively tend to see the economic agencies like the Special Fund, as subsidiary instruments of an institution whose important aims are political. The business of technical aid at the stage of pre-investment, when the effort is being directed towards filling certain gaps in knowledge about local resources or in the training of certain local skills, which will then make it possible to use capital properly, is generally unspectacular—if not positively dull. Certainly it does not have the glamour of saving Laos from communist infiltration or helping to prevent the disintegration of the state in Guinea.*

Of course there is bound to be some compromise between the political needs and the economic aims of an international organization. Mr. Hoffman with his earlier experience of similar problems, as the administrator of the Marshall Plan in Europe, seems to be expert at making the compromises as inexpensive as possible. At any rate during the first year of operations by the Special Fund he managed, with the help of his able deputy, Professor Arthur Lewis of the West Indies, to seize and hold the initiative in a way that no United Nations body had succeeded in doing before. He was even able in some measure to follow the vital principle of "unfair shares" in the distribution of funds among member countries. The Fund has gone out frankly looking for high returns.

That so much has been possible is partly due to the exceptional circumstances surrounding the person of the Managing Director of the Fund. He comes from right outside the hierarchy of the United Nations officialdom and is entirely free from the civil service inhibitions of this class. Taking on this job at the age of sixty-eight, a rich man with a record of great

* See pp. 97 and 100

achievement behind him, he had the freedom of manoeuvre of someone who does not have a career still to make. This kind of thing is quickly sensed in the inbred and highly competitive atmosphere of the United Nations headquarters in New York. However, having once established the broad principle that economic criteria were to be paramount, Hoffman was careful to avoid a show of intransigence. Indeed, he has been criticized for being too ready to allow money to be used in small amounts for projects which are unlikely to yield very useful results, in order to be left free from political pressures when the allocation of the large sums come to be decided.

One factor which has certainly had an influence is the general view among the undeveloped countries themselves that Hoffman is uniquely capable of collecting from Western governments the money that is required to finance the work of pre-investment. He therefore has a special status in their eyes as a kind of breadwinner, as well as dispenser of funds. Even so, there must be some doubt whether as the programme develops and expands, with perhaps a hundred or two hundred schemes going forward in various parts of the world, nations which feel they have been robbed of their share will be quite so willing to allow the Managing Director a free hand to concentrate money on some country of his choosing, just because he judges that there his projects are likely to open the way quickly to big investment opportunities. A lot plainly depends on the personality of the man in charge. Someone once described Hoffman as "a modest man, who modestly deals with governments as if they were people much like himself". That is the kind of approach needed—not overimpressed by the brute fact of national sovereignty—in order to assert an independent role in the business of economic development. It is probably a help to come from a big country, also not to be a professional civil servant.

### Impotent or Irresponsible Management

Still, personalities are only part of the story. However big the man in charge, it is unlikely that he would be able to conduct the distribution of funds with this degree of freedom and independence, if the amounts involved were themselves really big. That is the decisive factor. The Special Fund, although it has power over the distribution of larger sums of money than any other United Nations body before, still only deals in amounts which do not make a significant difference to the average country's foreign exchange budget. Only exceptionally will a country be able to draw more than a few hundred thousand dollars a year of equipment and services from this source. If the prizes were much larger, any undeveloped country which felt itself to be aggrieved or passed over by the Managing Director would not easily resist the temptation to use its vote to make life awkward for him.

In fact the main difficulty about any system of economic aid working on the United Nations principle of direct democracy, with an equal voice for all, is that it either makes the management impotent or irresponsible. Impotence occurs when the managers are so anxious about the dangerous repercussions of changing anything that they accept the principle that whatever is, is best. An example is the paralysis of the function of policy-making which has occurred in the Technical Assistance Board. This is not inevitable, as the U.N. Special Fund has now shown. So long as the amount of money that can be obtained by any individual country is not very large, member nations may be induced to surrender their power to interfere with the disposition of funds—if there is also a big personality about to surrender it to. It is true that Mr. Hoffman in the Special Fund is subjected to a Governing Council of eighteen national delegates of the United Nations who meet twice yearly and have to approve any new project proposed by the Fund, before any money can be spent. But the members of the Governing Council only have the power of veto, not of initiating projects. Moreover, since they are without expertise in this field, being diplomats rather than economists or technicians, their role is reduced to a speech-making one. There is no active participation in the making of decisions, like that of a committee of parliament, for example, in its relations with the executive branch of government. In such circumstances the executive is effectively responsible to no one.

This particular defect might be overcome if a different kind of person were chosen to deal with these matters within the

United Nations. It was indeed proposed at one stage that the eighteen Executive Directors of the World Bank in Washington, who are appointed by their countries for their special knowledge and are regarded by them as being sufficiently reliable to be given some limited power of initiative and decision (unlike most delegates at the United Nations), should take over the Governing Council of the U.N. Special Fund as well. That would have made quite a difference to the efficiency and the speed of operation of the Special Fund, for one of the big advantages of the Bank is that it can call its board together at a few days' notice, if there is some important matter to be discussed, and get a decision out of it. At the United Nations, six weeks is the minimum period of advance notice which members of the Governing Council require in order to be able to get the answers from their home governments, and besides, they meet only at set periods twice a year. However, the jealousy between the United Nations proper in New York and the very loosely associated "specialized agencies" of the United Nations in Washington—the World Bank and the International Monetary Fund which are totally independent in practice and anxious to mark the gulf between themselves and the *hoi polloi* presided over by Mr. Hammarskjöld—prevented this solution.

But the point to observe is that if it had been adopted, the rest of the member nations would have had to content themselves with the formal exercise of as little power as they now enjoy in the World Bank. There they are confined to an annual meeting lasting three or four days and a couple of set speeches each. Power is in fact exercised personally by the President of the Bank, Mr. Eugene Black, in consultation, whenever he deems this necessary, with the representatives of the important countries. He knows that in practice it will be awkward to do anything that the United States and Britain do not like. In the board meetings of the World Bank, it has never, I am informed, come to a formal vote among the eighteen members. The atmosphere is close and cosy; the meetings are private and it is generally agreed that the least useful thing that people can do is to make set speeches.

The question is whether it would be possible to run a big grant programme like the SUNFED scheme on similar lines, but without the system of weighted voting employed in the

Bank. If it could be done two things would almost inevitably happen. First of all, the management of such an organization would, as a matter of prudence, keep in especially close touch with the chief donor countries. If the United States provided 30–40 per cent of the money, as it does in most of the U.N. institutions, then it would clearly be recognized by any effective management that it was essential not to get at cross purposes with the U.S. government. After all there are annual budgets in most countries, and it is not unreasonable that the representatives of those national groups of taxpayers who put up most of the money should be especially interested in seeing that it is spent economically and efficiently. In other words, the effective power of veto is likely to reside with the main donor countries in such an organization, whether there is a formal system of weighted voting or not.

The second result of such an arrangement is bound to be the growth of the policy-making powers of the man in charge. If he is to do his job properly, he must, like a British judge, be virtually irremovable and free from the pressure of parliamentary questions. Thus the final effect would be to appoint a single man, or small group of men, to act for a stated period of years as the arbiter of world aid. Only in this way would it be possible to use the available funds effectively to speed up economic development. That, as we have seen, means accepting the principle of inequality among nations, so that large sums can be concentrated on particular projects in selected countries when the conditions are appropriate. But this of course is not what the countries which have been pressing for SUNFED are after. They want a jolly shareout, not a deliberate and ruthless concentration of aid in a few chosen countries— just because someone happens to judge that these countries are likely to use it more efficiently than others.

*Notes*

1. The World Bank's authorized capital is now $21 billion. Subscribed capital in 1960 was $19·3 billion.

2. The specialized agencies concerned are:
   Food and Agricultural Organization,
   International Atomic Energy Agency,
   International Civil Aviation Organization,
   International Labour Organization,

International Telecommunication Union,
United Nations Educational, Scientific and Cultural
Organization,
World Health Organization,
World Meteorological Organization.

The World Bank and the International Monetary Fund are also represented on TAB, but only as observers. (See organizational chart, Appendix II.)

3. The Executive Chairman of TAB disposes of funds from two sources:

(*a*) A Contingency Fund of up to 5 per cent of each year's financial resources (with an upper limit of $1·6m. per annum). This is drawn out of the Reserve Fund of TAB, amounting to $12m. Replacement of these contingency drawings in any year is a first charge on the following year's budget.

(*b*) A Planning Reserve equal to 3 per cent of the cost of field programmes, or about $750,000 at the recent rate of budgeting. This is intended to provide some flexibility in the technical aid programme, to meet requirements of newly independent countries and also to provide some extra finance for the smaller U.N. agencies like WMO.

The practical effect is that there is about $2¼m. out of a total budget of $30m.–$35m. which can be held back for use on the initiative of the man in charge of the U.N. Technical Assistance Programme. This is widely felt to be inadequate, and it has been agreed by the United Nations to increase Planning Reserve funds to 5 per cent of field programme costs when the "financial situation ... permits".

CHAPTER 8

# LESSONS FROM THE WORLD BANK

THE last chapter showed why it was that any international organization handing out large sums of aid was likely in practice to weight the opinions of some of its members—the big donors—much more heavily than those of others. An informal understanding of this kind has no particular advantage over the formal system of weighted voting used in the World Bank; it has the serious disadvantage that the countries responsible for providing large sums of aid would almost certainly refuse to accept an arrangement which did not formally recognize their special position. The World Bank has in fact been so much the most successful of the international bodies concerned with economic development that it is worth examining its work more closely to see whether it could not, after all, be used to fulfil the new and bigger task. There is indeed a body of influential opinion which believes that the Bank ought to be given the leading role in any enlarged programme of economic aid to the undeveloped countries.

That there should be this feeling is a justified tribute to the shrewdness and energy with which the Bank has conducted its business. It is not simply, or even mainly, that it is particularly good at "playing the market" in Wall Street—though Mr. Eugene Black, the President who is a former stock exchange man, is especially proud of his ability to obtain the capital he needs from investors, insurance companies or from foreign central banks on finely judged terms, presented just at the right moment. The more remarkable achievement is that the Bank has been able to evoke in many of the undeveloped countries themselves a feeling that it has genuine sympathy and understanding for their problems. This feeling is more widespread, it is fair to say, in Asia than it is in Latin America. But that the view should exist at all among people who have had requests for loans turned down, as well as accepted, by the Bank is a sufficiently notable circumstance.

This is not just the result of good public relations, though the Bank's characteristically American attention to that side of the business has certainly been a help. More important is the high calibre of the Bank's staff and the general mood in which it conducts its affairs. It is hard to say precisely how this question of mood affects the problem—or indeed to describe it precisely. Yet there is no doubt that it is an extremely potent factor. One way in which one notices it, as a visitor from the outside, is the frequency with which one encounters individuals of very high ability who are also the very slightest bit *odd*— or at any rate would stand a good chance of being regarded so by any organization which was really intent on getting itself run by a lot of "organization men". The Bank struck me as very un-American in this respect: the cult of individuality was certainly much stronger than one would expect to find in businesses of comparable size in the United States. And the atmosphere too is unhurried, indeed almost reflective: the local cult of the executive being overworked, and being seen to be so, has somehow passed by the spacious office block on the corner of H Street, Washington. The senior people here tend to behave rather like the traditional merchant banker, who knows that the important thing is not to pass pieces of paper, but to have one or two good ideas not too infrequently.

Bankers of this type, who are putting their money down on their judgment of other people's initiative, with an admixture of their own expertise, must above all be open mentally if they are to do their job well. They will not be able to do it if they are fussed by a too tightly packed timetable or a mass of routine work. It is encouraging to find that some of the 19th century banker's insistence on being unharassed, developed first in the City of London, has been carried over into this institution. It is worth remembering that George Grote, the historian of ancient Greece, was a London banker in the 19th century running his business in Threadneedle Street in such a way as to be able to do his writing and research in his spare time. That was perhaps carrying the pursuit of unclouded judgment, as well as the short working-day, a little further than it will go today. But the direction was right.

Yet the World Bank remains a very American institution. Right from the beginning the convention was established that of the two financial institutions set up at the Bretton Woods Conference in 1944, the International Monetary Fund should be predominantly controlled by Europeans with a European president, and the World Bank by the Americans. A couple of accidents helped the World Bank to recruit U.S. officials of such high quality in the middle ranges of the hierarchy. One was the Marshall Plan which produced a new crop of experienced young American administrators with an understanding of international realities; the other accident was the stream of distinguished refugees from the U.S. State Department and other offices of government during the McCarthy period in the early and middle 1950s. The World Bank seems to have gained a part, at any rate, of what the U.S. government lost in the strange debauch of the McCarthy witch-hunt, when many able people felt that they could not make a decent career as government officials. Incidentally it was during this period, when the United Nations was McCarthy's special target for persecution, that the U.N. headquarters in New York lost some of its best people, and, equally important, put off many more outside from joining the organization. The United Nations has still not quite recovered from the damage that was done to it then.

In the World Bank, especially since Mr. Black took over in the early fifties, the nucleus of American senior staff has been increasingly supplemented by Europeans of high calibre. This was a deliberate choice on the part of the President. Another advantage of the Bank over the United Nations is that Black, unlike Hammarskjöld, is under no compulsion to share out the manning of his headquarters staff on any principle of national fair shares. It is a common and bitter complaint inside the United Nations that some first class candidate for a post is turned down, because he belongs to the wrong nation (e.g. British or American), and the post has to be filled by a second rate man from a country with a claim to a quota of places on the staff. Furthermore, the United Nations is bound by a rigid set of salary scales—no longer high enough, with the progress of inflation since the war, to attract the right sort of people for all the jobs that need to be filled—whereas the President of the Bank makes his own decisions about the market price of any person whom he wishes to employ. All this helps to maintain the special mood of the Bank; the people about whom such trouble and expense are taken in selection are also likely to be allowed considerable initiative in action.

### *Position of Trust*

In several countries where there is a resident World Bank representative, he seems to have established a relationship with the government rather like that of an ambassador of a peculiarly intimate ally. Only unlike most ambassadors, he is also professionally equipped to understand the detailed working of the economic policy of the government to which he is accredited. Frequently he will have an office in the middle of one of the government ministries and be consulted as a matter of regular practice when major economic decisions are being taken. The working relationship is in some instances even closer. In Pakistan, for example, the World Bank put its representative at the effective disposal of the Minister of Finance, while he was engaged in working out a new plan of development, with the understanding that the man would act pretty much as the Minister's chief civil servant. His duties as a World Bank official were reduced to a minimum and he was engaged practically full-time in working for the Pakistani government—at the level where the crucial decisions for the next five years were being made.

This is not an exceptional case, though it is unusual to find it in so big and important a country as Pakistan. It is well understood within the Bank that there are circumstances in which the most useful work that can be done by a resident representative is to devote himself to helping a government to sort out its own problems. It is a form of technical assistance, not very different from a certain kind of pre-investment activity that might be undertaken by the U.N. Special Fund. For the Bank's idea is simply that if a government is helped to formulate a sound plan of development, containing a number of bankable investment projects, the operation will have turned out to be a good stroke of business. Before the U.N. Special Fund was thought of, the Bank was actively engaged in this kind of technical aid—perhaps the most useful kind, directly designed to increase a country's absorptive capacity for capital—but the work was always on a small scale. It should now be possible to use the U.N. Special Fund as a direct and fertile source of business for the Bank, with the two organizations working closely together. Mr. Black, the President of the World Bank, is one of the three members of the Consultative Board of the Special Fund.

From a long-term point of view the most important gain from a habit of successful cooperation of this kind would be to bring the World Bank into a more intimate working relationship with the United Nations. There is remarkably little sense of belonging among the specialized agencies spread through Europe, and even less in the two Bretton Woods institutions, the IMF and the World Bank, in Washington. It is ironic to reflect that Lord Keynes opposed giving the Bank and the IMF a home in Washington and suggested New York as the place where they would keep in close touch with the financial world; had he won his point, they might at any rate have kept in touch with the United Nations.

Admittedly, the President of the World Bank does have to make a formal report to the meetings of the U.N. Economic and Social Council. But his manner on these occasions is rather that of a visiting potentate about to receive an honorary degree; certainly it would be a serious shock if, after the ceremony was over, someone behaved as if it were an appropriate time to get him to answer some straight questions about his kingdom. It is indeed often maintained that the jealously guarded separateness of the Bank has been one of the secrets of its success. There is little doubt that it would have been much more difficult for Mr. Black to make his way as a successful borrower on Wall Street, if he had presented himself there as an agent of the United Nations. Quite apart from anything else, many investors would have been deterred, particularly during the early and middle 1950s, by the thought of Soviet influence on the disposition of their cash. Mr. Black was able to boast that he had no Russians on his board. The Soviet Union could, it is true, decide to join the World Bank at any time—it would have to subscribe a sum of money in gold, to the International Monetary Fund as well as the Bank, which, although substantial, would hardly impose a strain on the Russian reserves[1]—but presumably it feels that there is little to be gained from acquiring a comparatively small weighted vote in the councils of the organization.

The Bank did not achieve its present high reputation overnight. There were times, particularly during the early 1950s, when it was severely criticized for its failure to lend either on the scale required or to the nations most in need. Before that, during the period immediately following the war, the Bank had made a few big loans to West European countries for purposes of reconstruction—a function specifically recognized in its official title: International Bank for Reconstruction and Development. But once the Marshall Plan started, this type of lending ceased. There followed a period in which the Bank had very little to do. Even as late as 1956 its total annual lending—to all countries, not just to the poor ones—was only $400m.; and the insiders argued vigorously at the time that this was at or near the absolute maximum which the Bank could provide. Then all of a sudden Mr. Black found a lot of new customers; Bank lending increased by 75 per cent in one year, to $700m. It has remained at about this level since 1958.

Looking back over the whole story since the war, there is little sign of any continuous thread of policy running through the Bank's activities. After its early efforts to assist in postwar reconstruction were brought to a halt, it wandered about for several years with no clear sense of direction. At this stage it looked as if there would be few nations who were both needy and sufficiently creditworthy to recommend themselves to this new international lending institution. It was not, in fact, until the second half of the 1950s that the Bank began lending on any substantial scale to the undeveloped countries. Then it played a particularly important part in the financing of the Indian Second Five Year Plan. India became during these years the Bank's biggest customer; and by the end of the decade one-eighth of all the outstanding loans were in its hands.

# LESSONS FROM THE WORLD BANK

## Banker-Client Relationship

Nevertheless, taking the Bank's operations as a whole, it has been more important as a source of funds to the comparatively well-to-do, semi-developed countries, like Australia, South Africa, Italy and Japan, than to the really poor. Of course helping the semi-developed countries over their last financial hurdle, before they are able to move on their own into the ordinary capital markets of the U.S. and Europe and borrow the money that they need, is something well worth doing. And the World Bank does it extremely well, with the minimum of bureaucratic fuss about the detailed disposal of the cash that it makes available, relying mainly on personal contacts with the people in charge on the spot. The loans made during the 1950s to the Italian government in support of its programme for the revival of the backward agricultural region of Southern Italy were a model of this type of operation. Once the Bank had satisfied itself that the plan was well founded and that the man who had been put in charge of the operation and his immediate subordinates were competent and reliable people, it left the details alone. It conceived its task in this instance to be essentially that of a merchant banker who has found a good client with a project that looks like being successful: it is up to the client to decide how precisely to use the money offered to him.

That, however, is not the kind of relationship envisaged in the World Bank's constitution: it is only supposed to put up money for individual projects on their own inherent merits, the personality of the borrower has nothing to do with it. It is easy to see why the people who wrote the constitution should have been so eager to ensure that the new international lending agency should be no respecter of persons or nations. But, alas, the principle of equality among borrowers cannot be established as easily as that. The banker-client relationship, based on personal judgment of how different people are likely to behave, is of the essence of the lending business. As soon tell a banker to discard it as ask a physician to start prescribing for anonymous patients by post.

But of course the consequences of the World Bank's acceptance of the logic of its position as a banker has been that the semi-developed countries, with all sorts of attractive features to recommend them, including their anticipated ability to obtain capital on the basis of their own credit in the market in the fairly near future, have been allowed to get away with things that are strictly denied to the poor and untrustworthy and underdeveloped. In the Italian case money which the government borrowed from the Bank during the 1950s was not in fact required to meet the foreign exchange cost of equipment that it needed to buy abroad. The Italian government's problem was the broader one of keeping the total demand and supply at home in balance. If a lot of additional investment was to be undertaken in order to help the backward South, then plainly the existing balance was likely to be upset: more money would be handed out in wages to workers employed on the investment projects, without an equivalent increase in consumer supplies. One way to restore the balance, assuming that there is a friendly banker who is confident about the ultimate success of the investment plan, is to obtain a loan which will cover the cost of extra consumer supplies from abroad to meet the rise in home demand.

Unfortunately the Bank's constitution does not envisage the circumstances in which the provision of extra consumption goods might be a more important aid to investment than the supply of any number of capital goods. There is a semantic difficulty here, because of a widespread feeling that "capital" (austere and virtuous) must be wholly different from "consumption" (frivolous and enjoyable) and that it is wicked, as well as confusing, to suggest that virtue might accumulate by the simple act of purveying more enjoyment.

### *"Impact Loans"*

In practice the Bank overcame the difficulty in Italy by asking the government to pick out a few projects, for which foreign equipment was going to be bought anyhow, and to attach the loans formally to these. But this was a purely metaphysical operation: it had no practical meaning. The Bank made the loan on the basis of its view of the whole programme for the development of Southern Italy, and it would have been prepared to make the loan to help this programme along, even if there had not been any projects in it requiring the large-scale purchase of foreign supplies. It was for this reason that, right at the start of the Italian programme, a proposal was put up by the economist Mr. Rosenstein-Rodan, who was economic adviser to the World Bank at the time, that a new type of transaction, called an "impact loan", should be introduced to deal with the problem. This would give official recognition to the fact that the impact of investment expenditure at one point of the economy might be felt at a totally different point—in a shortage of consumption goods or in a balance of payments crisis caused by running down the country's foreign exchange reserve to pay for imports of such goods.

The need for a principle of this kind to guide Bank lending in the undeveloped countries has, as Rosenstein-Rodan fore-saw, become increasingly urgent. An early example, which shows the nature of the problem in its simplest form, was the request from Ecuador for a loan to help fight the disease of swollen shoot affecting its cacao plantations. In order to deal with the problem Ecuador needed a lot of organized labour for a systematic campaign to eliminate the diseased trees. But there was no surplus of local labour available, and to take it away from other agricultural occupations would have re-sulted in a shortage of food while the campaign was in progress. The obvious answer was a loan to finance some extra food imports, but the Bank's rules did not allow this. There was a short while in the early fifties when the World Bank did toy with the device of "impact loans". However, in the end the banker's instinct prevailed against the economist's argument. It was felt that to concede the point would be to impair one of the Bank's most powerful instruments for supervising the proper use of its loans to the undeveloped countries. Once it was formally granted that money could be borrowed to meet some general pressure on a country's balance of payments caused by internal expansion, there would, it was felt, be no defence against the most unreasonable demands by the most wasteful governments.

The World Bank's fears are understandable. But they hardly seem to provide strong enough grounds for a total refusal to consider some means of overcoming a profound weakness in the whole philosophy of lending enshrined in its rules. For the insistence on the use of money exclusively to buy foreign capital goods and technical services introduces a strange and self-defeating bias into the development programmes of the un-developed countries. After all, for many of them, particularly in Asia, the problem is how to find useful work for the large mass of underemployed labour: the best solution would be to put people to work on capital projects designed to raise the productive power of the country. That is, of course, precisely the method employed by the Chinese and other communist governments: labour used prodigally and subjected to total discipline allows them to build up capital assets, without foreign loans or aid. Because the countries which are friendly with the West reject this solution, it is wrong to drive them to the opposite extreme where they have an incentive to use large amounts of foreign labour-saving equipment—since this is something on which World Bank money can be spent—and so to limit the employment of the surplus of local labour. Nobody calculates the cost of the waste involved in keeping men idle and producing nothing. We have already noticed the case where in conditions of labour *scarcity* (in Ecuador) the Bank's rigid rules, disqualifying loans to finance food imports, interfere with the intelligent use of a country's resources. The harm is even more serious in the conditions of labour surplus which are common throughout most of Asia today.

## *Capital Replaces Labour*

The rules about the use of foreign capital serve to reinforce a strong bias that already exists among the new class of Western oriented technicians in most of the undeveloped countries. These men are instinctively attracted towards the labour-saving device: they see it as an essential part of the new cultural pattern, which they are hoping to impose at top speed on their own societies. And in a sense they are right; at any rate an attitude of mind which treats labour as something to be used economically and with care usually goes together with some degree of respect for the workman himself. But beyond this there is often the strong emotional preference—part aesthetic

—for the new, clean, manageable, quick machine, and against the semi-barbaric techniques of marshalling multitudes of primitive people and imposing on them the harsh disciplines which will make them work in an orderly fashion. Naturally the man in control of a development project will, if he can see a way out, try to avoid the responsibility for creating a mass of squalor while engaged in the grand enterprise of bringing his country forward into the brave new world of clean concrete structures, electric pylons and broad metalled roads. Often he does not even have to face the choice; he simply follows the advice given by Western technical consultants who unthinkingly apply their standard methods of reducing costs.

I described earlier the results that I saw at Bhakra dam in India.* This is by no means an isolated case or indeed an extreme one. In Northern Siam there is another great hydro-electricity project, the Yanhee dam; this one, unlike Bhakra, is being financed by a large loan from the World Bank, and the Bank takes a close interest in the whole operation. It is on an impressive scale. The high dam blocking the gorge on the Yanhee River will absorb a million cubic metres of concrete and carry an electric power capacity ultimately of over half a million kilowatts—that is five times the installed capacity of the whole of Siam at the moment. When I went there in late 1959 the project was well advanced and the total labour force was around 800 men, including the storemen for the great quantity of machinery, equipment and vehicles collected on the site, as well as the drivers, cleaners and the servants at the guest-house. The number of men actually engaged on the work of construction was about 400. It was a splendid American-type job, run, as if it might be something out of the American Far West, by a U.S. firm of engineering consultants. I put the obvious question to the American engineer in charge as he came out of one of the two main tunnels through the hillside, where perhaps a dozen men were at work, surrounded by bright arc lamps at the far end, making rapid inroads into the rock face with pneumatic drills: Why had he decided to run the job with so much machinery and so little labour? He looked puzzled for a moment. "Why", he said, "I just figured

* See Chapter 2, p. 15

# "SHADOW PRICES"

out how the job could be done most efficiently, and then added on the labour that I needed."

Of course, the idea that U.S. prices applied in costing the machines and equipment used on this site might be wholly inappropriate for determining the most economical way of employing Siam's resources is not something that would occur spontaneously to an engineer. But it should have been put to him by an economic planner—and it surely ought to have been in the mind of the international lending agency, which makes a point of concerning itself with the country's economic development as a whole. Foreign exchange costs are different from local costs, for as soon as any of the poor countries begin to press forward their development with any success the shortage of foreign exchange normally becomes the chief limiting factor on the pace of progress. The extreme example of this at the moment is India. There foreign-made capital equipment is enormously scarce, while indigenous productive resources in the form of labour are embarrassingly plentiful. The rate of exchange of the rupee in no way reflects the true relative costs of these things. That is only another way of saying that *if* India were compelled suddenly to pay its own way in international trade, foreign goods would become very scarce and expensive, while the export prices of Indian goods would have to be cut sharply in order to achieve even a modest increase in the country's earnings abroad. Measured in terms of what is really scarce or plentiful in India, it is clear that local resources and labour in particular—even at the present pitifully low wage level—are overpriced, while imported capital goods are grossly underpriced.

## *"Shadow Prices"*

The devaluation of the Indian rupee—which would automatically raise the domestic price of foreign imported machinery, as well as lowering the export price in foreign currency of domestically produced goods—might help to introduce some rational order into the planned use of resources. Mr. I. M. D. Little has pointed out how the present structure of prices gets in the way of rational planning in India.[2] Worse still, he says,

119

"in private industry, which follows the guide of profit without the correcting bias which planners can to some extent impose, all decisions tend to be slanted towards using too little labour, too much capital, and too many imports." Since it is unlikely that a government will willingly invite the political odium that seems to accompany a devaluation of the currency these days, it is up to the planners to use some system of "shadow prices", however rough the calculation, which would more accurately reflect the cost in terms of Indian resources of buying foreign goods.

The whole bias not only in the West but also in the Soviet Union is to arrange matters so as to substitute capital equipment for increasingly expensive labour. That is no doubt an exercise which India too will face several decades from now. But in the meanwhile its problem is how to use more labour and fewer machines than the developed countries. That means that planners must avoid, above all, being bamboozled into taking so-called "free market" prices, which reflect the balance of costs in highly industrialized countries, as the basis for the calculation of their own development costs and benefits. Even an arbitrarily determined "shadow price" will be better than that.

It would be a help if the World Bank took the lead by getting rid of the powerful built-in bias towards the employment of scarce capital goods and away from the use of surplus labour. For example, agricultural investment in the undeveloped countries barely figures in World Bank lending, except where there is a big conventional project, like a dam with an irrigation system to be built. Yet it is clear that, apart from these larger schemes, there is vast scope for an increase in the output of food in Asia, Africa and Latin America, if a small addition to the resources and know-how of peasants were applied in millions of individual agricultural holdings. It is this central problem which no international institution seems to be able to tackle at the moment. Part of the trouble is that what the peasant needs in order to increase his productive power is not readily indentifiable as capital. Thus it is all right to lend money to India to set up fertilizer factories to produce supplies which will eventually raise Indian agricultural output. Everyone agrees that it is an extremely useful investment. But if it is suggested that money should be borrowed by the Indian government here and now to buy fertilizers abroad, until the fertilizer plants are in action, that is not investment and so cannot qualify for a World Bank loan.

## Failure in Argiculture

It is worth observing that the whole conception of what constitutes "investment" and what does not has been shaped by the experience of industry, not agriculture. Fertilizer is treated, naturally enough, as the equivalent of an industrial raw material; it is therefore a part of the *current* costs of production. Nevertheless it is, together with irrigation, a necessary part of the long-term process of improving the productivity of the soil. What it comes to is that because we are used to thinking of machines as capital, we are ready to accept the action of a farmer who buys a tractor as "investment", and to give him a loan to buy it abroad. But it would be more difficult to persuade the World Bank that it ought, for example, to make a loan just as readily to pay for a series of imported consignments of improved seeds. The transaction in this case is viewed as equivalent to a raw material purchase for a manufacturing plant.

Yet the essential aim of these operations with seed and fertilizer is to anticipate by a few years the start of the long-term process of improvement in the productive power of the land. It is a very long process because peasants not only have to be taught what to do, but be convinced that it is worth while paying for the stuff. In a society of peasant proprietors where each man is free to grow more or less what he likes, exacting payment for fertilizer is often an essential part of the pressure that has to be exerted on the producer to induce him to market more produce. If he gets his fertilizer for nothing he is under no compulsion to sell more outside the farm. One promising way of dealing with the problem is to start off by offering the fertilizer or the improved seed, or whatever it may be, at a low subsidized price, but as soon as its efficacy has been convincingly demonstrated to the peasants, to charge the full cost. That was what was done in Yugoslavia with the recent introduction of the immensely successful hybrid wheat; after a period of suspicion and resistance the peasants started clamouring for the new seeds and even stealing them in order to improve their own output. But in more primitive societies than Yugoslavia, without the vigorous leadership of a government believing firmly in state enterprise, any similar operation is likely to take several years longer.

It is, however, the mobilization of labour for capital works which is the overriding problem of agricultural investment in undeveloped countries. The organized land drainage schemes, which are a marked feature of Chinese agriculture and which have been so dangerously neglected in India and Pakistan, are a case in point. Plenty of people are available to do the work, especially during the agricultural off-season. In China there is no problem. But in India the workers will have to be paid something extra, and that is bound to increase the demand for consumption goods, especially food. The planners are afraid to put a lot of money into this form of investment without some additional consumer supplies being made available, because that would disturb the overall balance of supply and demand. Plainly what is required to meet this kind of need is some form of "impact loan".*

What the World Bank has been able to do so far in the field of agriculture is little more than to tinker about on the periphery of the problem. The responsible officials of the organization are keenly aware of their failure, and have tried to do something by providing capital for services which are an adjunct to agricultural development, for example roads, which make it easier to market produce, and also some money for agricultural credit institutions. But there is little prospect, if the Bank continues to be guided by its present principles of lending, of any major contribution from this quarter towards raising the productive power of agriculture in the undeveloped countries. The following table shows the meagreness of the effort to date. Out of nearly $4 billion of development loans, only $124m. has gone into agricultural development in the underdeveloped world.

* See pp. 115–117

# THE PEASANT'S MIND

WORLD LOANS FOR AGRICULTURE TO
UNDERDEVELOPED COUNTRIES OUTSIDE EUROPE ($ million)
Cumulative to mid-1959

| Purpose | Latin America | Asia | Africa | Total |
|---|---|---|---|---|
| Farm mechanization .. | 26 | — | — | 26 |
| Irrigation and food control .. .. .. | 21 | 53 | — | 74 |
| Land clearance and improvement .. .. | 5 | 14 | — | 19 |
| Crop processing and storage .. .. .. | 1 | — | — | 1 |
| Livestock .. .. | 3 | 1 | — | 4 |
| Total agriculture | 56 | 68 | — | 124 |

## The Peasant's Mind

More money is needed in agriculture, not only to pay for supplies and capital works, but also in order to bring about a more fundamental change in social attitudes. Studies by the Food and Agriculture Organization have indicated that one of the chief barriers to increased production of food in Asia is the utterly passive attitude on the part of the mass of cultivators, the feeling that extra effort cannot be worth while, because life is fixed and determined. In the attempt to unravel these attitudes the FAO, like other observers, soon arrives at the ganglion knot of the village moneylender-trader-boss. This figure cannot be used as a comprehensive scapegoat for all that is wrong in the peasant life of the orient—the peasants contribute quite a lot themselves—but he is probably the most powerful factor making for immobility. People are commonly in debt to him throughout their lives. Yet it would be wrong to imagine that this makes him a simple enemy. The peasants have an ambivalent attitude towards him: he is after all the man to whom they can turn in case of need, and he does after all provide money on the strength of no more security than a promise to repay. He also tends to be viewed as a superior and powerful person with connections in the mysterious urban places.

As one FAO official put it: "The worst of it is that a townsman has only to come and start arguing with a peasant for the peasant to feel worried and inferior." And since the peasant begins with the assumption that he is likely to come off worst in any encounter with any representative of this alien world, but especially with a representative of the government, he is intensely suspicious of proposals from outside for change in his method of work or way of living. Besides, a simple calculation leads him to the conclusion that since he is already heavily in debt to the moneylender, who is also the trader handling his crop, any increase in his output is bound to benefit the moneylender and not himself.

This is one of the powerful reasons why extra effort, especially if it involves any expense that has to be paid for out of the peasant's pocket, is not believed to be worth while. A glance at the normal rates of interest charged for personal loans in a few Asian countries suggest how easy it is for people to get caught in a life-long financial thrall. The following rates taken from the ECAFE/FAO study "Credit Problems of Small Farmers in Asia and the Far East", are stated to be those "commonly charged by landlords, agriculturists and other moneylenders, relatives and village shopkeepers":

| COUNTRY | RATE OF INTEREST (*per cent per annum*) |
|---|---|
| India | 25 or over |
| Indonesia | 80–100 |
| Malaya | 50–60 |
| Philippines | 25–100 |
| Thailand | 28–45* |
| Japan | 5 |

* Relatives in Thailand are stated to charge an average of only 18 per cent.

The Japanese have entirely overcome the problem of the village moneylender by an effective system of cheap cooperative credit. This is the primary instrument of social reform on the land. But it is liable to be ineffective unless it is backed up by other means. Peasants will give credit to one another through the cooperative on the security of a certain amount of land; very poor peasants and share-croppers therefore tend to do badly under this arrangement. There has to be much more active intervention by the public authorities to break the stranglehold of the moneylender and his allies among the few well-to-do families in the village. A powerful weapon, as Japanese experience has once again demonstrated, is the system of guaranteed prices for agricultural produce. But here, too, the social obstacle has to be overcome before the guaranteed price can be made effective. Unless the government's man is actually there on the spot ready to pay cash for the crop, it still gets sold at a discount in the traditional fashion to the moneylender-trader. The peasant almost never has liquid funds and can very rarely afford to wait; and this is perhaps the main cause of his feeling of inferiority and of the sense of hopelessness that goes with it.

## Guaranteeing Farmers' Prices

One of the motives behind the much disputed Indian government decision to nationalize the wholesale trade in food grains was to try and overcome this difficulty; but little progress has been made so far. Moreover the Indian government has not yet been prepared to take on the burden of guaranteeing agricultural prices throughout the country. A start has been made in a few restricted areas on an experimental basis, but in this matter, as in so many others connected with agricultural reform, progress is held up by the lack of financial resources in the government's hands. It is afraid to print additional paper money and put it into the peasants' hands in return for their crops—although it would in the end be able to reimburse itself fully when the grain was finally sold in the market, so long as the guaranteed price had not been pitched above the market price. Indeed it would be reasonable to expect that if the authorities showed any trading acumen at all, they would be able to pay the peasants a good deal more than they get from the local trader at present and still show a profit on the final sale. What is required in order to allow a government the necessary room for manoeuvre to carry forward a programme of this type is, once more, a variety of "impact loan". Only in this case the money is needed as a reserve in case of trouble: the government should have at its disposal a fund of foreign exchange on which it can draw during the limited period of time between the purchase of grain from the peasants and its sale in the open market.

There is a tendency to confuse this problem of breaking the hold of the socially superior middleman class with the general problem of land reform. It is in fact quite wrong to imagine that land reform by itself will deal with the more profound social difficulty, which is a matter of building up the self-confidence of the peasant; reform is only the first step. Even the great revolutionary upheaval which accompanied the expropriation of the landowners in Mexico has still not succeeded in giving the Mexican peasant his rights. This is in spite of the fact that the Mexican government has established a system of guaranteed prices for maize, which is the staple food. Recently this has been some 600 pesos a ton. But according to the best information available to the government officials administering the programme in Mexico City it is rare for any small peasant to obtain more than 250 pesos a ton. This is because he sells it to the local merchant, whose main power in this case consists in having an effective monopoly of transport. The more remote the area, the more effective the control of transport is. These men are usually friends of the local political boss or of the provincial governor himself, and it is generally not worth while trying to challenge their power.

The final and tragic twist in this story is that even though the Mexican government, or part of it, might like to administer the programme of guaranteed prices in an honest fashion, it is at present inhibited by fear of the financial consequences. It would have to find or print the money to buy up much more maize. Hitherto it has had to buy only a small proportion of the crop at the guaranteed price; the rest moves into the market through the chain of middlemen. As one Mexican put it graphically: "There are tremendous profits to be made here just by plugging into the distribution network and tapping the current." But if the government really wished to make a reality of its guaranteed prices to the peasants it would have to come in with an initial expenditure of several billion pesos, perhaps as much as the whole of its present budget. The action itself would probably carry all sorts of social overtones, which would almost certainly cause some flight of capital out of the country. It is in fact unlikely that any government—except one which was in the first flush of power and over-confidence on the morrow of a revolution—would undertake so hazardous an enterprise without international backing.

This is where the World Bank or the International Monetary Fund, or both together, could most usefully make a loan in support of agricultural development. As the experience of the United States demonstrated first of all, there is no more powerful instrument for raising agricultural productivity than an effective system of guaranteed prices. In recent years it has even proved more powerful than the direct restrictions on the acreage of cultivated land or the bribes to farmers to take their good fields out of cultivation and put them into a "soil bank"; the crops have kept coming on. Nothing other than the abolition of guaranteed prices will, it seems, stop them.

*Notes*

1. Only 1 per cent of the enlarged quota subscriptions to the World Bank has to be paid in gold. The bigger item of expense would be membership of the IMF—which is obligatory on World Bank members—and requires a gold payment of 25 per cent of the national quota. For Russia this would amount to several hundred million dollars, which it would however be able to draw back from the IMF with the minimum of formalities if it ever needed to strengthen its reserves.

2. "The Strategy of Indian Development", by I. M. D. Little, *Economic Review, National Institute of Economic and Social Research*, London, May 1960. Mr. Little suggests that in order to avoid the incidental loss of export earnings on certain goods which are not overpriced at present, the Indians would have to accompany any devaluation by introducing export taxes "or similar discriminatory methods". The notion of "shadow prices" was mentioned by Mr. Little in a privately circulated paper.

# CHAPTER 9

# WHAT THE BANKER CANNOT DO

IT is fortunate that the World Bank has had enough imagination, as well as pragmatic spirit, to find ways of overcoming the ban on general purpose loans for development when it has a mind to do so. There is no more flexible banker than the World Bank—when it is dealing with business approximating to normal banking functions. It is unfortunate that the countries which mainly benefit from these favours are not the really poor and underdeveloped, but those which have arrived at the next stage of development. The reason why this is so lies in the nature of the normal banker-client relationship—and the habit of the banker to judge the individual client rather than the individual case on its merits. Clients differ enormously in their creditworthiness, as well as in the extent to which they can be left to use borrowed money without supervision. The two qualities are not the same—creditworthiness being related ultimately to a country's capacity to earn enough to make repayments, and trustworthiness to the general honesty and efficiency to its administration—but they sometimes go together. When they do coincide the Bank seems to be willing to stretch its rules a long way.

The outstanding recent instance is Japan. Here there has not even been the formality, on which the Bank had insisted in the past in its dealings with other semi-developed countries, like Australia, of presenting a shopping list of foreign capital goods required for an investment programme and attaching the loan to a number of random items. The Japanese have made no pretence of intending to use the dollars, which they have been lent so lavishly in recent years, on foreign capital equipment. Nearly all the equipment that they need is produced at low prices by Japanese industry itself; and the problem is usually to obtain enough raw materials to ensure that the available productive capacity at home is fully employed. The money obtained from the World Bank therefore goes straight into the government's reserve of gold and foreign exchange.

Of course that in itself means that the Japanese government —which is not traditionally a currency hoarder of the type, common in Europe since the war, which only feels happy with a great thumping stock of gold and dollars locked away—will be more disposed to loosen up its severe import restrictions and let more foreign goods into the country. To that extent the Bank's loans do have an impact on Japanese external trade. But that can hardly be regarded as a major achievement of international lending policy. A lot of other countries would import more if they had more foreign exchange at their disposal. The Bank attempts to cover all this with a face-saving device: the Japanese solemnly undertake to put out certain contracts, e.g. the motorway financed by a Bank loan in 1960, to international tender so that there is free competition with other countries for the resulting business; but this is not to be taken very seriously. The real object of making such loans a these is not economic: it is a matter of financial tactics. Japan's financial status is gradually and deliberately built up by the Bank; commercial banks and other institutions in Wall Street, Frankfurt, and so on, are encouraged to come in as partners in these loan issues. And then, more daringly, the Japanese are given the opportunity to use the occasion of a fairly small World Bank loan to make a much larger simultaneous issue of their own government bonds in the New York market. The investor is influenced to buy by a species of sympathetic magic. This happened in 1959; and judging by the response, the magic worked. By this time the American commercial banks, which had been made familiar with Japanese business in large part through the World Bank's effort, were acting independently of the Bank as underwriters for the $30m. bond issue of the government of Japan.

Here in fact is the World Bank behaving like a pushing merchant banker, much as Rothschilds or Barings did in the 19th century when they introduced the bonds of new countries to the City of London—only doing so on a much larger scale. The association of the Bank with a country is also taken to provide some assurance of international good behaviour— something that the Rothschilds were distinctly unable to guarantee. At any rate it is generally believed that a country would hesitate many times over before it deliberately sacrificed its international goodwill by defaulting on a World Bank loan. And this has made it possible for the Bank to channel private investors' money into strange places, where it would otherwise have been reluctant to go.

At the same time it is able to act as a kind of shield to foreign companies which want to develop some mineral or other natural resource in a distant spot, but are anxious to be protected against the political risks that are run by a rich and isolated alien concern operating in the territory of a poor nation. Thus for example the American steel companies, who wanted to develop the manganese deposits of Gabon on the west coast of Africa, were able to avoid a direct connection with the business, because the Bank took the initiative, once the American interest in the manganese had been firmly established, and made a loan—knowing that it would be able, almost immediately afterwards to sell rather more than half of the loan obligations to American insurance companies, who were standing ready to buy. These combined operations of the finance house, the large industrial corporation and the Bank are an interesting extension of modern investment practice. It is clear that some of the big American aluminium companies, who are taking an increasing interest in Africa as a source of bauxite and cheap power, would now like to move in under Mr. Black's umbrella. In time this may, indeed, become the standard formula for large-scale company investment in the natural resources of an undeveloped country—a formula which seems much preferable to the old type of arrangement, with its overtones of anxiety and arrogance and its undertones of political intrigue.

In all this, however, the Bank's role is less that of a lender on its own account than that of an organizer of other people's loans. It has never got anywhere near the figure of $1 billion a year of loans to undeveloped countries which was suggested as a reasonable target for the Bank back in 1951 by the group of economists who prepared the report to the United Nations on "Measures for the economic development of underdeveloped countries".[1] The current rate of disbursement of loans to all countries is somewhat under $600m. a year,[2] and of this the undeveloped countries receive around $350m. Hitherto the semi-developed countries have absorbed a lot of the Bank's money: four of these, Australia, South Africa, Italy and Japan, hold close on one-quarter of all the outstanding loans. It is natural that the Bank should want to keep a high proportion of "good financial paper" of this type in its portfolio. But it is noticeable that an increasing number of the solid and respectable borrowers, whom the Bank has nursed along since the war, are now able to look after their own needs in the international capital market. The most recent arrivals to adult financial status are Australia and Italy; and it should not be long before Japan follows. Then what? Apart from Mexico it is hard to see any country that it likely to qualify soon for the Bank's favourite treatment.

## Lending Becomes More Difficult

Indeed, it is clear that the period of the 1950s was an exceptionally favourable one for the type of conventional lending operation which the Bank performs most readily. Its high prestige today owes something to the special circumstances which provided on the one hand a number of fairly advanced countries ready to be launched quickly, and on the other hand a lot of straightforward commercial business from undeveloped countries, whose "creditworthiness" had not yet been impaired by heavy foreign borrowing in support of their development programmes. From a lender's point of view the world of the mid-1950s was like a field of ripening corn waiting for someone to turn up with a combine harvester. But looking ahead, it is hard to see a repetition of the crop.

The chief beneficiary of the increased lending to undeveloped countries during the late 1950s was India, and the Bank plainly does not expect to make a comparable contribution to Indian economic progress in the 1960s; its normal standards of creditworthiness would prevent it. Indeed, senior officials of the Bank make no secret of the fact that they regard the present proportion of loans outstanding to India, around 12 per cent of the total, as about the maximum for comfort. Even so, there would still be scope for some additional lending, as the instalments on existing Indian loans from the Bank fell due for payment. This would have the same effect as the proposal made earlier to increase the "period of grace" on bank loans before a borrower is obliged to make any repayments of principal:* the Bank would re-lend enough to stave off the day of debt settlement. However, in the meanwhile the money would make no contribution towards covering the cost of the additional capital goods that the Indians will need to import for their Third and Fourth Five Year Plans.

The problem in the rest of Asia outside India is generally not so much the unattractiveness of the potential borrowers as the difficulty of finding sufficient projects of the type to which the Bank has restricted itself. There is, however, no reason, other than self-imposed convention, why it should not lend money for a much broader range of activities, including basic social services like schools and housing or a wide variety of manufacturing industries. Hitherto the Bank's approach to factory investment has been hardly more helpful than to agriculture. In some ways it has been even more restrictive, for in agricultural development it is at least clear that there is a strong desire within the Bank to find some formula for more active lending, while in manufacturing industry there is a definite ideological bias against anything but the occasional transaction as a junior partner of private enterprise in a limited operation. Although the instincts of Mr. Black and his senior staff are powerfully against government enterprise or any public participation in the business of manufacturing, when the Bank does make a loan to a private firm, like the Tata Iron and Steel Company in India for example, it has to carry a government guarantee. That almost inevitably means that the state's influence over the private concern receiving the loan is reinforced.

Ideally the Bank would like to leave private enterprise business in the field of manufacturing to its small affiliate, the International Finance Corporation. This is an organization with some $90m. of subscribed capital, which invests directly in private enterprise without requiring any government guarantees. It concentrates even more than the World Bank on the merchant banker function—lending fairly small sums on

* See Chapter 7, pp. 91–2

its own account, and in this way stimulating others to invest in promising businesses on a larger scale. It also aims to make much bigger profits; indeed one or two countries have found its terms so stiff that they have refused to use this source of finance for development. But the main point is that the actual contribution of money by IFC towards the establishment of new factories in undeveloped countries is too small to make a difference one way or another to the general progress of industrialization: in the four years since its establishment in 1956 it has lent a total of some $20m.

One of the obvious ways in which manufacturing industry could be helped forward in the undeveloped countries is by the establishment of industrial investment banks to provide liquid funds for small and medium businesses. In many of these countries there is no functioning credit mechanism to support the small factory establishment, which can only grow if it can obtain borrowed money readily for materials, for new machinery, sales promotion, etc. Working capital for these unfamiliar purposes is scarce. Moreover, the discipline imposed by the professional banker on the entrepreneur, making the latter present his case for a loan in a systematic fashion with the relevant facts marshalled and considered, is itself a contribution to development. Bankers in fact have an important creative role to play in enforcing business habits—of an alien, unattractive and tiresome kind—on the enterprising people of an undeveloped country. A really able banker will do more: he will find the profitable idea himself and then persuade an enterprising character to execute it—on a loan from the bank.

## Mr. Black and Private Enterprise

Development banks have been set up with the aid of World Bank money in India, Pakistan, Persia and other Asian countries. In Latin America, however, despite the need for precisely this kind of help in a number of developing industries, the World Bank has done hardly anything at all. When I asked Mr. Eugene Black why this was so he replied laconically, as if the answer were self-explanatory: "But they're government banks." In Asia the new investment institutions, which the

World Bank has helped, are managed by representatives of private investors, even though most of the initial capital is provided out of public funds. The sharpness of Mr. Black's objection to the Latin American alternative of public enter-prise taking charge of the management public funds put me in mind of a slightly malicious parody of World Bank attitudes, which had been produced impromptu by Dr. Prebisch, the head of the U.N. Economic Commission for Latin America, over a dinner table in Santiago. "Consider what would have happened", he said, "if Christopher Columbus had tried to put up his scheme to Mr. Black—always assuming that he would eventually have got a hearing, as he did, after all, from the Spanish Royal family. I imagine the reply would have been something like this: 'It seems a very risky business. Can you produce any concrete evidence? And what can you tell me of the political situation over there—on the assumption, of course, that there is something on the other side, which I don't admit?' "

The skit does not, as Dr. Prebisch himself would be the first to admit, provide a fair description of the whole man—only of one particular mood in which certain of his prejudices are uppermost. Eugene Black has achieved one of those remarkable transitions fairly late in life (which one has come to associate with some of the best men in American public life) from a conventional and successful career of an entirely uninspired character to a major role as an innovator in an unfamiliar and difficult field of endeavour. To establish the World Bank in the leading position which it came to occupy in the 1950s required both imagination and sensitiveness of a kind of which there was little overt evidence in his earlier career—beginning as an investment man selling bonds in Georgia and going on to become vice-president of a solid, orthodox New York bank. His formal education ended at the age of eighteen. At first sight, with his very tall, gangling body, the smallish head, the friendly, light blue eyes, he almost suggests one of those American boys of the type who age without growing up. But all this is quickly belied by his manner—mature and polished, with all the aplomb and ease that go with belonging to a well-established, well-to-do family in one of the southern states of America. His father was governor of the Federal Reserve Bank of Atlanta, Georgia, and also served as head of the Federal Reserve System in Washington.

Black has overcome many of the prejudices that might be expected to be firmly in the possession of a man past fifty— which was his age by the time he took up his appointment at the World Bank—emerging from such a background. He has in generous measure the American virtue of being pragmatic, and he retains the refreshing national faith in the power of people, properly organized, to produce more and more wealth. There is nothing brash about this however—rather the opposite: it has been remarked that Black's manners are so good and attentive that he makes people going away with a refusal feel that they have really got away with something. Nevertheless he is not one of the wholly liberated American spirits—the type of businessman who is associated in the European mind with the Marshall Plan phase of U.S. history—who manages to slough off a whole lifetime's accumulation of conventional ideas at the touch of fresh experience. His limitations appear most obviously in his attitude towards socialism and state enterprise. Black, at any rate in certain moods, is inclined to talk as if there were some kind of exclusive relationship between political freedom and private enterprise, and as if he believed that his main task is therefore to defend the only true economic faith throughout the world. It is no accident that the right-wing opposition movement in India, led by Mr. Masani, has adopted a slogan taken from Mr. Black: "People must come to accept private enterprise not as a necessary evil but as an affirmative good." The statement appears in a frame on the inside cover of all the pamphlets published by its propaganda organization, "The Forum of Free Enterprise".

All this goes back to a famous exchange of letters in 1956 with the Indian Finance Minister of the day, Mr. Krischna-machari, in which Mr. Black took him to task for putting too much emphasis on public enterprise in industry in the Second Five Year Plan. The Indian minister felt constrained to make the following point in his reply: "I am aware that your views and ours about private and public enterprise do not altogether coincide, though the differences are not quite as great as seem to appear in public debate. We are, of course, not convinced that the motive of private profit is the only one which can ensure efficient operation of an industry; nor do we believe that private enterprise is inherently superior to state enterprise. Indeed, the short experience we have had with state enterprises leads us to believe that they can often be more efficient than private units."

It is fair to say that after this curious exchange of ideological niceties, Black proceeded to lend money on a generous scale to assist in carrying through these Indian plans. He followed this in 1958 by calling together India's main creditors—U.S., Britain, Germany and Japan—to arrange a series of long-term bilateral loans. Some have suggested that in his earlier exchange with Krischnamacheri the President of the Bank was, like some latter-day Pilate, washing his hands in full view of Wall Street. Yet as late as 1960 he said to me, when I made the obvious point that Indian attitudes had changed in recent years and that the authorities were now actively fostering the growth of small and medium-sized businesses in private hands: "But do the Indians really *want* private enterprise?" I answered that they were certainly acting as if they did, which he countered by saying that this was only because they had found themselves forced by circumstances to do so. Evidently that was not in his view enough; private enterprise was the one subject on which it was insufficient to be a good pragmatist, moved simply by the logic of events to support it.

These views have not prevented the World Bank from having amicable relations with governments professing socialist aims. There is the occasional friction—the Mexicans claim that their request for a development loan for PEMEX, the state-owned petroleum industry, was turned down by the Bank for ideological reasons, and there has been further trouble about the division of investment in electric power between the private foreign company, Mexlight, and the nationalized power corporation. But this has not, so far as is known, led to the frustration of any single important development project. The effects are general and negative. The Banks fails to make any significant contribution to the advance of manufacturing industry in the undeveloped countries. It is inhibited in its attitude towards industrial investment banks in Latin America, which could, in some countries at any rate, be a potent engine of useful enterprise—and private enterprise at that. It appears that the Bank has not grasped the fact that in undeveloped countries the introduction of government enterprise in unaccustomed fields can often be the means of stimulating private business initiative which would not otherwise have emerged. This is plainly true of India today and also, though to a lesser extent now than in the past, of Mexico. Starting with Japan, it has become normal in modern times for the state to provide not only the groundwork of capitalism but also some of the initial superstructure in the early stages of development.

## Zero by 1968

The problem of breaking out of the restrictions, which at present impede the activities of what is after all the most important single instrument of world economic development, will become increasingly urgent during the coming years. If the World Bank simply continues to make new loan agreements at the 1958/9 rate of around $700m. a year (of which two-thirds are loans to the undeveloped countries), the actual *net* contribution of money from the Bank towards the finance of economic development will diminish steadily during the 1960s. This is because the volume of annual repayments on outstanding loans, together with the cost of interest and other charges, will be rising as the amount of debt owing to the Bank is added to each year. In 1959 these servicing costs which the borrowers had to pay had already reached $220m. It can be shown that if the Bank proceeds to lend money at a steady rate of $700m. a year, servicing costs will increase to the point where the net contribution to development is reduced to zero by 1968.[3]

In itself that would not necessarily be tragic, if it were possible to assume that a series of fully developed countries, finally launched by the Bank, would be paying the money back on their old loans, so that it could be passed on to the next lot of undeveloped countries coming forward—though it would argue a certain lack of business initiative to stay put at this figure of lending in a world of expanding capital investment and development. It would mean at the very least that the Bank's share in the finance of development throughout the world would be falling. But in fact the problem is more serious, for as we have seen, there is now little prospect of another lot of semi-developed countries being rapidly floated off to economic independence—like Australia, Italy, South Africa and Japan in the 1950s. The new generation of borrowers coming forward in the 1960s are, possibly with one or two exceptions, going to stick in the mud much longer than the comparatively well-to-do clients of the Bank during the past decade. So by the late 1960s, when the net lending of the World Bank is reduced to zero—assuming that there is no increase beyond the current rate of making loans of about $700m. a year—the situation will be that a lot of undeveloped countries will be re-borrowing from the Bank each year just about as much as they pay back to it.

Another way of looking at the problem is to ask what the Bank will have to do in order to go on making at least the same *net* contribution of money to international development as it did in 1959. By the middle of the decade, say the end of the financial year 1965/6, its annual *gross* lending would have to be some $400m. higher; that would bring it above $1 billion a year. By 1974 the Bank will have to be lending as much as $1,600m., in order to maintain the same level of *net* economic aid for development as at the end of the 1950s.

All this serves to emphasize the need for the World Bank to think in terms of new forms of business—and also to develop a new spirit which will induce it to take bolder risks. It is understandable enough that the Bank should have adopted an ultra-cautious policy of lending during its early days, when it was trying to establish its reputation with the people on Wall Street as just another hard-faced banker. But by now it is much the biggest banker in this field. It is also extremely rich. By the mid-1960s, if it just continues ticking over with its annual rate of gross lending at about $700., its total reserves will have risen to just short of $1,200., and its annual net income, including commissions, will at that point reach the high figure of $136m. after meeting all expenses (measured at 1960 price levels). But before then perhaps some simple-minded banker, with no pretensions to being especially hard-faced, will be wondering why Mr. Black, or his successor, should be left to enjoy the monopoly of this peculiarly profitable and riskless line of humanitarian business. That is the main reason for hope. There are two things which are likely to move Mr. Black to the discovery of novel ways of doing business: one is competition and the other is the desire to keep his own business expanding.

*Notes*

1. E/1986, United Nations, 1951.

2. New loans made (i.e. agreed to) by the World Bank were close to $700m. a year during the late 1950s, but actual disbursements were lower. In the financial year 1959/60 loans made (i.e. commitments) to all countries fell to $659m. and disbursements to $544m.

3. Actual disbursements of money by the World Bank have never yet reached $700m. a year; this figure is the rate at which new loans have been undertaken. However, the projection of net lending up to 1968 assumes that the rate of disbursing money will rise, and catch up with the rate at which new loans are being contracted —if the latter does not rise above the level of $700m. a year. There is usually an interval of time between obtaining a loan for a new capital project and drawing on it heavily to finance the most expensive phase of the operation. That is why a sudden jump in the rate of lending does not immediately place an equivalent financial burden on the lender. See for example the Soviet case (Chapter 2, pp. 10–11).

The forward projections of the World Bank's operations are based on the assumption that the average cost of interest and commission charges together will be 5 per cent. By 1960 the rate of interest charged by the Bank had gone above 5 per cent; adding on the 1 per cent commission charge levied on all outstanding loans, the effective cost of new borrowing was over 6 per cent.

# CHAPTER 10

# GENEROSITY FRUSTRATED

I N the new mood which began to make itself felt towards the
end of the 1950s, partly as a result of the growing Soviet
effort in the undeveloped countries, but also under the straightforward philanthropic impulse of Western countries, keenly
aware of their own rapidly growing prosperity and its contrast
with the unrelieved misery of the majority of mankind, governments came to face the need for supplementing the armoury
of weapons of economic aid. The first result was the International Development Association, on which agreement was
finally reached in 1959. It was designed essentially to do something more for the underdeveloped countries than the World
Bank; but everyone was anxious that it should do it by applying
some of the techniques that had been successfully evolved by
the World Bank for distinguishing between a worth while
investment project, capable eventually of paying its way, and a
proposition with less substance. Indeed the nations concerned,
led by the United States, were so impressed by the Bank's
achievement that they decided to leave the job of designing the
new institution, as well as its actual management entirely to
Mr. Eugene Black and his staff.

That turned out to be a mistake. Although it appeared to be
a good idea to go to the most successful of the international
institutions in the field for advice on how to take the next step
forward, the chosen advisers naturally tended to concentrate
on the particular difficulties which had bothered the Bank
during a special period when it was still a fledgling institution,
nervously feeling its way towards a position of respectability in
the world's capital markets and at the same time trying to
establish a position of trust, as well as authority, among its
clients in the undeveloped countries. As I have already
indicated* there is a strong *prima facie* case for reconsidering
the Bank's own methods and trying to evolve a more flexible

* See Chapter 9

system of lending in the 1960s, which will deliberately confront the problem of the diminishing creditworthiness of a poor country trying over a period of some years of difficulty to establish the basis for self-sustaining economic growth. In a way the advent of the IDA allowed the World Bank to duck a problem which it would otherwise have been forced to face.

It would, for example, have been compelled to think of some way of at least maintaining its assistance to India at the level of the late 1950s, in spite of the fact that India is bound to become less creditworthy after 1961, when the cost of servicing its external public debt will rise above the banker's conventional peril point of 10 per cent of export earnings. There is, in fact, nothing absolute about being creditworthy. If, for example, repayments of the loan are spread out over a longer period, so that the annual servicing bill is smaller, or the period of grace before repayments begin is extended, then the whole arithmetic alters. Or there may simply be a change of view about the prospects of a country endowed with good natural resources, because it has a new and more efficient administration. Thus the World Bank was prepared to make funds available to Colombia in the later fifties, although its debt servicing ratio was over 20 per cent at the time. The decision to do so was, among other things, a reflection of confidence in the honesty and ability of the new government which took office in 1958 after the successful revolution against the previous dictator, General Rojas Pinilla.

Lending of this kind is bound to be, in part, a matter of political judgment. There is, of course, a pretence that for any organ of the United Nations this consideration is irrelevant. The constitution of the IDA, for example, says specifically that decisions about loans are not to be influenced by the political character of a borrowing country; only economic considerations are to be taken into account. Yet it does surely matter that India has a stable government which is capable of carrying out a clear line of policy over a number of years, while for example Argentina, so far at any rate, has not. It might also be a qualifying factor in the mind of any prudent lender that there is no obvious successor to Pandit Nehru as the Indian Prime Minister, who would be able to command the same stable political support in the future. Plainly, an international institution should resist the belief, which is the familiar sin of diplomats and the Foreign Offices which they serve, that it has some sure-fire system of political intelligence or, worse still, of political intuition to guide it. But there are some political judgments that it must make boldly—whether for example in India, or in Colombia for that matter, supposing a rather long period of grace is allowed before repayments of the principal of a loan have to begin (say ten years instead of the usual maximum of five), there is likely, after that time has elapsed, still to be a government in power which will be prepared to pay up. The question is, of course, only worth asking in this form, if another affirmative judgment of an economic character has already been made—that the country's export earnings, or its ability to save imports, will have improved sufficiently by the 1970s, as a result of its development programme, to make it *possible* to meet the cost of foreign debt service payments without intolerable hardship.

### Banker's Charity

Without IDA, the World Bank would at any rate have been forced to consider whether a rather more generous interpretation of creditworthiness was not appropriate in the 1960s—even at the risk of an occasional default. It does not seem an altogether wise policy for an international institution, which has been given the leading role in financing development, to be quite so obsessed with avoiding this risk. The Bank now has a very substantial reserve fund, made up of its own accumulated earnings, quite apart from the iron reserve of interest-free country subscriptions in hard currencies amounting to well over $1 billion. Indeed, unless some luckless country defaults soon, someone will begin to ask awkward questions about what the Bank wants such a big reserve fund for. The rich countries might even inconsiderately suggest that it should distribute a dividend.

But temporarily at any rate the IDA has provided a convenient receptacle for the World Bank's problems. The Bank has no need to face the awkward question whether some undeveloped country ought not, after all, to be allowed a delay

in the repayment of the principal of a loan until its balance
of payments has had time to benefit properly from a long-term
programme of investment, which the loan has helped to finance.
IDA has been told that it can meet just this need, under the
charter prepared for it by the Bank. The Bank does not have
to worry any more about interest rates and other charges
being too high for less-developed countries with a limited
capacity for earning foreign exchange—for IDA has been told
that it can make loans at lower than market rates of interest,
right down to zero. Finally, it is unnecessary to start thinking
about new fields of social investment, because IDA has been
told to look after these.

However, lest anyone might be encouraged to think that
IDA's main role was to be a true innovator, opening up a new
world for the productive use of capital, the official memorandum
setting out its purposes (prepared by the Bank), says: "It is
expected that a major part of the Association's financing is
likely to be for projects of the type financed by the Bank".
On this interpretation the whole institution seems likely to be
used chiefly as a kind of a bargain basement for the World
Bank, where customers are sent when the man in charge of
credit ratings finds that it would be awkward to make a loan
on ordinary commercial terms. Of course that, too, has its uses.
Some institution capable of providing ordinary loans on somewhat longer or cheaper terms than the going commercial rates
is needed by the undeveloped countries. The argument in the
earlier part of this book was designed to show that *in addition*
to funds required for social investment, e.g. in education, on
which it is generally accepted that a commercial return
will not be forthcoming, quite large sums of money will have
to be made available somehow to support the balance of
payments of countries during the early stages of development,
when there is very little chance of their earning enough,
through exports, to service ordinary bank loans. IDA could
deal both with the problem of social investment and with
the residual gap in the balance of payments, caused by low
exporting power.

It differs from the original idea of SUNFED* in not having
the power to make *outright* grants of money to undeveloped

* See Chapter 7, p. 93 *et seq.*

countries; but there is enough latitude allowed in fixing the terms for "soft loans", so that a country may never have to pay any interest at all or have to bother itself for many years about finding the money for any repayments of principal, to ensure that this missing element will not seriously impair its ability to be generous—providing the management wishes to exercise generosity. Nor can there be much quarrel about the form of organization, identical with that of the World Bank, chosen for IDA: as we saw earlier, some system of weighted voting, either formal or informal, is inevitable in an institution where a small minority of donor countries are handing out large sums of money to a majority of the needy. Indeed this conclusion had come to be accepted by the more realistic backers of the original SUNFED proposal.

There is no doubt either that the World Bank will be able to give IDA a great deal of useful guidance on techniques of making loans and supervising the use of the money in the borrowing countries. But it is quite a different matter to hand the new institution over lock, stock and barrel to the head of the World Bank, who is *ex officio* the President of IDA, to be run by his staff as part of their general business, with no separate offices at all. It is noteworthy that the much smaller International Finance Corporation, established also as an affiliate of the World Bank to make loans to private enterprise,* was treated much more respectfully and given an independent president of its own, although Mr. Black formally retains the ultimate power of sanction as Chairman of the Board of Governors. The difference between remote Chairmanship of one body and the active role of President of the other reflects, among other things, Mr. Black's personal predilections. He was reported as saying, during the early stages of the discussions on IDA, that he had never liked the idea of "soft loans", but if they had to come he was going to make certain that he was the man who handled them. Plainly he was not moved by any corresponding anxieties about the purposes of IFC, when that organization was being established. Mr. Garner, the President of IFC, is in the matter of the religion of private enterprise rather more catholic than his pope.

* See Chapter 9, pp. 132–33

## A Miniature IDA

A "soft loan" operation is bound to require more capital than ordinary banking. That is because a bank can rely on a revolving fund of money which is paid back and re-lent to the next lot of customers, while at the same time its own reserves are constantly reinforced by the annual payments of interest and other charges. IDA will have to wait longer than the World Bank to get its money back from borrowers and will also charge them lower rates of interest. It is indeed apparent that if the development problem were being treated with the urgency that is required in order to make an impression on world poverty during the decade of the 1960s, IDA would be the senior partner of the World Bank. Even if the Bank were prepared to adopt the bolder lending policies outlined in the last chapter, it is unlikely that it would be able to find sufficient bankable propositions to keep up with an IDA which was vigorously tackling its job.

It is the small scale of IDA which is the most serious distortion that has been imparted by its subjection to the World Bank. It should have been conceived from the beginning as a giant—but in that case how could the Bank have treated it as if it were its kid brother? The solution finally adopted was to turn it into a dwarf. Its theoretical capital is $1 billion, to be subscribed by member countries over five years. In practice rather more than one-fifth of the amount is useless, because it will be provided in the currencies of undeveloped countries and will not be available to buy goods elsewhere.[1] During the first five years when the members' subscriptions are to be called up by annual instalments, the maximum sum of usable currencies at the disposal of IDA will be something under $160m. a year; and no doubt it will want to hold back something to build up its reserves. This amount is equivalent to less than half of the World Bank's annual total of lending to undeveloped countries.

IDA is, it is true, not necessarily fixed in this minature mould for ever. Its governors can, if they wish, expand it to a size more in keeping with the task that it has been set. But the trouble is that once having started out as a dwarf, IDA has only to put on a few inches for everyone to clap their hands in an ecstasy of self-congratulation and say: "See how fast it's growing!" What is really needed now is not growth but transformation. Even if, for example, the member nations decided in two or three years' time on a 50 per cent increase in the size of the organization—which would be counted a remarkable gesture, in view of the fact that the first lot of subscriptions (the $1 billion) are only to be paid up finally by 1965, and the rules moreover leave each individual nation free to pay up or not after a majority vote to expand the organization—the maximum rate of lending that it would then be able to undertake would still be under $250m. a year.

Mr. Eugene Black has argued placidly against the critics of IDA's smallness, that the institution will grow as the need for its services and its experience in meeting them develop. The argument is as good an illustration as one could find of the limitations of the banker's approach to this problem. Experience is the last thing that is necessary to establish the need for a massive inflow of capital to the undeveloped countries, most of which cannot possibly be in the form of ordinary bank loans, over the next ten years or so. Certainly experience would be a help—and it ought to be obtained as quickly as possible—in developing new techniques for lending money on a much larger scale than hitherto and for purposes which the World Bank has hardly touched. But IDA is not well designed to serve this purpose. The chief missing element in all this is the sense of urgency. What is required now is not the slow accumulation of experience on a series of pilot projects, but a political act of will on the part of the rich countries about the quantity of resources that they are ready to devote to raising the submerged majority of mankind. As IDA has turned out, it has become the means of enabling the rich to evade the essential problem rather than to solve it. The decision about the appropriate relative sizes of IDA and the World Bank implies the belief that the main issue can be dealt with by means of orthodox bank loans; what is left over, as not fully bankable, is treated as a marginal problem only. It is, in fact, the central issue.

## U.S. Balance of Payments

It will, however, be difficult to make a fresh approach to the problem now, partly because IDA is a *fait accompli* and consciences are to that extent salved, but more important, because of the change that has occurred, during the interval since the idea was first conceived, in the economic circumstances of the main donor country, the United States. The launching of IDA and the new mood of more urgent practical concern in the West about the undeveloped countries also happened to coincide with the end of the long postwar period of overwhelming American financial dominance in the world. The United States has not ceased to be much the richest country; in terms of what its citizens could afford, it is plainly capable of providing a lot more aid to poor nations without causing any noticeable hardship to itself. The new factor which appeared at the close of the 1950s was the sudden awareness on the part of the Americans of the limits imposed on their freedom to spend abroad by their external balance of payments. Up until the late 1950s this was never a serious consideration. Any argument about American spending was always conducted in terms of the internal taxes that it would involve, never in terms of the burden on external payments. It was thought to be a matter of indifference whether government spending took place at home or abroad: if America could "afford" the money, it could afford to spend it equally in either place.

All that was changed by the events of 1958–9. In the first of those years there was a huge outflow of gold from the United States. This was at least partly due to the gathering momentum of American investment abroad. But in 1959, when the capital outflow slackened, the underlying situation got worse, and for the first time in many years the United States registered a small deficit on its balance of payments on current account (i.e. on the international exchange of goods and services). The cause was one that was only too familiar everywhere else outside the United States—a sharp rise in imports without a corresponding increase in exports. There were, it is true, a number of special and temporary factors which helped to aggravate the trouble; moreover the total deficit on current account was very small— a matter of $100m. or so. But none of this helped to moderate the emotional reaction to the discovery that the Americans were now consuming more than they were currently earning abroad. It meant that the United States was faced, at the moment when its national product was making fresh records, with a new limitation on its power to spend—in foreign countries, not at home.

Of course the economic change which led to this result was not nearly as sudden as it appeared to be. The process of restoring the balance of competitive power between the United States and the rest of the world had been in progress over a number of years, but it had barely been noticed. It was in any case unreasonable to expect that a country, however rich, could go on acting forever as if it need not think at all about its balance of payments with the rest of the world. But when the realization came that America was not, after all, armed by Nature against all possible anxiety about currency reserves and foreign trade deficits, the U.S. government took it very hard. Although it still held half the world's stock of gold, it began to think in the characteristic mode of a country which believes itself to be threatened by an imminent foreign exchange crisis. The economic policies of the last two years of the Eisenhower Administration, 1959/60, with Mr. Robert Anderson in command at the Treasury, were guided above all by fears about the balance of payments. The Secretary of the Treasury left no one in any doubt that his main preoccupation was to frustrate any political proposal which would add one cent to the foreign exchange obligations of the United States.

Since the United States is directly responsible under its own foreign assistance programmes, for two-thirds of all the economic aid in public loans and outright grants going to the undeveloped countries,* as well as providing the bulk of the funds for the international flow of capital from the World Bank, the new mood in Washington presents a serious impediment to any new big push for world development. One obvious way out, which the United States has been urging on other Western nations, is that they should use part of their new-found prosperity to take over a larger share of the burden of aid to poor countries. It is reasonable to expect that this will happen in the long run. However, in the short run the amount of aid

* See Appendix I

forthcoming from other countries will depend not only on the availability of resources, but also on the habit of generosity towards people in remote places. It requires a little time and practice before a government of a newly rich country like Germany comes to take the habit for granted. Unfortunately, the two European nations where such habitual attitudes are well established, Britain and France, both enter the 1960s with their freedom to spend abroad circumscribed by the difficulties of their balance of payments, in much the same way as the United States. In France it is simply the cost of the Algerian war, coupled with the substantial aid expenditure already being incurred in a crumbling colonial empire.

## Ceiling on British Aid

In Britain the problem is the recurrence of the familiar post-war pressure on the balance of payments, after a brief interlude in 1958/9. In these two years British aid to the undeveloped countries of the Commonwealth, chiefly in the form of long-term loans, was substantially increased; the feeling in London by 1960 was that, allowing for commitments already undertaken which would mature in later years, the ceiling on the foreign aid programme had already been reached. The essential limitation is that a sizeable amount of Britain's overseas earnings is already pre-empted to finance foreign investment in Commonwealth countries; and to this has been added, more recently, the flow of British capital to Western Europe, attracted by the opportunities offered by the European Common Market. Since the movement of investment funds overseas is subject to very little control—if it is directed to the sterling area to no control whatsoever—this outflow of private capital is a first charge on the balance of payments; the government with its public aid programmes to the undeveloped countries is a kind of residual legatee. If the balance of payments weakens or, alternatively, the volume of private investment increases in the favoured countries of the Commonwealth with white settler communities, it is the government's aid programme which has to make room. Worse still, the government knowing that it faces the risk of sudden pressures on the country's balance of payments, either from these causes or as a result of one of those sharp movements in international sentiment which affect a worldwide currency like the pound sterling, tries to avoid danger by holding down its long-term commitments to a minimum.

Indeed the contribution that can be expected from Britain towards any new attack on the problem of poverty in the undeveloped countries is bound to be small—so long as the present obligations that go with the maintenance of the sterling area system and the management of the pound sterling as an international currency remain fully in force. As regards the international position of sterling, the difficulty is that having encouraged everyone around the world to hold and use pounds as much as possible, Britain is then in a constant state of nerves about the possibility that the holders may arrive in a body all of a sudden and demand to have their pounds turned back into foreign exchange. The contingent liability to pass out huge sums of money from the gold reserve at a moment's notice, which the British government accepts in running sterling as a major international currency, prompts it always to try to reduce the inevitable risks that go with economic expansion at home or with economic aid programmes abroad.

This is, in my view, a lamentable situation. The only excuse there can be for running a worldwide currency is the possession of large enough reserves not to feel the strain. As we have now seen, it is doubtful whether even the United States, with its vast hoard of gold and its unrivalled productive power both in industry and in agriculture, can afford the luxury of running an international currency single-handed. A nation which does this must, in order to make the system work, distribute enough of its currency in the hands of foreigners around the world to permit them to use it as a ready medium of exchange. In doing that it also distributes more and more hostages to fortune; in the end it becomes involved in a psychological game, which the Bank of England has been desperately playing for years, aimed at deterring foreigners from demanding cash (i.e. gold) for their holdings all at once. That is essentially the reason which has prompted the proposals that have recently been made, particularly by Professor Triffin of Yale University, to establish a world currency system, which will be independent of any individual national currency unit, and will be managed by an international agency like the International Monetary Fund.

But America at least does still possess sufficient quick reserves to deal with any sudden run on the dollar—although we have seen the U.S. Administration already beginning to show the characteristic signs of anxiety neurosis of a nation which feels itself no longer fully in control of its own destiny. Britain has wholly inadequate reserves for the task that it has undertaken, and this provides a solid reason for trying to avoid any fresh commitments. Another disadvantage of the present financial arrangement is that there is a built-in tendency to divert any surplus of foreign exchange that Britain invests in the sterling area, away from the places of most urgent need and towards those where the need is less. To understand why that happens it is necessary to look for a moment at the mechanism of the sterling area. The most important element in it is that in return for holding the bulk of their currency reserves in pounds sterling in London, the members of the system, who include all the members of the Commonwealth except Canada, are given free access to British capital resources. No controls whatsoever are placed on the movement of any funds out of London into sterling area countries—not even so much as a statistical check, which would allow Britain to estimate more accurately than it is able to do at present how much capital does in fact go out this way.

Such facts as are known come mainly from the receiving end, where there are no such inhibitions; and these make it clear that the white dominions and the white settler communities, notably Rhodesia, attract most of the money. There is nothing surprising about that; these countries, after all, offer a European businessman a convenient and attractive form of investment, where he feels he is dealing with the kind of people he understands. Besides, the political risks of overseas investment are less than in an underdeveloped country under native control. Nor is it remarkable that the other big draw for sterling investment is the oil sheikdom of Kuwait, one of the few sterling area countries which is not a member of the Commonwealth. The concession here, which British Petroleum shares with an American company, has probably been the most profitable of all British oil investments in recent years. But in terms of

Britain's contribution to the progress of the main body of the underdeveloped world such investment is less helpful. Kuwait has a population of about a quarter of a million and Rhodesia perhaps five million; these two countries together have probably absorbed the bulk of British private investment in all underdeveloped countries, which is estimated at a total of about £100m. a year.

All told the outflow of British capital and aid to foreign countries, developed and underdeveloped is officially stated to be some £440m.[2] a year, one-third of which is public funds and two-thirds private investment. It seems to be the official view in London that this is at or very near to the tolerable maximum of British capital exports—unless the balance of payments suddenly improves out of all recognition. Britain seems to be unable, at any rate judging by the performance of the late 1950s, to achieve both a satisfactory external surplus and a high level of internal activity. The good years for the balance of payments are the bad years for economic growth at home, and vice versa. This is a specifically British, not a universal, problem. That there is no automatic connection between the two—that a country does not necessarily live on an economic see-saw with one end marked "home" and the other "abroad" —was demonstrated once and for all by the German performance in 1959/60, when with booming production and a level of unemployment as low as anything that Britain has achieved since the war, Germany earned a balance of payments surplus (on current account) twice as large as Britain's record figure, attained during the recession of 1958.

But for practical purposes what matters is that the experience of the 1950s has created a mood of anxiety in Whitehall about anything which might involve further exports of capital. In fact even the present outflow can only be sustained because there is a steady inflow of capital into the United Kingdom, from the United States and elsewhere, which helps to keep the balance of payments in equilibrium. The outflow would be less if Britain relied on its own earning power to finance capital investment overseas. As matters now stand, about half of this capital goes to underdeveloped countries, including the £100m. of private investment mentioned earlier. If the need for a more determined attack on the problem of development is accepted, one way in which Britain could contribute would be by making the public authorities assume some measure of control over the substantial export of capital from this country, amounting to one and a quarter billion dollars a year, in order to direct it more purposefully towards the places of greatest need. But if the balance between public and private capital is to be altered, in favour of the former, it will be necessary to impose retrictions on the export of private capital to the sterling area, and the authorities are plainly afraid that this might spell the end of the sterling system in its present form. Honesty should however compel them to recognize that the sterling area, as it now stands, prevents Britain from making as effective a contribution to the undeveloped countries as would be possible without it.

### The Cost of Empire

Thus British and French policies, in spite of important differences of attitude towards their diminishing overseas empires, do have this basic resemblance—that the traditional imperial association with a particular group of countries gets in the way of a more purposeful international programme of aid to the underdeveloped world as a whole. The Americans for their part pride themselves on being blessedly free from colonial or post-colonial distortions of a similar kind. There is however the costly legacy of America's postwar (non-colonial) sphere of influence in the Far East, which, sadly for the Americans, produces effects which are barely distinguishable from the others. There the United States has managed to accumulate all the expensive disabilities characteristic of an imperial nation in decline, without ever having enjoyed the sweets of empire. That is no doubt the penalty that has to be paid by a world power which presides over a series of necessary but unpopular territorial partitions, aimed at preventing a major war.

The American "ward countries"—the left-overs of the three Far Eastern wars with the communists: South Korea, Formosa and the southern half of Indo-China—have been absorbing close to one-third of all the dollars expended by the United States government in economic aid. Because of the preponderant size of the American contribution to world economic development, the result is that this small group of nations captures a sizeable slice of all the money going to the undeveloped countries. Only one of them, Formosa, has anything much to show in the way of economic progress for the vast sums that have been expended. For the rest, the combination of recalcitrance and feebleness in these allies of the United States has allowed them to extend a blackmail hold over American foreign aid policies. Measured in terms of straight strategic gains, the cost is almost certainly excessive; but sentiment, fear of loss of face and a certain emotional inertia have come to play an important part on the American side. It is possible to assert with confidence that if the amounts devoted to the American "wards" had been spent elsewhere, in countries chosen for their economic potential rather than their strategic position, the investment would by now have added something pretty substantial to the productive capacity of the underdeveloped world.

The conclusion that emerges is that a sizeable part of the money required to start up a vigorous international programme for the low-income countries could be obtained by eliminating the national and political bias in the aid programmes of the three main donor countries of the West—the United States, Britain and France. I am not seriously suggesting that these countries will be persuaded to give up their established traditional policies on that account. But they ought at least to start by recognizing that when they talk virtuously of their present obligations and the limits which these impose on their ability to provide more help, they are really setting up their individual national predilections as insurmountable obstacles. And it is reasonable to hope that the spirit of self-examination pursued along these lines might lead to some adjustment of the extremes of present national aid policies—sufficient perhaps to make available some extra funds for the work of an institution like the International Development Association.

Indeed there is an unofficial proposal, which has attracted some support inside the U.S. Administration, that the work of the Development Loan Fund—the agency set up by President Eisenhower in the late 1950s to make cheap long-term loans to poor countries—should eventually be transferred to IDA. The Development Loan Fund at present has $500m. a year to spend

—three times as much as the maximum amount that IDA has in prospect from all its regular sources—and if that were handed over, it would transform the whole character and scale of the international effort. No doubt only a portion of this money would be siphoned off to IDA initially; but even this gesture might well prompt other countries to look at their own national aid programmes more critically, and consider whether it would not pay them—assuming the aim of *part* of their expenditure, at any rate, is straight economic development regardless of any particular national interest—to follow suit. Plainly there is no chance that nations will prefer to use an international agency to conduct all, or even the greater part, of their present programmes of bilateral aid. These programmes are in any case an important contribution to development. All that can reasonably be suggested is that the balance which is at present struck between national and international aid programmes ought to be shifted somewhat in favour of the international effort.

## *Spreading the Burden*

The idea of streamlining the national programmes of the donor countries and bringing them together into some kind of joint effort began to take hold in 1959. It led to the formation of the Development Assistance Group[3]—a kind of club consisting of the richer nations of Western Europe together with North America and Japan, which meets periodically to compare notes on economic aid. The original inspiration for this scheme came from the U.S. State Department, where Mr. Dillon, the Under-Secretary of State, was anxiously looking for ways of sharing the burden of financing development more equitably between the United States and the prosperous countries of Europe. With the novel experience of a balance of payments problem in the United States and the emotional reaction to it, the question of spreading the load of international responsibilities among America's allies had become a big national issue. Britain with its chronic anxiety about its own balance of payments and a feeling that its record, with over 1 per cent of the national income being devoted to public and private investment in the undeveloped countries, was a good one, enthusiastically supported the proposal. Indeed it was soon made quite evident that the chief target of these Anglo-American manoeuvres was Germany. The Germans had achieved a larger surplus of current earnings on their balance of payments than any other country—it was bigger than the British and American surplus combined—but unfortunately they had not yet become accustomed to exporting capital to poor countries or to dispensing government aid to them. Germany in fact was behaving like a thrifty apprentice who had just made his pile; the problem was to persuade him to start spending it quickly on unfamiliar good works.

The Americans and British also had hopes of inducing some of the even newer *nouveau riche* countries of the Development Assistance Group, Italy first of all and to a lesser extent Japan, to enlarge their contributions. Italy's progress during 1959, when it managed to add so abundantly to its gold reserve that it ended the year with the third largest stock in the non-communist world, was spectacular. Japan, too, showed an immensely strong balance of payments and an impressive foreign exchange reserve by the end of the 1950s. However, both countries still have to overcome the problem of mass poverty in parts of their own national territories; their first priority is surely going to be to build up the productive capacity of their domestic industries to the point where they will provide employment and a decent standard of living for their own people. Admittedly, this need has not prevented either Italy or Japan from investing substantial sums of money in certain enterprises abroad, but these have usually had a specific national purpose, e.g. the investment in Middle East oil, where the aim is to reduce the foreign exchange cost of fuel imports. It is doubtful whether they will be ready for some time yet to make available any substantial sums of money to promote development for its own sake in the poorest countries of the world. Their own poverty is too much with them at home to encourage generosity towards outsiders.

What emerges from the preceding survey of balances of payments and states of mind in the leading countries at the start of the 1960s, is that, apart from what Germany may provide, there is no substantial net addition to the resources for development likely to be forthcoming from the Development Assistance Group. The Scandinavian countries and Benelux could do more, but they are unlikely to act without a decisive lead from America and Britain; and the American and British governments both believe that they are doing as much as can reasonably be asked of them, given their present economic circumstances. We must face the fact, therefore, that we are not going to get anything like the sum required for a crash programme, which will begin to make an impact on the extremes of world misery in the 1960s, and then push them steadily back in the '70s and '80s—if we have to rely on the existing conventional methods of giving aid. I conclude that if we are in earnest about this task, a new way of mobilizing the resources of the developed countries for capital investment in Asia, Africa and Latin America must be found.

*Notes*

1. IDA subscriptions are divided into two parts: $763m. from developed countries in fully convertible currencies, and $237m. from the undeveloped countries, of which only 10 per cent is convertible. The rest of their subcription may be used only in their own national currencies. So that the total of internationally usable funds at the disposal of IDA, including the $24m. from the undeveloped countries, is $787m.

2. White Paper on "Assistance from the United Kingdom for Overseas Development", Cmnd 974, March 1960. Official U.K. aid figures include funds made available as Britain's subscription to the World Bank, which then appear again as World Bank lending. Normally money transferred to the World Bank is omitted from country aid totals, and that is the convention followed in this book (see Appendix I). Also certain capital expenditures of a quasi-military character, e.g. in Kenya, ought to be excluded. After these deductions the British total of public and private investment abroad comes to slightly over £444m., of which some £200m. goes to undeveloped countries.

3. The original members of DAG were: Britain, France, Germany, Belgium, Italy, Portugal, U.S.A., Canada, Japan. The European Economic Community (Common Market) is also separately represented, although four of its six members belong to DAG, because of its potential interest in the undeveloped countries through the European Investment Bank (subscribed capital: $1,000m.).

# CHAPTER II

# HOW TO GET MORE AID

THE grand inhibition on generous conduct in the Western world towards the poor countries is the anxiety of each of the donors about its balance of payments. This applies most obviously to the United States and Britain, but also in fact to most of the others, including Italy and Japan. These countries, for all their impressive looking reserves, are afraid to do anything which might tilt the balance of trade against them; if Italy, for example, handed out money to the undeveloped countries, which was used by them to buy capital goods, say, in America, the final effect would be to transfer part of Italy's reserves to the United States. It would be exactly the same as if more American goods were imported by Italy without a corresponding increase in exports. Thus any gift or loan of money to a poor country, to which the ordinary practices of international trade apply, is complicated by the danger that the way in which the gift is used may upset the giver's balance of payments with another rich country. Multilateralism, it seems, makes skinflints of us all.

Now consider the cases where the balance of payments fear does not apply. The two outstanding ones are Germany and the Soviet Union. We confidently expect an increase in aid to the undeveloped world from both of these countries during the coming years. Why? They are not richer than the rest of us. The standard of living of the Russians is still well below a normal West European level, and in Germany, although standards have risen very fast in recent years, there is some way to go before they catch up with those that are well established in Western Europe, e.g. in Sweden or Britain, let alone in the United States. Germany's strength lies in the fact that its exports are considerably in excess of its imports, and its selling power in foreign markets is such that it expects to capture an increasing share of any additional export trade that is freely open to international competition. In other words, the Germans feel confident, when they put up any money for an international aid programme, that it will come back to them in the form of export orders for their industries. *It is as good as if they actually tied the money in advance to German exports.*

The difference in the Russian case is that the money is formally tied to Soviet goods. The Russians contend that it would otherwise be exceedingly difficult to fit any large amount of foreign aid into their system of planning. Even in normal export trade they have always preferred the strict bilateral arrangement, with shopping lists of goods laid down in advance on both sides. The element of market uncertainty is, indeed, one of the powerful economic factors which hamper the growth of trade between Soviet Russia and the capitalist world. (Some of the Soviet satellite countries, like Poland and Czechoslovakia, seem to be more ready than the Russians to accommodate themselves to the problems of marketing part of their produce in the free-for-all of the capitalist world.) Even if the Russians are now prepared to engage in rather more of this unplanned trading activity—in order to be able to buy some Western know-how not available at home, as they have done recently in the chemical industry, or in order to deal with some particular shortage of supplies, whether foodstuffs or raw materials—they will not be willing to spread the area of uncertainty over a further substantial part of their industrial order books at home just for the sake of a foreign aid programme. Why should they put up large sums in cash for the undeveloped countries which might be used by the recipients to buy goods elsewhere, so that the final effect of the transaction would be a drain of gold out of the Soviet reserves benefiting the capitalist nations supplying the goods?

The Russian leaders would regard it as quixotic—suspiciously so—to introduce gratuitously an element of risk to the national balance of payments into an act of generosity towards the poor countries—like gambling with a hungry beggar instead of giving him the piece of bread that you carry in your hand. They would point out with some justice that once this risk is there, a country's urge to be generous is bound to be enfeebled. Moreover, they would no doubt add, an undeveloped country which was seriously bent on progress ought to have a systematic plan of investment, which would enable it to state its requirements for capital goods, and a rough timetable for their delivery over a period of years, well in advance. If this is done the supplier can then fit these orders into his own production schedule, using his plant efficiently and cutting down his costs.

### More Tied Loans Needed

These arguments deserve to be taken seriously. It is interesting to observe that the undeveloped countries themselves, far from resenting this Russian insistence on physical supplies, rather than aid in the form of freely spendable sums of money, seem often to feel that they have obtained some special benefit from it. They have got a solid Soviet steel mill or an engineering factory, not just a lot of American dollars. The Americans themselves understood this well enough during the Marshall Plan, when they insisted on identifying each consignment of goods going to Europe at the expense of the U.S. taxpayer with a special label or flag.

There is a certain intellectual confusion in the West about this whole problem of aid, which will tend in the long run to make us less effectual than the Soviets. We insist on treating aid transactions as if they were simply a sub-category of normal international trade, subject to the same rules about the free convertibility of currencies provided by donor countries and the usual conventions of international competition for the resulting business. The consequence is that when we are asked to put up some money for an international aid programme we tend to react in the same spirit of anxiety as we would to a proposal to let in a lot of extra imports: we are worried about finding the foreign exchange to pay the bill.

It was precisely this which led the American government in 1959 to introduce a rule that money provided from the Development Loan Fund must, wherever this is possible, be spent on American goods. One cogent argument which was used by the Americans in the subsequent storm of indignation over this departure from two important religious dogmas at the same time—multilateral trade and currency convertibility —was that in practice German grants or loans were tied to

German goods, because this is what the undeveloped countries invariably bought with their Deutschemarks, and in addition that the Germans mopped up a fair share of the American dollars. If there were less American money available for buying German goods, the argument went on, the Germans would be compelled to put up more Deutschemarks in order to enable the undeveloped countries to finance the same volume of purchases from them as before.

The implication of this American argument was that by introducing the principle of the tied loan, i.e. tied to American goods, the total amount of economic aid from all sources would be increased. This was because it was assumed, rightly, that a nation like Germany would be willing to increase its aid programme so long as it was assured that the additional money would be used for buying German exports. Unfortunately the argument was only deployed (by officials in private) as a slightly shamefaced tactical excuse for an action which was felt to be inherently wrong; its strategic implications were never brought out into the open and properly examined. The basic lesson in strategy for the undeveloped countries is that, if they are to abtain substantially more economic aid, they must take an active interest in protecting the balance of payments of the donor countries. It is not enough to point to the wealth of the donors and say that they must surely be able to afford to give something more to the poor. The analogy with human charity diverts attention from the real problem. A country can be very rich and still have a balance of payments so vulnerable that it is afraid to give money away for purposes of which it approves.

There are in fact various safeguards used by other donor countries besides the United States. The Germans move in with more credits *after* they have been assured that the money will be spent on Germans goods; the French fix it so that the aid given to their colonial territories is spent in francs; and the British have recently taken to using the machinery of the Export Credits Guarantee Department (a government agency) as a channel for aid to Asia, so that the credits can in fact only be spent on British goods. But all this is done in a furtive, under-cover spirit, with governments trying hard to avoid any overt act which would allow them to be pilloried for the unspeakable crime of bilateralism. Everyone is officially in favour of aid freely given and orders freely competed for among the supplying nations; yet there is little doubt that the volume of aid would be less than it is now if these principles were enforced. Ever since the Western countries made their currencies convertible at the end of 1958, they have been so concerned with their reputation for purity that they behave like a rich old spinster who is afraid to be seen giving presents to the man next door —for fear of what all the other rich old spinsters in the district will say. What seems to be overlooked is that the object of the exercise is not to run a competition in self-sacrifice among the well-to-do nations, but to collect the maximum amount of useful things that the poor need and the rich are willing to spare. It would be a help if the recipients of aid applied themselves more actively to finding uses for some of the things which the donors would be ready to part with on request.

The pity is that the undeveloped countries have been so willing to enter into the spirit of this Western exercise in purity of principles, and have failed to see that if there are five countries, each of which is worried by the possibility that its gift of aid may result in export orders for one of the others, they will all try to cut their risks by offering little. One of the factors which influences the undeveloped countries is, paradoxically, the continuing anxiety about being subjected to imperialist exploitation by Western countries in their new guise as providers of long-term capital. Most of them are convinced that they were kept poor for many years by imperial masters, who, because of their exclusive economic control, were able to sell goods to them at high prices or take goods from them at low prices or charge them excessive rates of interest. The fear now is that under a bilateral aid arrangement they will be lent money in order to pay excessive prices for goods that could be obtained more cheaply elsewhere, and then be saddled for years with interest charges on loans which are bigger than they ought to have been. International competition for the orders financed by economic aid is seen as a safeguard against this kind of exploitation.

These fears are not entirely idle. We have already seen in Chapter 3* how the cost of servicing a loan can use up a

* See pp. 28–29

formidable proportion of a country's export earnings, once it tries to push through a big programme of development fast. Indeed what emerged unmistakably from our examination of the arithmetic of debt servicing was that no large-scale programme of help to the undeveloped countries, capable of making an impact on the problem of world poverty, could possibly be financed on commercial terms. If the donor countries once accept this—and the signs are with the establishment of IDA that they may have started to do so—then the fears of the recipients about being charged too much lose their force. And if the donors do not accept it, it will be impossible to keep the aid programme even at its present level, as poor countries exhaust their credit as borrowers—let alone increase it. Some undeveloped countries may, however, be slow to see the point. Unsophisticated people are easily obsessed by prices; they have even been known to argue that food which they obtain from the Americans under their surplus disposal programme might have been obtained at lower cost elsewhere—regardless of the fact that the standard American practice in a poor country nowadays is to turn at least four-fifths of this "loan" into a gift. They do this by taking the local currency, which is paid to them by the receiving country for this food, and giving it back to the government for use in its development programme. It is perhaps silly that the Americans have to go through the motions of making a loan in order to carry out their intention of making a gift; but it is even sillier for the receivers of this bounty to start telling themselves that they might have got a better bargain from someone else in the free market.

## Good Obsolescent Machines

Not everyone fortunately is taken in by this ritualistic commercial play-acting. Just because Western countries, and the United States in particular, feel a compulsive urge to act as if they were involved in conducting a hard business deal, it does not necessarily follow that beneficiaries feel compelled to act as if they thought they were suckers. The Indians in particular seem to know what they are about. They have even on occasion recently gone so far as to make suggestions to donor countries about particular lines of goods that they would be willing to accept on easy terms—having first discovered that these were goods which the donor country was particularly anxious to dispose of. German ships are one example. But this has been done on a small scale and on the initiative of individual officials. It suggests, however, the much larger benefits which the undeveloped countries might obtain if they took an intelligent interest in the pockets of surplus productive capacity that keep appearing in the industrial countries, and asked themselves constantly how they could make use of these for their own advancement.

There is an obvious opportunity of this kind at the moment in the heavy electrical industries. With the change of power station design, leading to the use of much larger generating units in the advanced countries, Britain and other producers have spare capacity for making traditional types of electric power equipment which the undeveloped countries need. Similar situations are certain to occur frequently during a period when exceptionally rapid technological progress, as well as the frivolities of fashionable change in technical design, make machines idle and ready for the scrapheap long before their useful life has been exhausted. Again there is the instinctive emotional hostility of the undeveloped country to overcome: national pride insists that nothing which is regarded by the advanced nations as a second-best product is acceptable. Only the very latest thing will do. The truth is, however, that much of the equipment required during the early stages of an industrialization programme could be readily provided second-hand—if people on both sides made a positive effort to exploit one of the assets of the advanced industrial countries that is at present subject to the greatest waste.

It would be necessary first of all to break down the strong prejudice which exists in the undeveloped countries against buying second-hand machinery abroad. The main fear is that something will go wrong and that there will be no help to be obtained from the seller of the machine, who will have neither the sense of responsibility nor the servicing facilities of the original maker. Besides, it is felt that to cope efficiently with the vagaries of second-hand machines and in particular to keep them operating at full capacity, in the face of an assumed likelihood that they will be subject to more frequent faults and breakdowns, must require the services of more trained technicians than would be necessary for new equipment. If this is true, then there is a strong case for a programme of technical assistance to be concentrated on this problem, possibly as part of the work of the United Nations Special Fund on pre-investment. It would be an obvious economy to train a few more technicians in order to bring down the capital cost of plant. In addition, arrangements would have to be made for any large second-hand plant to be run in with the help of foreign technicians, just as any new industrial works is.[1] However, there should be no similar problem about running in the ordinary small machine tool or motor bought second-hand—at any rate judging by India's experience in the past few years. There the typical small workshop nowadays starts up with a well used machine, often in a fairly battered condition, and quickly learns the tricks of improvisation, which seem to keep it running and producing against all odds. But these are machines obtained, at high prices, from other Indian entrepreneurs. The government has never gone into the trade and acquired cheap seondhand equipment abroad for sale to enterprising Indian businessmen. Everything has to be new.

But an even more fertile source of industrial goods than the actual transfer of second-hand machinery would be the use of idle or under-employed manufacturing capacity in the capital goods industries of Western countries to supply certain kinds of equipment for which the original customers have dwindled or completely disappeared. The loss of customers may be due either to a change in investment programmes or to the fact that the product is regarded as technologically obsolete. Of course the idea that one should try to supply poor countries with products suffering from technological obsolescence is liable to cause the kind of reaction that might be aroused by a proposal to use the United Nations to promote international traffic in narcotic drugs. But often what makes a machine obsolete in a Western country is the fact that another machine has been developed which uses less labour and the high level of wages makes it economical to replace the original one. If wages were as low as they are in India, Mexico or one of the other undeveloped countries, no one would have thought of doing so.

The old model of machine will do very well, and at this stage, when it has lost its normal market and the manufacturer making it has written off the cost of his plant, he is often willing to execute a further run of orders at a much lower price. We became familiar after the last war with the fact that in the last stages of a very long run of a motorcar model a manufacturer is able to offer an unusually cheap product; the same applies to other industrial goods coming off a production line.

There is one sphere where the high rate of technological obsolescence might offer the undeveloped countries special opportunities, and that is agriculture. In the West shortage of labour and high wage costs have brought about a mechanical revolution on the farm, and the result is that many simple and efficient pieces of equipment, previously in use, are no longer worth producing. New ways of saving labour are constantly being discovered and old machines discarded. A recent report on Indian agriculture commented: "The intermediate forms of agricultural development using animal power with improved implements, still practised in some places in Europe, might be of interest to India, which does not have the capital to adopt the latest machinery immediately and everywhere."[2] But the Indians will have to hurry. Sources of supply are dwindling. The report suggest that "some models of animal-driven machinery which were formerly used in Western Europe and the United States can still be obtained for demonstration and study from countries in Eastern and Southern Europe."

### The Principle of Mutual Convenience

My proposal, in short, is that the principle of mutual convenience between giver and recipient ought to be the starting point for any new and enlarged programme of economic aid to the undeveloped countries. Hitherto the only place in which any principle of this kind has been openly and consistently pursued is in the American surplus food disposal programme. It is extraordinary that the force of currently fashionable dogmas about multilateral trade and free markets should have been such that this programme, instead of being treated as one of the solid contributions that the West has made towards the attack on world poverty, has come to be almost a matter of apology. If the American government were less wrapped up in its feelings of guilt about its failure to bring its farm programme under control, it would have taken more notice of the good that it has done.

India is perhaps the outstanding case. There the import of two to three million tons of food grains a year out of the American surplus has made it possible for the authorities to exercise some control over what is traditionally a volatile and pitiless market for food. The Indian government has been able to throw in its reserves of grain at those points where shortages were driving up prices. The effect has been not only to limit price fluctuations but also to curb the hoarding of food, which is the normal response of traders to a rising market. Admittedly the control exercised by the government has been uncertain and intermittent, and during 1958, after a poor harvest, it failed altogether in many places. But without the reserve derived from the American farm surplus it is at least doubtful whether India would have been able to make the orderly economic progress of the late 1950s on the basis of fairly stable prices. It is encouraging that another 17 million tons of American surplus food grains have been promised for the Third Five Year Plan.

Perhaps in the long run the political consequences of the surplus food programme are likely to be its most important aspect. If the experience of India and other Asian countries in recent years is any guide, we must assume that during the early stages of development progress in agriculture will lag far behind the industrial advance. That is not because the technical possibilities for a rapid rise in agricultural output do not exist; on the contrary, the yield of food grains per acre in India and other countries of South Asia is only a fraction of what the Japanese achieve on soil which starts out by being no better. The trouble is that to increase the productive power of a backward agricultural system requires a revolution in people's habits of mind. Capital investment is the lesser part; new forms of organization and, more profoundly, the spiritual revolution, which brings peasants to believe that real progress is possible through the rational application of experimental knowledge, make the decisive difference. This may take years. Say in the meanwhile food output rises about in line with the increase in the number of mouths to be fed—which would mean by 2 per cent a year in a country like India, quite a fast rate of agricultural expansion by historic standards—then the very rapid rise in town populations, accompanying the growth of industry, may well create a crisis. For the marketable food supply in a poor peasant country does not increase automatically as members of farming families migrate to the towns; those left on the land tend to consume more. Broadly, the threat of starvation in the towns can be met either by allowing food prices to rise, and so making it more attractive for the producer to sell, or by forced deliveries from the peasants. No doubt in a crisis other methods would be tried, starting with rationing and price control; but these expedients are most unlikely to work in the long run unless they are backed by compulsion over the peasants.

To make such compulsion effective over a long period will probably involve the whole paraphernalia of a communist tyranny. Yet it has to be conceded that if a policy of industrialization is pursued with rapidity and success, while a traditional and overpopulated agriculture lags behind, there is no gentle way of ensuring that the towns are properly fed. If the method of raising food prices is chosen, rather than forced deliveries, this means that the standard of living of the industrial worker is forced down, while that of the peasant who markets his produce goes up at the townsman's expense. Thus if the West were to mount a big surplus food programme, it might make a decisive contribution towards easing the violent pressures that seem likely to accompany the years of transition in Asia. Unless India manages to carry through a revolution of agricultural techniques in its 500,000 villages much faster than now seems likely, considerably larger imports of food will be needed as the programme of industrialization goes forward. The Third Five Year Plan is based on the opposite assumption; it postulates the complete cessation of food imports by the mid-1960s. But to achieve this without imposing intolerable austerity and political strains on the Indian people will require unusually powerful leadership in agriculture and a readiness to respond on the part of the peasant, of which there is no sign so far.

*Agrarian Revolution*

The food problem of the transition period in Asia is of a special kind; there is no historical precedent to look at for guidance. That is partly because of the scale of the problem, with a simultaneous upsurge of demand impending from a large number of overpopulated countries, all pushing forward with programmes for industrial development. Moreover, the industrial revolutions of the past have usually been preceded or accompanied by an agricultural revolution; indeed it has usually been the increase in agricultural output which has made the initial development of industry possible. Over most of non-communist Asia today the industrial revolution is being imposed, so to say, from above, and the only hope is that it will not be necessary to wait too long for the response from the sluggish agrarian substructure of these traditional societies. But there is no doubt that it will be necessary to wait.

However, the fortunate coincidence of the second agricultural revolution in the West—the revolution which since the war has applied modern technology to farming so successfully that there has been a rising quantity of food produced each year with fewer and fewer men working the land—offers the means of coping smoothly with the menace in Asia. It happens in any case that most of the Western nations are determined, for reasons of social policy, to keep a substantial farming community on the land and to buy their produce at remunerative prices. Since these modern farmers have acquired the knack of becoming steadily more productive, governments keep desperately casting around for new devices to curb their energies.

It is arguable, however, that this is a self- frustrating approach and that by imposing artificial restrictions on output, production costs are increased and the burden of the farming subsidy is made heavier. At any rate, it is interesting that recent experience in the United States suggests that removing restrictions on the acreage permitted to be sown can have the effect of both reducing costs and greatly expanding output. This is what happened to maize when the restrictions were lifted and the support price was lowered in 1958. The sudden jump in output, by 17 per cent in the following year, indicated the existence of a huge reserve of highly efficient productive power, which probably extends over a wide range of agricultural produce. This is borne out by other evidence about the structure of American farming. The larger farms, amounting to 45 per cent of the total, produce 90 per cent of the output.[3] These are the efficient producers, and the available information suggests that they do not on the whole depend for their profit on official price supports; on the other hand their output is held back and their costs raised by the acreage restrictions. It is noteworthy that even within the straitjacket of controls and output disincentives, productivity in American agriculture has risen during the 1950s much faster than in the rest of the American economy.[4]

One important advantage of American agriculture as a source of additional supplies for the undeveloped countries is that it can be made effective at once; there is no need to wait while production is being built up. The existing U.S. stocks of food grains (estimated at 67 million tons at the end of the 1959 season) are considerably larger than the whole of a year's exports of all these commodities from all sources in the world. The Americans should indeed be encouraged to draw down these stocks straightaway as part of a concerted policy to increase the volume of consumption resources available to undeveloped countries, who would use it to mobilize more labour and pay it a living wage. It was pointed out in an earlier chapter* that investment in public works for agriculture is held back at present by the fear of the inflationary consequences of handing out more wages to workers employed on such projects, without a corresponding increase in the available supplies of consumer goods which these workers would want to buy. One of the chief failures of Western aid programmes so far, and of the World Bank in particular, is that they have not confronted this crucial problem of mobilizing the only plentiful resource in the undeveloped countries of Asia—labour.

In India, for example, according to the data collected by the Government's National Sample Survey, the average rural worker in 1953/4 spent between 140 and 150 days of the year unemployed.[5] It was officially estimated that allowing for sickness and other reasons preventing people from working, the

* See Chapter 8, p. 122

genuine unemployment was around 70 days a year. There is nothing to suggest that the situation has got any better since then. If such people were given work and earned wages during the slack season, the two things that they would buy in larger quantities would be food and cloth. The extra cloth could be readily obtained from domestic production; and the additional demand would probably act as a healthy stimulus to the whole economy. It is the vast suppressed hunger for more food and the fear of the effect on prices of letting it loose, which holds back public enterprise on the land. We have seen that the Chinese communists, because of their absolute control over wages and people, have no difficulty in mobilizing their surplus labour to improve the productive power of the soil. One of the most useful things that the Western countries could do to help the Indians and others to match the Chinese effort, without the total regimentation and the destruction of basic human rights, would be to offer them large quantities of food specifically in support of a new programme of public works in agriculture. Food in this instance would be the means of increasing food production.

But the principle should not be confined to this single commodity. There is, for example, a need for the type of goods which will attract more teachers into the villages and more agricultural extension workers of high quality; certain kinds of sophisticated Western products would be an effective draw, giving the educated man exiled in a primitive village for a few years some compensation for his hardships. Again, in India, there is a class of intellectual unemployed which could be used fruitfully in a drive for literacy, if the authorities were in a position to offer these people the necessary material inducements. But to begin with, we on our side must get rid of our rigid notions about the distinction between capital and consumer goods, which at present inhibit a rational approach to these problems. It is not the physical nature of the goods, but the consequence of using them which is solely worth considering. A radio set or a motor scooter, which make up the wages of a teacher in a remote village and help to keep him there, may contribute as much to economic development as a steel plough or machine tool.

# HOW TO GET MORE AID

## An International Clearinghouse

It may be thought that this emphasis on tied loans and aid in the form of earmarked physical supplies must result in shifting the balance towards the bilateral arrangement and away from an international development programme. So it is interesting to find that aid in the form of some $300m. worth of American surplus food figures prominently in so international a venture as the World Bank Scheme for the Indus Waters. In order to divide the Indus Water supplies fairly between India and Pakistan, Pakistan has to undertake extensive works on three rivers which will cost a total of $1,000m.; this money has been offered jointly by a number of friendly governments together with the World Bank. The United States provides the lion's share, and about half of it is to be in surplus food. It is extremely doubtful whether the Americans would have been prepared to give nearly so much, if they had been asked to make the whole of their contribution available in free dollars. As it happens the Pakistan government needs to apply about 50 per cent of the expenditure on this vast scheme to meet domestic costs, mainly to pay the wages of the great army of workers who will have to dig and build around these rivers for ten years; and so it is quite convenient to receive additional supplies of food, on which the bulk of any wages is likely to be spent.

Plainly it is possible for an international body to use and distribute physical supplies of goods made available by donor countries under the arrangements outlined above. But it would be more difficult work than dealing with development problems neatly in money terms, and then going out to shop comfortably for the goods required. The kind of management necessary would be more like that of an army commissariat in wartime than that of a bank or a business. The organizers would have to think constantly about ways of organizing the second-best, marrying what is readily available in the way of capital goods and supplies with the endless succession of needs at the other end, seizing the opportunity for making constructive use of some temporary surplus of manufacturing capacity as a particular programme of investment in a developed country—it might be on the railways or in electric power or in farm mechanization—begins to run down. Or it might be that disarmament will make redundant ordnance factories and massive quantities of materials and plant designed for war purposes available for productive use. One of the incidental virtues of this scheme would be that it would bring powerful pressure to bear on the governments of undeveloped countries to think ahead intelligently about their own plans and limitations.

However, in practice arrangements such as these are most likely to emerge out of the initiative of pairs of governments actively trying to dovetail their needs and resources; and the role of the international body would in the main be to act as a kind of clearinghouse, record-keeper and adviser. So far as the International Development Association is concerned, the most that can probably be hoped is that it would be willing to engage in pyhsical aid programmes of the simplest sort, involving what is probably the most important commodity of all —food. Surplus food disposals do indeed offer a convenient way out of the problem, which has so far defeated the World Bank, of giving general support to the balance of payments of undeveloped countries which want to invest at home and do not need more than a modicum of capital goods from abroad, but are deterred from going ahead by fear of the inflationary consequences of domestic expansion.

To make these arrangements work—either on a bilateral or a multilateral basis—will require physical planning on an elaborate scale. That will not pose any special difficulty for most governments in advanced industrial countries, who already make it their business to know where surpluses of productive capacity and labour are likely to occur in the years ahead, and engage in long-term strategic programmes of investment to mitigate the social consequences. The only practical problem that is likely to arise here is that this mode of constructive thinking in physical terms is alien to most of the officials who concern themselves with international trade. Perhaps the most sensible course would be to take the new programme of aid right out of their hands, and let the other type of official, who has learnt how to cope with such long-term questions in domestic policy, deal with it. The worst obstacle is likely to be a lot of doctrinal prejudices—above all the feeling that such a programme will have an anti-capitalist bias in the undeveloped countries themselves, that it will encourage state enterprise in all sorts of fields where it is dangerous to let it in, and that by compelling a government to take an interest in the physical details of investment, in countries where business is weak and private investors are few, the West is giving hostages to fortune. The proposal would probably be less objectionable on ideological grounds, if it were simply concerned with making use of temporary surpluses of production as and when they occur. But that is usually much too late. The aim is that both parties to the deal should get into the habit of looking ahead, exchanging information and planning to do things which require government action well in advance.

### Technological Leavings?

It is easy to parody this whole proposal as a policy of giving the undeveloped countries the technological leavings of the rich. The first point to observe is that the programme is not intended to take over the existing forms of economic aid but to supplement them. The receiving countries should treat these additional foreign supplies of capital goods and food in the same spirit as they would treat the discovery of some valuable natural resource within their own territory—as a piece of luck to be exploited to the full in furthering the country's general economic development. The particular natural resource discovered may not be the one which the country would ideally have chosen; it may be located in some remote spot, so that awkward adjustments have to be made to the national system of communications—still no one is likely to suggest that it is not worth bothering with. Indeed a purist might well argue that an element of distortion is introduced into the development of a country, when, say it is found suddenly to possess some rich deposits of copper: capital pours into the copper mines and large resources have to be devoted to roads and harbours and houses to serve the copper industry—while all the time the country may be wanting to invest in agriculture or the development of consumer goods industries. If it has any sense, however, it will recognize that it must make full use of any asset that looks like producing more wealth quickly.

The second point is that even though arrangements are made to absorb from the rich countries those goods that they can make available with comparative ease, the citizens of these countries will not find it a completely painless operation. They will have to make some real sacrifices, especially at times of domestic boom and high employment when these supplies to the undeveloped countries—even if they are made in plants that would otherwise be redundant—have to be forced out of an already fully loaded economic system. In such circumstances the developed countries providing aid have to face a choice between inflation and higher taxes. One way or another it involves some discomfort. Indeed it should be made clear that the convenience sought for the donor countries by the system of aid tied to goods is partly social convenience, partly financial (in giving direct protection to a country's balance of payments and gold reserve), and partly the opportunity of doing a useful service at a lower economic cost than would otherwise be possible. But it is undeniable that under this programme taxes in the donor countries, or savings, will have to be higher than would otherwise be necessary.

The main purpose of the exercise is to allow for the fact that awkward changes caused by economic pressures are occurring on both sides—in the advanced as well as in the backward countries. The problems resulting from very rapid technological change in a comparatively rich society can also be pretty formidable to those who have to suffer them. We should not adopt the attitude that because we are rich we are invulnerable, and therefore ought to be ashamed to ask the poor to help us in making our charitable enterprises less difficult for us. On the contrary, we should encourage the poor countries to regard us as people with problems—not just as tourists with unimaginable amounts of money or as remote nations living a chromium plated existence, armed with the limitless power of modern science. There is no reason why they should be less willing to adapt themselves to our needs, than we are to theirs. Above all, we should not be too proud to ask them.

*Notes*

1. A Swedish businessman, Mr. Langenskold, founded an organization in 1960 which is intended to deal with this problem of after-sales service of second-hand machinery in the undeveloped countries. The organization—a non-profit making body which is called *Industrial Coordination Bureau* with headquarters at Geneva—plans to establish a number of regional inspectors at key points in Asia, Africa and Latin America. ICB proposes not only to act as a kind of technical middleman between sellers and buyers of second-hand machinery, but also to help the latter with credits to finance the deal. It is reported to have the backing of some Swedish banks.

2. Report of a community development evaluation mission in India, United Nations, TAO/IND/31, 1959.

3. "Towards a Realistic Farm Programme", Committee for Economic Development, New York, 1957.

4. "Economic Report of the U.S. President", January 1960. During the decade 1948/58 the average rate of growth of productivity in U.S. agriculture was 2–3 times as rapid as the average for all other branches of activity.

5. National Sample Survey Report, No. 14, March 1959.

*Part III*

# THE ROLE OF THE UNITED NATIONS

*(Together with Zuzanna Shonfield)*

# CHAPTER 12

## THE MISSING THRUST

IT seems improbable, even on an optimistic view of the changing attitude in the West towards undeveloped countries, that the bulk of any enlarged flow of funds for economic development will be transferred to international control. Large-scale investment is not a function in which the United Nations is likely to be able to make a successful bid for outright leadership. There are too many obstacles. On the one side, there is the money contributed by private investment—which will go exactly where its owners feel like sending it, or will not go at all. On the other side, there is the large block of public funds which governments put into their economic aid programmes, guided in part by political considerations. The politics may be a very small or even negligible element at any single moment of time; but donor governments are liable, not unreasonably, to resist the idea that they should surrender altogether the right to use these funds to further the welfare of particular countries, to whom an international agency might give low priority.

Turkey, one of the favoured recipients of U.S. aid, is a clear case in point. It happens that Turkish relations with the World Bank are bad; an incident occurred some years ago when the Turkish government summarily ordered the World Bank representative out of the country. There are in fact cogent reasons for the World Bank's view that strong international pressure ought to be exerted on the Turks to put their own house in order, before they are given any more money over and above the large sums that they have already obtained. On the other hand, it is hard not to sympathize a little with the comment which was made to me on this subject by a U.S. State Department official in a moment of irritation: "You don't expect the United States government to stop helping one of its allies, just because the country doesn't happen to appeal to Eugene Black."

The essential point is that governments—and the voters who elect them—would almost certainly be loth to hand over several billion dollars of taxpayers' money, at this stage, to be disposed of as an international agency saw fit. That is not to say that they would not be willing to put more resources through the International Development Association, especially as the interests of the big donor countries here are safeguarded by the system of weighted voting. It is also clear that the World Bank could obtain more investment funds for use in underdeveloped countries on the basis of the extensive government guarantees at its disposal, which make the Bank's bonds practically a riskless investment. But even assuming that both IDA and the Bank break through the limitations which now confine their activities, and substantially enlarge their present scale of lending, the amounts are still likely to constitute a relatively modest addition to the existing flow of economic aid from all sources to the undeveloped countries.

*Technical Assistance*

In the field of technical assistance, on the other hand, there is every reason why the United Nations should assume the dominant role. This is precisely the kind of work that demands the active leadership of an organization which is entirely independent of national interests, and known by everyone to be so. The reason is that a poor country, attempting to acquire new techniques and modern methods of conducting its business, tends at the early stage of development to find itself in a position of spiritual dependence on outsiders. It is bad enough to be poor; to have to rely on another man's bounty for ideas as well is liable to turn even a normally sensible personality awkward and stubborn. The whole relationship is eased if the technicians do not appear as a pack of foreigners belonging to some remote and superior nation, rich enough to spare a consignment of instructors and experts as an act of charity, but come in as the emissaries of a worldwide organization of which the poor country is an equal member on a par with everyone else.

The point is that although people may resent having to receive capital aid from a particular country, they may yet invest it very successfully; but if there is an emotional barrier to communication, for example in the teaching of new methods of farming or in advising on reforms in government organization, the obstacle can be insurmountable. This is especially so when the foreign expert is suggesting radical changes in accepted ways of doing things. To make an effective impact, he must on occasion be absolutely firm, in the knowledge that this may irritate the people whom he is trying to help. That is another risk which officials of a national government, providing aid under a bilateral programme to a friendly country, are very loth to take. International officials, who should not be so concerned about the political repercussions of ruffled feelings, ought to feel freer to be bold. I am not suggesting they they do invariably, or even usually, feel like this at present; but that is due to the particular weaknesses in the way that the United Nations now goes about the work of technical assistance. The possible remedies will be discussed later.

## Investment in Ideas

But first it is necessary to define more closely the range of activity covered by the term "technical assistance". It is not in fact an exact term, and there is plenty of room for argument on the borderline whether something is technical assistance or straight capital investment. In part, the distinction is a matter of the relative proportions of productive equipment and technical know-how in the operation. Broadly, investment means installing new physical assets of a productive character; technical aid means introducing new procedures leading to the better use of existing productive assets. However, it is immediately evident that the two activities constantly overlap. If someone attaches a small and inexpensive device to a machine which allows the operator to double his output after he has been taught how to use the machine in a new way—is that investment or technical aid? Presumably the latter, because the main factor is taken to be the new *method*, for which the additional device provides a vehicle. But it is plainly not a hard and fast distinction.

Then there is the whole field of pre-investment, in which the technical aid itself often consists largely of special equipment —e.g. for surveying mineral resources, or measuring the hydro-electric potential of a river—while the contribution of human expertise represents the smaller part of the cost. Is pre-invest-ment therefore capital investment under another guise? The extreme case perhaps is the pilot factory, which, once estab-lished, provides an addition to the country's productive capa-city, indistinguishable from any other investment in manufac-turing industry. The United Nations Special Fund, faced with this tricky problem, and with the temptation of some govern-ments to try and use the resources of the Fund as a roundabout way of obtaining investment capital, laid down the principle that a pilot factory would only be regarded as an acceptable project if it contributed some new facts about industrial methods or potentialities, e.g. new ways of using local raw materials, which were not available from any other source. The uniqueness of the problem was what counted, and the end-product which justified setting up a production unit was not the manufacturing output of this plant, but the knowledge that it provided. The important distinction is that the product of investment is extra goods and services, while the product of technical assistance is ideas and new modes of behaviour.

However, it would be unwise to press even this broad dis-tinction too far. How, for instance, is one to classify the highly successful programme of world malaria eradication which has been conducted in recent years by the World Health Organiz-ation? It is conventionally regarded as a programme of technical assistance—on the ground that the expert comes in from outside with his equipment and helps with advice and leadership in the campaign against the mosquito. It is a service, or a piece of technical instruction, rather than an investment. Yet consider the case of a completely passive population—made passive perhaps by generations of malaria—where the experts working their equipment do the whole job over a period of years and thus add permanently to the country's productive power and welfare, in the same way as if they had built new schools or provided some other form of social investment. Perhaps the reason why one is, nevertheless, reluctant to classify this as investment proper is the crude fact that no new physical assets are added in the course of the operation—only a physical nuisance permanently subtracted.

When it comes to the creation of social capital, the very notion of pre-investment is difficult to place. Or alternatively one might say that the whole of social investment is pre-investment, in the sense that it prepares a country for the stage when it will be able to use capital for productive purposes. That is the view that has been taken by the U.N. Special Fund. The important practical point, however, is that the international effort in social investment has so far been very weak; and it is as well that the Special Fund has not been deterred by terminological considerations from moving promptly into the field. Once IDA is more active in this sort of work, it might be worth contemplating a new lot of more precise definitions, which would emphasize the Special Fund's particular function of easing a technical bottleneck in a specific operation.

All told, the technical assistance programmes being conducted in the undeveloped countries today are thought to add up to a cost of around $300m. a year—compared with $5½ billion for all forms of investment and aid.* The figure for technical assistance is necessarily very approximate, because of the difficulty of identifying each operation and distinguishing it from other forms of development activity. Close to half of the money spent is provided by the United States programme. In this instance the American effort is not concentrated in particular countries where there are special strategic interests —as it is in the main grant aid programmes—but is spread fairly evenly around the world. In most of the undeveloped countries it is several times as large as the United Nations Technical Assistance Programme, which is also, incidentally, dependent on the United States for 40 per cent of its funds.

## Colombo Plan

Britain and the other colonial powers concentrate the greater part of their technical assistance in their own colonies. Britain spends some $15m. (£5·2m.) under various programmes, including the Colombo Plan. This last was established in 1950

* See Chapter 2, p. 8

as a Commonwealth scheme[1] for furthering the development of the countries of South Asia, and has managed over the years to acquire unusual prestige. The public image is one of unqualified success, as was shown during the 1960 Commonwealth Prime Ministers' Conference in London which suggested, as a special contribution to the problem of African development, the establishment of a so-called Colombo Plan for Africa.

It is slightly mysterious where the inflated reputation of the Colombo Plan comes from, for it carries out no planning and very little spending. Perhaps its very modesty is one of the things which makes it so popular with its members, since it sets out principally to provide an atmosphere and an annual occasion when they can talk together amicably about their problems. The image of the Colombo Plan must be regarded as one of the more remarkable public relations jobs of the British government—and even that, like the rest of the exercise, has been done on the cheap, with a couple of information officers, an administrative secretary and a director to staff the office in Colombo and deal with the problems of South Asia. In practice the work mainly consists in filling in some of the gaps left by other, more active programmes; the job of the Colombo office, which is rather grandly called the Bureau of Technical Cooperation, is to put anyone with a problem in touch with a donor government that is thought likely to be able to help—and then to leave the pair of them to sort it out. The final transaction is strictly bilateral, with Colombo acting as a kind of post-office. The work is done with the minimum of fuss, and there is usually some money that can be found in a hurry to support a sudden request from some South Asian government to send people off on a specialist technical course in Australia or Britain or to obtain the services of a foreign expert in an emergency. In this the Colombo Plan compares favourably with the ponderous and slow-moving procedures of the United Nations Technical Assistance Programme.

But the operation is essentially a marginal one; the whole of the technical aid provided comes to slightly under $10m. a year,[2] which is less than the amount spent by one of the charitable foundations, like Ford, on work in the undeveloped countries. In part the reason for the prestige of the Colombo

Plan is semantic. When Commonwealth countries, like Canada, run their own separate economic aid programmes and give money to India or Pakistan or Ceylon, they go out of their way to label the various development schemes for which aid is given, "Colombo Plan Projects". The projects have in reality no connection with one another or with Colombo, other than the fact that Canada provides the money for them. But what probably counts most in the end is the marked Commonwealth talent for handling the talking end of the development business. In no time at all after the start of the Colombo Plan the British were able to create something of the atmosphere of a club at the annual meetings. There is here a sense of active participation on the part of the undeveloped countries, who sit round the same table with representatives of the donor nations, U.S.A., Canada, Britain and so on, and discuss the problems of aid as equals.

This sense of participation and equality is one of the virtues which the Commonwealth system shares with the United Nations. Unfortunately it is also, in both institutions, accompanied by a lack of thrust and effective purpose. But whereas the Commonwealth spirit, expressed through the Colombo Plan, consciously eschews the purposeful role, asserting its preference for the club over the boardroom, the United Nations' failure is due in large part to its own structural weakness at the centre. In consequence its energies tend to be dissipated at the periphery.

### Fragmented Effort

The main source of this weakness has already been referred to in Chapter 7: briefly, it is the fragmentation of the work of the United Nations in the social and economic field, and the claim to complete autonomy by each one of the fragments. Although to any stranger, coming on the system from the outside, it has a deliberately self-stultified look, the arrangement is fully accepted by the insiders who have grown up with it as part of the order of nature—perhaps not the best of all possible worlds, but then who, with any sense of history, expects to achieve that? Part of the trouble is, in fact, this historical view which does make, if not sense, then not total nonsense either, of having a set of world agencies specializing on different subjects and working in completely watertight compartments. The role that each of them was given at the start was to provide a comprehensive repository of information on a particular range of subjectmatter and a world forum for periodic discussions. Their business was to cultivate their own plot of garden. At the end of the War the International Labour Organization (ILO), which was transferred readymade to the United Nations with a proud history of independent achievement behind it, set the tone. Its watchword had always been: freedom from outsiders.

Of course no one thinks it strange that a body like the World Health Organization, for example, should carry out its programmes without trying to integrate the work into some closely knit structure of United Nations policies directed from a central point. That is because the objectives of a health department are generally clear; and when there is some controversy about medical policy, it is usually the kind of thing that has to be settled by medical experts. This applies to a department of health inside a national government, as well as to an international agency. Except in an emergency, the policy of the health department tends to come up for general consideration only once a year, at budget time.

It may be argued that even in WHO's work there is more room for the formulation of an overall international policy in the underdeveloped countries, combining medical with economic and social advance, than the medical experts generally allow. Plainly if a country like Ceylon embarks on a thoroughgoing campaign for the elimination of malaria, the people concerned with economic planning ought to be forewarned about the probable timetable of rising population pressure on the land. This points to the crucial issue of contraception and its possible role in raising income per head by curbing the rate of population growth. It so happens that WHO has been specifically forbidden by a lamentable decision of a religious majority of its members to take any official interest at all in this subject. But there are other matters, for example its latest campaign to improve environmental sanitation by providing everyone in the world with enough clean water to wash with, as well as to drink, on which WHO could act in closer unison with its sister agencies. Still by and large there is sufficient agreement about the need to keep as many people as possible alive and in health to allow the organization to get on with tasks of its own choosing, without seriously cutting across other technical aid programmes.

This is far from being so with the other U.N. agencies. Their work in the undeveloped countries ought to be one integrated operation, responding flexibly to changing needs, with a single responsible authority answering for the direction and performance of each project. In practice the specialized agencies negotiate together over any piece of work involving their collaboration in the high manner of independent sovereign states, whose basically friendly relations are constantly in jeopardy because their spheres of influence abut on one another. It is not that they fail to collaborate in the end; they do get together. But too often it requires the most elaborate formal preparations; there are delays while the commanders parley with one another and the battlefield waits; and finally when the allies do join up for the battle they will surrender no power at all to a commander: each insists on retaining complete control over his own troops. There are certain conventions about seniority, but they affect status rather than power. At the United Nations in New York officials set great store on a convention that in any inter-agency work that includes the Technical Assistance Office of the United Nations headquarters (UNTAO), the latter can automatically claim the senior role. But in practice any pretensions to leadership from New York are vigorously rebutted by the other members of the U.N. family.

### Community Development

The best that can be hoped from this procedure of coming together as independent entities to collaborate on a project, which ought to have been conceived from the start as a single piece of business, is that it does ultimately produce a reasonable working arrangement in the field between the technicians who are trying to get on with the job. At its worst, it results in years of delay while a problem clearly recognized as crucial is tinkered with, instead of being tackled. This is the sad story of the United Nations' effort on "community development"—one of the most striking examples of wasted opportunity. The term "community development" suffers from vagueness, but it broadly covers any programme of leadership and education in primitive villages which uses labour and other resources readily available on the spot to raise the standard of living. An obvious example is the introduction of a cooperative system of contributing work by villagers towards the construction of a local road or a rat-free warehouse for storing grain, which will serve them all. The outside technical expert comes in with advice about methods and materials—but also, if he is to be effective, in a much more awkward role, as the original pebble cast forcefully into a stagnant pond.

Plainly this kind of work by its very nature involves an element of quasi-revolutionary activity in the village, since its overriding aim is to force the pace by bringing in the untraditional and more productive methods of agriculture—and that in turn almost inevitably involves social change, disrupting first of all the old patterns of behaviour and respect towards the landlord, the trader and moneylender. To be successful it requires special talent in the man on the spot and a very carefully thought out campaign by the organization in charge of the programme, with lots of tactical variations in readiness to deal with special circumstances. The idea is, after all, to find a voluntary answer to the problems which the communists solved by forced collectivization of farms, backed up in China by the further military regimentation of the peasants. There could hardly be anything more ambitious than the attempt to set up a free working alternative to the juggernaut.

It has not been done. The idea of a controlled and non-violent agrarian revolution has attracted a lot of attention, particularly in India, but the results of several years of much publicized effort are extremely meagre. Of course there are show places where the visitor can see with his own eyes that peasants have struggled out of their apathy and got together to create a village hall or school. But judged in terms of the effect on average living standards—and that must mean in Asia its effect in helping to increase the output of food—the experiment has got nowhere. And one of the reasons is that each country has been largely dependent on its own local experiments and blunders in going forward with the programme. The mass of information that might have been brought to bear on the problem, through an intelligent use of data drawn from the big agrarian changes that have taken place in other countries, has not been effectively applied.

As late as 1959, seven years after the big Indian community development programme was launched, one finds a mission of international experts, sent by the United Nations, pointing out the following things to the Indian government.[3] First the programme has failed to concentrate sufficiently on the main object, which is to raise agricultural output, and has allowed the energies of its officers to be diverted into marginal activities of a social and cultural character—partly no doubt because these seemed easier to do. Secondly, and connected with this, the programme has not made contact with the minds of the poorer peasants. Because the official coming from outside tends to look for people with a modicum of education to make the cultural and social bridge between himself and the established order in the village, community development comes to be viewed by the ordinary villager as an alliance between the government man and the existing ruling class. The report concludes that if the programme is to succeed in raising agricultural production, "it must win the confidence of the majority of the people by avoiding too exclusive dependence on the more well-to-do persons in the villages and by not being afraid to take up the cudgels against social abuses, against infringements of the law—such as the kind of share cropping in which the farmer receives one-third of the crop—and against usury and speculative sharp practices."

# THE MISSING THRUST

*Reasons for Failure*

Here is precisely the kind of issue on which the United Nations should have been in a unique position to provide expert guidance and direction right from the start. It is bound to be a delicate operation, trenching as it does upon sensitive areas of a nation's cultural heritage and on its spiritual inadequacies; to be of any value, an outside adviser must feel strong enough to use the critical freedom and the sharp practical approach to the problem of stirring up the villages, which is so well expressed in the independent report from which I have just quoted. Yet most of the time the various agencies of the United Nations, which have made their piecemeal and separate contributions to community development, have tagged along behind other people's ideas, almost as if they were afraid, more than anything else, of being accused of *wanting* to exercise leadership. It is noteworthy that the Ford Foundation, finding this obvious gap waiting to be filled, has now decided to put some $10m. into a series of big experimental projects in Indian community development with the aim of answering a number of urgent questions on policy for the future.

Why has the United Nations not made better use of its opportunities? In this instance there was the special disability caused by the presence of UNESCO (U.N. Educational, Scientific and Cultural Organization) in a leading role. UNESCO coined the term "fundamental education" for what it conceived to be the main function of village training in this sphere, and the result was to emphasize out of all proportion the simple and relatively easily organized activities of village life, the folk art and the group leisure activity, diverting attention from the stern realities of the agrarian revolution which is the main object of the exercise. Unfortunately this approach fitted in only too well with the fuzzy attitudes of many of the national officials who were initially drawn into community development work; the whole operation became a hunting ground for fuddy-duddies. It would be wrong to suggest that UNESCO failed to contribute anything useful— help in the organization of village schools constructed by local voluntary labour was plainly valuable—but what was entirely lacking was a sense of priorities, and an effort to focus on precise practical aims. Luckily UNESCO's original pretensions to assume command of world community development —on the strange ground that since this was a new bit of social science, it obviously belonged to it as the supervisor of international scientific effort—have been scotched. But there are still two expensive Fundamental Education Centres, one in Egypt for the whole Middle East and another in Mexico for Latin America, which absorb funds that could be much better devoted to other purposes. The Mexican centre alone costs close to $250,000 a year to run and turns out thirty graduate "instructors" in that time. At $8,000 a head that makes it an expensive kind of finishing school for people who are supposed to take the lead in organizing the simplicities and the rough-and-tumble of village life.

However, it would be unfair to put the whole blame on UNESCO for the inadequacies of the United Nations in the work of community development. The chief cause of the failure is that there have been altogether too many different bodies involved in the business, all acting in their characteristically independent manner. WHO is concerned with elementary health education in the villages; the International Labour Office provides technical aid on how to use labour more efficiently in cottage industries; the Food and Agriculture Organization (FAO) looks after farming problems; and the Technical Assistance Office (TAO) is supposed to provide the authoritative ideas and studies through the U.N. Bureau of Social Affairs. As early as 1953 it became evident that these organizations, together with UNESCO, were treading on each other's toes, and the U.N. people in New York (TAO) exercising their rights of seniority, called a conference of the interested parties in an effort to agree on one coherent programme, with a rational division of functions among themselves. They all met in Geneva; but compromise was found to be impossible at that time. It was not until the late 1950s that the various agencies were able to reach a working arrangement, which shared out the tasks in a clear and sensible fashion.

The defenders of the present United Nations family system point out that the agencies do, in fact, work together successfully on a number of projects and that there are very few examples of complete stultification through overlap. It is true that the open quarrelling is much less—and so is the covert sabotage—than it was some years ago; the machinery for dealing with demarcation disputes, which now operates under the control of a committee of the heads of the independent agencies and the U.N. Secretary-General,[4] meeting twice a year, works pretty well. And it is supported, lower down, by the working groups of departmental heads from different agencies, who meet together informally in Geneva once a year. The trouble is that each one of these acts of coordination is a *tour de force*, and what emerges is a series of compromises about the way to handle a tricky development problem, rather than a single vigorous push for development itself.

### American Methods

The techniques and the spirit of the whole thing are closely in line with traditional American methods of administration.[5] American ideas, as well as American administrators, were completely in the ascendant when most of the U.N. agencies came into being just after the war. It is not wholly surprising therefore that they accept the principle of the fragmentation of authority as a way of life. The notion of checks and balances is at the centre of all American thinking on the use of executive power; and the solution when things become difficult is, as an American official once said to me, "to bring everyone you can think of into the act". The troubles of the United Nations family may therefore be regarded in some measure as a relic of the constitutional prejudices of the Founding Fathers. And within the individual U.N. agency there is more fragmentation and independence, so that FAO, for example, has its budget so rigidly divided between the main departments that it is difficult to manage a transfer of funds from one purpose to another (in a different department) after the start of the budget year. Some time ago the island of Haiti wanted the services of a technical expert on animal husbandry; but when this request was put through the machine FAO discovered that its technical aid funds for this department had already been committed for that year—so it generously offered to pay the Haitians out of another pocket for a rural dietician instead!

One defect of the system, then, is waste, particularly of skilled manpower. The other is muddle. At no stage has anyone formulated a clear and rational division of functions inside the United Nations, which would provide the undeveloped countries themselves with a simple guide to what is available and with an efficient system of obtaining it with the minimum of fuss. The U.N. agencies are the prisoners of their history. They were, after all, set up originally to deal with quite other problems than those of underdevelopment, on which we now expect them to focus their main energies. Each in turn was given a broad area of human activity and assumed the task of covering it in a spirit of comprehensiveness worthy of a world authority on the subject. Thus, for example, UNESCO, because it sets out to be the world leader on scientific research, runs a big and expensive programme of investigation into the problems of "arid lands", regardless of the fact that this ought to be the concern of the Water and Soil Division of the Food and Agriculture Organization. The end result of giving rein to its scientific ambitions is that UNESCO is left with too little money to deal with what should be its main task in the undeveloped countries —primary and secondary education.

FAO, on the other hand, does not get the resources that it needs to cope adequately with one of its main problems, the proper use of irrigation and land in poor peasant communities. It has another rival here—the U.N. Technical Assistance Office (TAO) in New York, which is in charge of river development and "ground water". Each organization employs a staff that is struggling to keep up with many of the same technical problems. Finally, in an effort to put an end to the constant outbreaks of bickering between the rivals, U.N. headquarters in New York set up a "Water Resources Centre", to share out the work and decide on lines of demarcation between agencies in particular projects. The senior U.N. official in charge of this venture is an able Jesuit priest, Father de Breuvery, and it has been widely remarked that this will provide a testing exercise for his metaphysical powers. Certainly, the rationale of the exact division of operational functions between TAO (in charge of "groundwater") and FAO (in charge of irrigation) eludes the ordinary man—as it does presumably the ordinary government of an undeveloped country, looking for a simple guide on whom to ask for what. Surely the simple view is right, that normally the problems of water in an undeveloped country are a matter for the Food and Agriculture Organization; if there happens to be some problem outside its range, e.g. hydro-electricity or river transport, FAO should call in the services of other bodies which have the expert knowledge. It does not really need the ingenuity of a Jesuit priest-economist in an office in New York to sort that one out.

## Reforming the System

More serious than the waste is the effect on the quality of work of the United Nations and its agencies—the lack of sharp initiative and coherent leadership in tackling new problems, like community development. However, there is no hope of reforming the system overnight; power has been dispersed, and it can only gradually be retrieved at the centre. The first salutary moves were made when the Special Fund was set up in 1958.* One of the decisions of Mr. Paul Hoffman, the first Managing Director, was that he would have dealings with only one "executing agent" for any given project, and that this agent would be responsible for *employing* anyone else in the U.N. family. This is the opposite of the usual technique of "bringing everyone into the act". But the Special Fund can only exercise authority in this way—forcing the practice of leadership and integrated operation on the U.N. agencies—because it keeps the purse-strings firmly in its own hands.

The next step is to tackle the U.N. Technical Assistance Programme in the same spirit. The discussion of the problem in Chapter 7 showed just how strong are the forces of inertia, preventing any initiatve on the part of the head of the TAB. He is in fact only the chairman of a committee in which the heads of the other U.N. agencies have an equal vote. In order to exercise effective authority at the centre, he must be able to use a substantial sum of money with the same freedom as the Managing Director of the U.N. Special Fund. The amount at his disposal at the moment (7–8 per cent of a total budget of

* See Chapter 7, p. 101

something over $30m.)* is insufficient. Admittedly the projects in the TA Programme projects are usually fairly small—rarely more than $50,000 compared with the normal minimum for the Special Fund of $250,000—but to obtain some freedom of manoeuvre the head of TAB probably needs at least $5–6m. for central disposal, say some 20 per cent of the present fund. And as more money is made available to the United Nations to further the work of technical assistance in undeveloped countries, the centrally directed fund should be steadily enlarged.⁶

The TA Programme could then be fused with the U.N. Special Fund in a single organization. The division between "pre-investment" and "technical aid" is useful as a broad practical concept, but it is evident that the two frequently overlap. For once, indeed, the United Nations has made an extremely sensible and unbureaucratic arrangement, putting the heads of the two programmes to work in offices next door to one another in New York; the two programmes operate in close concert and even pass over money from one account to the other without the usual obsession with mine-and-thine.

Of course, the new Technical Assistance Programme, like the Special Fund at present, would spend most of its money in employing the services of the specialized agencies of the United Nations. But it would be their master: it would designate the controlling authority in any operation and compel the other U.N. bodies engaged on the job to act like subordinate departments of a single organization. Its ultimate sanction over them would be its power to ignore them—and to go right outside the United Nations family for experts and consultants, if this were found to be necessary.

Leaving aside the Special Fund and TA Programme, the United Nations with its technical agencies (excluding the financial institutions, the World Bank and the Internationl Monetary Fund) spends around $110m. a year on economic and social activities.† Of this considerable sum less than half is used to forward the technical progress of the undeveloped countries. If UNICEF, which is simply an organization for distributing supplies, is left out of account, the proportion is only one-third. The first step, if the United Nations is to assume

* See Chapter 7, p. 101 and 107
† See Appendix III

the leading role in this phase of the work in the undeveloped countries, is to alter this unbalanced distribution of the load in its regular budget. It must learn to drop things, if it is to be more adept at taking on new responsibilities.

That does not mean, for example, that the FAO should be asked to give up its function of providing an international forum for the discussion of agricultural problems or of compiling its useful statistics of world trends in output and consumption of different commodities. But at the moment it is plainly trying to do too much about too many things. In the vast block of offices which it occupies near the Colosseum in Rome, it employs no less than 1,200 people, and of these 700 are professional staff. That is twice the number of professionals employed by the World Bank for all its operations.

It is not that the people in FAO are underemployed; on the contrary, the visitor can hardly escape the impression that in many offices in the building overwork is carried to the point of dangerous strain. He also arrives at the firm conviction—if he proceeds to follow some of FAO's activities around the world— that something is basically wrong, for its reputation in simple matters of administration, like paying cheques and giving instructions on time to the experts whom it employs, is frankly poor. I have come across no evidence to suggest that the reputation is unjustified. On the other hand, there is no question about the high technical performance of the men and women of this organization on almost any subject that they tackle. The real danger is that, by trying to cover too much, it will spread its resources too thin.

However, nobody inside FAO responds to the danger by suggesting that it might retreat from certain obscure corners of the great terrain originally allotted to it. On the contrary, officials there, as in other agencies, react with a strong sense of shock to any proposal that they might do a little less at head-quarters; the bug of comprehensiveness has bitten deep. The obvious remedy, they point out, is to build up the staff, and they can usually present a strong case for doing so. It is only possible to argue against them, if one starts from the assumption that the United Nations ought today to be doing different things, and to be using the bulk of its resources in quite different ways, from those that were envisaged when the first plans were made immediately after the war. The assumption, once stated, seems incontrovertible.

*Notes*

1. It has since been joined by the U.S., Japan and several South Asian countries outside the Commonwealth.

2. £3·1m. according to the last report for the year 1958/9.

3. Report of the Community Development Evaluation Mission in India, referred to earlier (Note 2, Chapter 11). The members of the mission were Mr. M. J. Coldwell (Canada), Professor R. Dumont (France) and Dr. Margaret Read (United Kingdom). The Indian authorities felt keenly enough on the subject to publish the report verbatim as a government paper in Delhi, in spite of its strictures on their own programme.

4. This is called the Administrative Committee on Coordination (ACC). See Appendix II.

5. See, for instance, an essay by W. W. Rostow in "The American Style", edited by Morison, 1958.

6. How exactly this change is to be accomplished is a matter for bargaining with the U.N. agencies. Clearly they will not like it, nor perhaps will the member nations who at present are favoured with fixed allocations of funds under the Technical Assistance Programme to use as they see fit. In practice the agencies retain a good deal of effective power over the use of the money: they can "under-fulfil" a programme in one country and "over-fulfil" it in another. When dealing with matters so complex as the personal movements of individual technical experts, endowed with some obscure speciality —and sometimes an obscurer private life—it is not easy for a government to exercise real supervision. It is, in any case, often prevented from doing so by rivalries between its own departments and ministries, each with its pet U.N. agency in tow. As we have seen, the strong centralized administrations, like Yugoslavia and Israel, tend to come off best.

The way to persuade these countries to vote for a reform, by which they will seem to be surrendering some control over their programme, is by making this the condition for a big increase in the programme of technical assistance. The U.N. agencies will probably have to be bribed into submission: they might for instance be granted a series of fixed allocations of TA funds for extended periods of time (say three years or so) to allow them to get on independently with their own longer-term programmes in the undeveloped countries. These programmes would still be subject to some degree of co-ordination through the action of the U.N. Resident Representative in each country, and governments would be able to turn to him (and to the substantial fund behind him in New York) if they felt they were not receiving satisfactory treatment from the agencies. This, like any piece of institutional horse-trading, is not wholly satisfactory; but some price will have to be paid if the U.N. family is to be turned from the present loose confederacy into something approximating to a unitary state.

# CHAPTER 13

# UNRAVELLING THE TANGLE

A<small>N</small> international organization whose job it is to give expert advice may approach its task either in the spirit of a university or of a consultancy business: it may take the view that it ought to aim at being the complete authority on all subjects within its allotted area or alternatively it may decide to vary the degree of its expertise in proportion to the needs of its customers. An industrial consultancy firm does not keep full-time experts on every conceivable phase of industry on its staff. It will concentrate its resources on a number of subjects which are in heavy demand from its clients and in addition, possibly, on one or two matters on which it reckons to have a special contribution of its own to make. For the rest it will be content to maintain a generally high level of technical competence at headquarters, sufficient to ensure proper supervision over the outside experts whom it employs to deal with particular tasks. The argument of the last chapter indicated that this ought to be the model for a body like the Food and Agriculture Organization in its approach to the problems of the undeveloped countries.

It will require a big wrench. Neither FAO nor UNESCO nor any of the other international agencies will readily surrender the ideal of a university which they were given at their birth. FAO indeed took over the prewar International Institute of Agriculture in Rome. (It also incidentally obtained its splendid headquarters, land and buildings, for an annual rent of $1 from the Italian government, which offered this bargain after the war with its eye on the foreign exchange income produced by the presence of an international organization, running periodic conferences with lots of foreign visitors. It so happened that the site had been designed to house Mussolini's new ministry for the Italian overseas empire, and so could readily be spared.)

In UNESCO, because of the vast terrain offered to the

organization—the whole of science and culture, as well as education—the ideal of a university has been the excuse for a wild and arbitrary diffusion of effort. Moreover, since it is not after all a university, following the ideal of patient and unspectacular intellectual activity, but a normal go-getting bureaucratic organization anxious to make a splash, the results of its work seem often not to justify the money put into them. There is something depressingly middlebrow and pretentious about many of the documents which the organization puts out —indicating clearly that the one thing that has not been acquired is the consistent standards of a university. Perhaps this too is the result of excessive diffusion of effort, leaving too little time and manpower for effective editorial direction and supervision. Like everyone else, UNESCO feels it is short of staff at headquarters and needs more people.

But that is surely not the solution. What is required first of all is to give this organization a clear and a strictly limited brief. Its main business, if it is now to be reoriented towards the needs of the undeveloped countries, is education of a pretty basic kind; science and culture should frankly be regarded as subsidiary matters, where UNESCO should not attempt to lead, let alone to create, but should confine itself to encouraging other people's work. The best solution indeed would be to take the "S" (for science) and the "C" (for culture) out of UNESCO, and put these subjects into a separate organization whose task would be similar to that of one of the big private foundations, like Ford or Rockefeller, which promotes intellectual activity. The headquarters staff would be small, and its main task would be to help in providing the vehicle for the communication of scientific ideas across national frontiers. It is particularly important to keep the new scientists who are coming up in the undeveloped countries in touch with what is happening in the main centres of experiment and research. This is a valuable task which UNESCO at present performs. But it is hard to see anything of comparable worth in UNESCO's work on culture. What ought to be done here is to limit the field to a narrow and well defined sector of international activity—contacts between museums and the like—to make the budget modest, and to insist that most of it be spent on subsidizing outside activities, not on work done by the organization itself.

*Education to Some Purpose*

The aim of this austerity programme is to save money in order to concentrate resources on a really powerful drive for basic education, focused on the specific tasks of speeding development in the poor countries. So far the United Nations, through UNESCO, has failed to get to grips with this problem. There are a few good ideas that have been tried out by isolated individuals, some useful films, and a number of excellent people doing a sturdy job as teachers and organizers. But what emerges in the end is little more than would come out of the efforts of a good charitable or religious order with a mission to educate the black and the brown man. The chief criticism—apart from the inadequate share of its total funds which UNESCO devotes to straightforward education—is that the outcome depends almost entirely on the individual calibre of the man on the spot. It is obvious that with the tiny number of such teachers and experts in education available, compared with the vast populations which have to acquire some knowledge of rudimentary modern techniques in order to move forward, little will be achieved unless there is a radical departure from orthodox methods of teaching.

What is required is a systematic approach to the task of making the undeveloped peoples learn in twenty or thirty years what it has taken the societies of the West a century or more to acquire. Many of these undeveloped countries start, moreover, at a disadvantage compared with the pre-capitalist Western societies: they have a smaller proportion of trained intellectuals to provide the initial cadres of teachers, who will train other teachers. Against this they have the advantage offered by the existence today of vastly improved equipment for mass teaching —films, gramophones, television, and even reading machines— and a mass of modern experience on techniques of accelerated instruction. But they have to be shown what to do by people who believe in quick learning. Presumably the Russians would have some useful ideas on this subject, after their experience of conquering mass illiteracy and rapidly forming a big nucleus of highly competent technicians out of the body of a backward peasant society.

The kind of question on which an undeveloped country

needs guidance is this: Assuming that there are only limited resources that can be applied to education, will it pay to concentrate the main weight of the teaching effort on secondary education, at the expense of primary, even though this may mean allowing the mass of the people to remain illiterate for a few years longer? How important practically is the knowledge of reading, and who must have it, in order to speed up the early stages of economic growth? Perhaps wealth would increase faster if a society were endowed with a good supply of moderately educated foreman types, rather than a very large number of people who can just read and write. Those are the questions put in their broadest form: specifically, a government wants expert guidance on where to direct a particular educational drive—what subjects and what methods to use—in order to move towards the attainment of certain economic and social ends.

By agreement among the U.N. agencies, this type of practical training with particular economic ends in view is left to soil the hands of the International Labour Organization, which has always concerned itself with apprenticeship and has now extended its activities through the whole field of technical training, industrial productivity and so on. It is only when technical instruction is put into the context of a university or an ordinary primary or secondary school that it comes under the authority of UNESCO. And that usually means that it gets pushed into the framework of the traditional mould of Western classical education; this is particularly true at the university level. Often, as ILO points out, the approach is wholly inappropriate, for what the undeveloped country probably requires is to spread the knowledge of a number of specific skills and disciplines as fast as possible in order to raise productive efficiency. This is what Yugoslavia has done (using ILO) with the help of a United Nations training scheme for industrial foremen. But perhaps the worst consequence of the present division of the field is that UNESCO has not been compelled to face its main job which is to educate people to some purpose, and to do it fast.

*Assault on Traditional Culture*

There is another and more delicate problem which has to be confronted. It sometimes happens that a major impediment to economic growth is presented by a strong traditional culture, which in various oblique but effective ways inhibits the acceptance of attitudes that are a prerequisite for a modern productive society. We have already come across this issue in relation to the community development programme.* It may appear in a more intellectual guise—as for instance in the initial refusal of many of the old universities of South America to teach modern economic techniques. The U.N. Economic Commission for Latin America deliberately set itself to fight against this particular manifestation of the Hispanic spirit, and proceeded to establish its own little faculty in economic planning, drawing many of the ablest economists of the Continent into its courses of instruction. The resistance of the intellectual reactionaries is now beginning to break down.

Often indeed there is no alternative to a frontal assault on some part of the local cultural pattern. Of course there are risks involved in these spiritual upheavals, and the United Nations must start by deciding whether it wants to get seriously involved in the work of education for development. If it does, it is bound to find itself quite frequently cast in a radical role, and siding with one political or social group against another. There is, of course, an alternative view on this whole question, the consciously conservative view put forthrightly by Mr. George Kennan: "Anyone can see why the underdeveloped countries are terribly interested in this problem of economic growth. . . . I personally think that they are making a great mistake to wish to change their societies with the speed with which they actually seem to wish to do this. It is my own belief that if you change the lives of people so rapidly that the experience of the father, the wisdom of the father, becomes irrelevant to the needs of the son, you have done something very dangerous—you have broken the organic bond of the family, and you have created emotional trauma in the minds of young people."[1]

There are many people engaged in the business of education

* See Chapter 12, p. 188 *et seq.*

who hold, covertly and partially, the views which Mr. Kennan puts with such forthrightness. They have no place in the kind of programme which I am suggesting here; and it is essential, if the work on education is to become an effective component of a programme of economic development, to begin by recognizing that there really is a serious conflict of opinion on this issue. Of course in some countries it will not be possible for an international organization to act in a radical spirit, because the government will not permit it. In such cases, I suggest, the United Nations ought to quit the field and leave the job of education there to one of the national aid programmes (like the American ICA), whose primary job is to please, even more than to help. Certainly the United Nations will not get anywhere in this work unless it is prepared at least to take the risk, every now and then, of official displeasure.

## Role of FAO

In the Food and Agriculture Organization the need is not for a major upheaval, as in UNESCO, but for a reduction in the size of certain departments, combined with the much greater use of outside consultants.[2] At the same time other departments, which are concerned with the most common and urgent needs of the undeveloped countries, e.g. irrigation and fertilizers, ought to be expanded. What an international organization of this kind needs, above all, is a complete and up-to-date register of the world's experts in each small subject, an intimate knowledge of their personal capabilities, and a close enough relationship with them to be able to call readily on their advice. That is the kind of asset that the World Bank has built up in subjects like hydro-electricity and water problems, in which it takes a special interest. It will always try to avoid employing its own staff, if outsiders can be found to do the job.

There are, however, certain subjects on which the FAO is the world authority—and ought to be so. A typical case is the control of rinderpest, one of the fatal diseases of cattle which was until a few years ago common throughout Asia and has now been largely eliminated. It is immensely contagious, and the FAO has developed a 48-hour service of reporting around the world, in order to keep it under control. Since neither cattle nor herdsmen are respecters of frontiers, this has to be an international service, controlled from one sensitive nerve centre. There are several other matters like it.

But the great bulk of the work of FAO is not of this kind. Yet it is all treated as if the elaborate system of checks and reporting was equally necessary. The outside expert, taken on under contract to do an ordinary job of work in an undeveloped country, is made to render a monthly written report to headquarters on what he is doing; this is the standard procedure, and it is a source of dreadful bureaucratic overload in Rome, as well as being a nuisance to the man who is trying to get on with his work in the field. In fact the great flow of paper pouring into the head offices of this and the other U.N. agencies cannot possibly be absorbed and digested: it tends to pile up like in some bureaucratic nightmare imagined by Kafka where an excessively suspicious police force invent a system of reporting so perfect and so full that they are unable to get any information out of it at all.

Much of the time the very idea of having a man at headquarters who is more expert than the man in the field, and capable of giving him technical instructions, is a mistaken one. It is another relic of the university atmosphere: the head of a department must know more than the junior demonstrator in the lab. In fact the need at headquarters is for someone like the manager of a business or a senior civil servant in a ministry, who has sufficient expertise to understand what his subordinates are doing and to know where to *get* them advice if they need it, but is not more expert than any of them. The most effective way of exercising control over the immensely varied activities of a technical agency in the undeveloped countries is to send out the headquarters men to make periodic spot checks; they do not have to know so much in order to ask the right questions, though they must have the administrator's talent for asking them.

# UNRAVELLING THE TANGLE

## *The New Ambassadors*

There is also the permanent Resident Representative of the U.N. Technical Assistance Programme in many of these countries. His role is akin to that of an economic ambassador of the United Nations to the government of the country concerned; and he should, at the same time, be the local eye of all the U.N. agencies on the technical experts employed by them under contract. There are some thirty-five of these representatives of the United Nations economic interest in different countries, and the cost of the whole establishment, with local office staff, is borne jointly by the Technical Assistance Programme and the U.N. Special Fund. Potentially they and their outposts in the undeveloped countries offer an important means of asserting the independent initiative of the United Nations in the economic sphere.

In practice, however, most of them are today treated as little more than post-offices by the independent U.N. agencies. Again it is the extreme jealousy surrounding each sovereign bureaucracy which makes the agencies insist on their own separate chains of command between themselves and the man in the field. My first direct contact with the full pettifogging force of the system as it now stands came in El Salvador, in Central America, where the United Nations Resident Representative happened to be engaged in trying to send an agricultural expert across the frontier to cope with something that required to be done in Guatemala. The U.N. Representative was officially accredited to all five republics of the Central American bloc; but it emerged that he could not authorize the $18 fare which this expert required, without referring the request to the Food and Agriculture Organization. There is a regional office of FAO in Mexico City, but it is thought to have little power in such matters; so the request, which was urgent, had to go by telegram to headquarters in Rome. Cable costs must in the end have added a fair amount to the expert's travel bill.

This is by no means an extreme example. Instead of engaging in a joint effort to raise the status and the authority of the local economic representative of the United Nations family, the agencies seem often to be doing their best to downgrade him. If they have their own man on the spot they usually ignore the U.N. man altogether. One of the Resident Representatives pointed out that he had even lost the authority that goes with handing out salary cheques to the people working in the field— "which is an important psychological matter", he said, "in the relationship with outside technical experts, who are only on short contracts with the United Nations."

Indeed it is clear that the first step in building up the status of the U.N. economic ambassador would be to give him power to spend money on behalf of all the agencies. This may seem a small matter of official routine, but it is really of decisive importance. All money transferred from any part of the United Nations family to an expert working in the field should pass into the account of the Resident Representative. He should be endowed with a small working reserve and be responsible for salary payments, local travel expenditure and so on; and the agencies would then reimburse his account. If they disapproved of some piece of expenditure—like any other local manager he would have a ceiling on the amount that he could authorize without reference to headquarters—they would take it up with him, and tell him of their wishes for the future.

The essential reform is that there should be no person acting for any part of the United Nations family in a country, who is not subordinate to the Resident Representative. This may sound simple and obvious, and so it is; but it would involve a revolution in the accepted way of doing things. In India, for example, where the United Nations has its biggest single country programme, each of the larger agencies runs an independent headquarters, which rarely takes any notice of any of the others. This applies even to the United Nations Children's Fund (UNICEF), whose job consists almost entirely in distributing useful supplies, like milk for child welfare or D.D.T. for an anti-malaria campaign, supplementing some larger programme of aid. But it, too, insists on having direct and independent relations with governments. I asked the U.N. Resident Representative how often he held a meeting of the local heads of all these branches of the United Nations family. "Once a year," he said, "over lunch."

It so happens that the offices of the U.N. Representative in

New Delhi are located in the same building as part of the Ministry of Finance. The Indian government department which looks after the coordination of all foreign aid programmes is in the Finance Ministry, and so, as a result of propinquity and personality, there are close and amicable relations with the United Nations' chief across the corridor. Indeed, this is in practice the only way in which any coordination of the various U.N. programmes within the country is achieved—at second-hand, by the Indian government with the informal advice of the Resident Representative. The paradox of this type of situation, in which so many of the U.N. Resident Representatives find themselves, was put rather well and rather bitterly by another one of them, this time in a Latin American country: "We start off by trying to represent the United Nations with the government to which we are accredited, but we end up by representing the views of the government to the U.N. agencies."

It is wrong in principle that the United Nations should be dependent on the accident of a government's goodwill towards the person of the Resident Representative for bringing some order into the activities of its agencies. But it is noticeable that where a government has an efficient system of coordination of its own departments and keeps them under a firm unified control, the U.N. Representative does have the opportunity of exercising some authority. The outstanding case is Yugoslavia. The government there refused to accept independent representation of agencies like FAO—that did not fit in with its own ideas of central planning—and insisted that everything connected with the Technical Assistance Programme of the United Nations should be controlled by the single office of the Resident Representative. It is partly because of this, though partly also because of the energetic and discriminating use that the Yugoslav government itself has made of the technical assistance available, that the work done here is one of the showpieces of the United Nations programme.

# AN ECONOMIC BOSS

*An Economic Boss*

Going round and asking several of the Resident Representatives about the idea of turning them into full-scale economic ambassadors of the United Nations, I found that they almost invariably expressed anxiety on one point. They were afraid that with their enhanced diplomatic status they might be expected to get involved in a political role on behalf of the United Nations. This, they thought, would confuse the issue, and would mean the loss of the intimate and informal relationship which quite a few of them had succeeded in establishing with the economic departments of the governments to which they were accredited. In some countries they have actually become one of the instruments of planning by the government itself. If they were now to be instructed to act in an entirely detached spirit as the "United Nations presence", and conduct delicate political negotiations on behalf of the Secretary-General, their carefully nurtured relationship was bound to suffer.

It seemed to me, on closer examination, that their anxieties referred back to a deeper need to sort out the different roles at the centre of the United Nations—the need to distinguish more clearly in the making of policy between political and economic objectives, and to allow the economic side an independence which it at present lacks. To be independent it has to be able to stand aside from the political preoccupations of the U.N. Secretary-General, even deliberately ignore them, if they conflict with some major long-term economic objective. At present the Under-Secretary in charge of the Economic and Social Affairs Department is just one of seven senior officials of equal status who make up the second layer of the hierarchy. There is not even an officially appointed second-in-command to Mr. Hammarskjöld, endowed with powers to deputize for him while he is away from headquarters on the frequent occasions when he is needed at a moment's notice in some more or less distant place to assert the "United Nations presence". The structure of the organization would be strengthened if there were a clear delegation of power while the Secretary-General is absent, and decisions could be made by one appointed man, in case of need, without reference to him. But in addition the independent policy-making powers of the head of the economic side of the United Nations need to be greatly enlarged. The man in charge of this work ought to be in full control, exercising initiative over the whole field, subject only to the Secretary-General's right of consultation and ultimate power of veto.

*Notes*

1. *Encounter*, March 1960. Interview with Melvin Lasky.

2. For instance the resources devoted at present to forestry and to all the phases of the use of wood products, right down to paper and board, seem to be excessive. There is a powerful pulp and paper industry which does the pioneering work in this field; all that is required of FAO is the middlemen's function of providing a forum for an occasional international meeting. It should not attempt to maintain a staff of experts able to challenge the industry on its own ground. The same is true of certain problems of dietetics, where the FAO might rely more on outside consultants' services and less on its own expertise.

# CHAPTER 14

# STRENGTHENING THE CENTRE

WE have seen how the competitive atmosphere inside the United Nations family tends to produce an obsession with status and independence in the individual international agencies. This is enhanced by an uncertainty of function at the centre. If there is to be a reform which will gradually reverse the process of fission and diffusion of effort, the Secretary-General, Mr. Dag Hammarskjöld, must start by deciding whether he really wishes the United Nations to make a bid for world leadership in that part of the field of economic development where ideas and techniques count (i.e. technical assistance and pre-investment) or whether its proper task is, after all, to concentrate on an international salvage job, providing the ultimate line of support for those few undeveloped countries which, owing to special political circumstances, find themselves in a state of total distress. Hitherto Mr. Hammarskjöld has concerned himself, above all, with the lame ducks—Guinea after independence from France, Bolivia after the revolution of 1952, Laos in 1959,* the Congo in 1960—and by now they seem to have acquired an exclusive grip on the imagination of the policy-makers in U.N. headquarters in New York. On the 38th floor, right at the top of the skyscraper, where the Secretary-General and his immediate staff hold sway, the lame duck seems to brood over the whole scene like some tribal fetish.

That is not, of course, how the matter appears to the immensely reasonable men who are in charge up there. As they put it, the role of the United Nations is "to concentrate on the problem countries of the post-imperialist era", and they have their eyes particularly on Africa. The implication is that the U.N.'s special task is not in the exercise of economic leadership, but in providing a kind of ultimate reserve, to be used when all ordinary methods have failed. This corresponds to the U.N. function in the political sphere; but surely in the struggle for

* See Chapter 7, pp. 97 and 100

world economic development it is capable of a bigger role than that.

The attitude at the centre adversely affects relations with the rest of the U.N. family. When for example the Secretary-General made a request in 1960 for a special $2½m. fund to cope with the problems of the newly emerging states in Africa, this at once encountered resistance and suspicion from the other U.N. agencies. They saw it as a move to obtain some special advantage for the Secretary-General's own operating agency in New York, UNTAO, and much preferred the idea of putting someone else—the chairman of TAB or the head of the U.N. Special Fund—in charge. These people would, they felt, look after the whole U.N. family, not just one bit of it.

The Technical Assistance Office (UNTAO) at U.N. headquarters has a different official status from the other agencies, but for practical purposes it is indistinguishable from them. It covers a wide range of subjects which are crucial for economic development, beginning with the whole field of industrialization; then there is transport, all metal and mineral resources, water, techniques of government administration, and finally the complete gamut of social welfare—from prisons to child care. This variegated collection of activities came together largely as a result of a series of historical accidents, and the organization in charge of them has suffered from the usual trouble of diffusion of effort.

Apart from considerations of the right tactics for the Secretary-General, there is therefore a straightforward practical argument for reform of the present set-up—that TAO is not a sufficiently powerful instrument to cope with several of the major tasks of economic development which it has undertaken. The outstanding failure has been its inability to provide a satisfactory service of technical advice on industrialization— the subject that the undeveloped countries regard as most important of all. They have made it clear that they are dissatisfied. And no wonder: until 1959 all the work was in the hands of a modest industry "section" and it was only in that year that it was upgraded to the level of a "branch".[1] Even after that promotion there were less than half a dozen full-time professionals employed on the subject. TAO suffers from the opposite complaint to the other U.N. agencies: it is grossly understaffed. Its full-time professional staff numbers forty-six people. Here again there is the disadvantage of its special relationship with U.N. headquarters, where it is subjected in common with all other offices to the manpower squeeze decreed by the Secretary-General. Mr. Hammarskjöld, with the laudable intention of imposing some check on his already vast administrative machine, has put a ceiling of 4,000 on the total staff—and TAO is part of the staff.

The theory is that it also benefits from its special position at U.N. headquarters, through the work done on its behalf by the experts of the United Nations Department of Economic and Social Affairs. This makes all the difference in certain subjects, for example statistics, where undeveloped countries need a great deal of technical aid, and in other matters of public administration, like giving advice on the design of tax systems. Indeed it is in this range of subjects, connected with public policy and administrative methods, that the U.N. shines; moreover it is often on these matters that an undeveloped country is most sorely in need of help—and most loth to ask another national government to help it. The problems in this field, connected in one way or another with the broad issues of economic policy and planning, are those in which the U.N. Department of Economic and Social Affairs has over the years developed a special interest and expertise.

However, this is not true of several of the other major topics included in the ragbag of highly technical responsibilities of TAO, listed earlier. On the contrary, the broad and generalized approach, which is natural to the economic staff at U.N. headquarters who are mainly concerned with broad policy issues, is usually not what is required to cope with the hard specific problems of industry or mines or construction techniques in undeveloped countries. If the trouble with most of the U.N. agencies is the malady of excessive detail and comprehensiveness, the trouble at UNTAO is a propensity to the olympian, where grubby detail is what is required. And the reason is readily understandable: the professional staff tends to think of itself as being first and foremost U.N. H.Q. and only secondarily as TAO.

*Pushing the Industrial Revolution*

The result is that the United Nations' effort lacks punch and drive precisely at the point where it ought to be pushing the industrial revolution in the undeveloped countries. They can get detailed technical guidance readily enough on health, on nutrition, on agriculture, on public administration; but on industry and the attendant mass of social and economic problems that go with industrialization and the emergence of new, closely packed communities in the towns, they have stopped looking to the United Nations for an effective lead. It is a little like the trouble over the community development programme which was discussed earlier:* the task of formulating coherent policies is evaded or it is dealt with in such general terms that the result has little practical worth.

What the developing countries want to know is how to build up their industries as fast as possible, while at the same time mitigating the worst social evils resulting from rapid industrialization. They need realistic and even harsh advice, which will not pretend that they will be able to avoid the social consequences of searing poverty and unemployment in the cities—which will tell them, for instance, how many extra prisons they ought to plan to have built in five years' time, or at what stage it is sensible for them to try and suppress the use of child labour in certain kinds of work. The trouble, too often, is that these social questions are approached quite independently of the central problem of economic development, by experts in social welfare who are naturally dominated by their views of minimum human standards. The bitter truth is, however, that once involved in this hothouse economic revolution, the advisers from outside must expect to make their compromise with the brutality and the filth which are the inevitable concomitants of the upheaval. The new gaols will almost certainly not meet the standards normally regarded as the minimum needed to protect the human dignity of the prisoner—prisons after all have to compete with many more obviously worthy objects for a share of the limited public resources available— but they still have to be constructed.

Perhaps the outstanding single failure so far, which has

* See Chapter 12, pp. 188–191

cropped up in several different contexts in this book, is the absence of constructive guidance on ways in which poor countries could use more cheap labour and less machinery to cope with the problems of their capital-starved industries. Belatedly TAO has begun to concern itself with the theoretical aspects of the question, but what is really needed is a body of almost drill-book techniques—an enormous variety of them applicable in different industries—for economizing equipment by the employment of extra workers at low wages. Technical advisers should, wherever the production process makes this possible, deliberately introduce an opposite bias to that which normally guides the design of tools and production methods in Western industry—a kind of neo-Luddite bias. This is something which the ordinary industrial expert will have to be pressed to do by the organization employing him, for it will go against his nature.

### ILO's Toughness

There is one U.N. agency which does seem to be applying some of this astringent spirit to at least part of its work in the undeveloped countries, and that is the International Labour Organization. Broadly the sphere of activity which I have been discussing—industrialization and its attendant social and economic problems—is shared by TAO and ILO. Through its concern with wage-earners' conditions and the efficient employment of manpower, ILO has come to assume responsibility within the United Nations family for labour productivity and vocational training (i.e. education for specific jobs).* In principle all problems of industrial machinery and equipment are dealt with by TAO, and labour by ILO. In practice this has come to mean that ILO looks after most of those industrial questions where human efficiency is the decisive factor in output, and that, by a further extension, has made it the authority on small-scale workshop industries, while TAO confines itself to large-scale industry.

One of the things which I found most striking in the ILO experts' approach to the problems of small-scale industry was

* See Chapter 13, p. 202

their awareness of the crucial need to allow big profits to be made, even at the expense of labour, during the early stages of capitalist development, when the industrial entrepreneur is still an unusual character who has to be encouraged. In spite of ILO's own record in fostering social welfare legislation and in defending workers' rights, it has helped to place a salutary curb on the enthusiasm of some undeveloped countries for advanced social security laws before their economies are ready for them. At this stage the exploitation of workers, producing high profits for reinvestment, is often an instrument for speeding up development.[2] That, of course, is not a blanket excuse for unlimited exploitation, but the point that was properly stressed by ILO was that it is more important to secure high profits than high wages at the beginning of industrial development. The ILO experts pointed to the success of Hong Kong, where they said it was normal for a small entrepreneur to make enough profit to double his original capital within three years, after allowing for his normal personal and family expenses during that period. They were telling the governments of undeveloped countries that five years was about the tolerable maximum for the normal turnround of capital—producing a rate of profit which is notably higher than in the ordinary business in established industrial societies—and that neither wages nor taxes on business should be allowed to eat into the essential margin of profits.

This kind of thinking has to be set against the background of ILO's own history. Its heroic period was in the 1920s and '30s, when it was breaking new ground in setting international labour standards—often at the expense of profit margins. It has required a revolution in its habits of thought to look at the problems of labour legislation from the point of view of undeveloped countries, who are desperately short of entrepreneurial capital and have a vast surplus of labour—a revolution indeed which only one half of the organization, the younger half, has accomplished. The other half tends to go on reliving its past glories, behaving as if the Western world of the second half of the 20th century were still the great arena of the struggle over workers' social rights that was fought to a finish in the inter-war period.

Indeed the visitor to ILO's Geneva headquarters, set rather

apart from the main body of the United Nations offices in the Palais des Nations, at the end of a road down by the shore of the Lake of Geneva, can hardly escape the impression that the organization is firmly imprisoned in its past. The building, as one approaches it, breathes the drab, conscious modernism of the early 1920s, when it was put up—all rough cement and narrow huddled windows, surmounted by a curious square ornamental structure with four gawky funeral urns in concrete at the corners. The whole effect is reminiscent most of all of the kind of architecture that an enlightened German employer, say a Krupp, might have used to house his local employees in the early years of the Weimar Republic. Of course it is unfair to blame people or institutions for the design of houses in which they have to live. But there is a widely held view that the architecture of ILO has entered into its soul. To some extent this is true. ILO was slower than almost any other of the U.N. agencies to begin to turn its attention away from its traditional preoccupations to the problem of the undeveloped countries. Even now the process has not gone very far.

However, the work on which ILO does engage in the un-developed countries is marked by the high standards and meticulous honesty which have been characteristic of all its efforts right from the beginning. In the competitive contest among the U.N. agencies it has been as jealous as anyone else of its own prerogatives, but it has not pushed to extend its empire; on the contrary it has tried to avoid taking on new responsibilities, whenever it looked as if its own resources might be insufficient to attain the highest standards of quality. The quality is not merely intellectual. The attention to detail, the good calibre of office organization and the inner confidence of an institution which habitually masters its subject, give ILO a kind of toughness in dealing with governments—or oppositions —which other U.N. agencies might emulate.

When, for instance, it provides one of its experts to help in preparing a basic piece of social security legislation, it is ready to have the man defend his text clause by clause before a hostile parliamentary committee. Take what happened in Burma over such an issue during the 1950s. The ILO expert who had been brought in took the view that an effective law could only be introduced slowly in stages, with the first stage being very modest indeed. It would no doubt have been better public relations to have produced a piece of legislation which looked good but which nobody bothered to obey. The ILO man, in fact, remained after the passage of the legislation to advise the authorities on how to use the courts to ensure that the law was enforced against powerful employers. But before that, he had to meet the accusation from the trade unions and from some politicians that he was a reactionary, opposing the interests of the working class. His proposal was that to begin with the law should be confined only to the capital, Rangoon, and that there should be sickness and accident compensation and payments for funerals, but no unemployment benefit or old age pensions. This was finally accepted. His arguments were severely practical: apart from the doubt whether the country could spare the economic resources required for a big advance in social welfare, it was clear that without labour exchanges or proper records of any kind it was impossible to operate an honest unemployment insurance system at this stage. A further modest step has now been taken and the social security law has been introduced into a second city, Mandalay; other places are to follow, as the administrative machine is able to absorb them.

### A New Agency

This instance is worth recording in detail because it shows clearly how technical aid, if it is properly conducted, does sometimes mean taking sides with one political group in a country against another. Moreover the job of the expert may turn out to be not just to help a government to perform some task which it has set itself, but to educate the government in the art of the possible. The *esprit de corps* of the people in ILO and their intransigence when they are up against what they conceive to be ultimate issues of policy are major virtues. The vices of the organization, as has been already indicated, are that it tends to be a little spinsterish in its old age, pedantic about unimportant matters, and passionately jealous of its own exclusive competence. It tends to run dangerously to the delusion that its experts in the field ought to be puppets at the end of a string manoeuvred from Geneva.

But for all that, it is an effective international institution with a strong personality, waiting for serious work to do which is commensurate with its powers. Its original job as the instrument for establishing minimum standards of social welfare in the Western world has run down, and by now too much of its energies are engaged in the long sterile quarrel with the Russians about the status of communist trade unions in the ILO committees where representatives of employers and organized labour sit together. It would be a pity to allow an international asset of this kind to be wasted, the more so as its work impinges all around on the field of industrialization, where the performance of the United Nations has been weak and urgently needs to be improved.

The simple way out would be to create, out of a merger of ILO and TAO, a new agency which would take effective command of this neglected area. One immediate gain would be the creation of a single coherent entity to cover the whole range of problems thrown up by the impact of modern industry on the undeveloped countries, corresponding to the work of FAO in agriculture. There would then be three main technical agencies of the United Nations working in separate well-defined spheres—education (UNESCO in Paris), agriculture (FAO in Rome) and industry (ILO/TAO in Geneva)—all of them incidentally located in Western Europe. In addition there would be WHO, standing rather apart from the mainstream of the technical aid programmes, and the smaller agencies, like the World Meteorological Organization, whose technical aid programmes could be administered for them by the new organization in Geneva.[3]

Under this arrangement, what would be left in New York would be the broad policy-making functions of the United Nations with the offices to serve them—notably the economists who report on world economic trends, the big statistical office, and the experts on taxes and other matters of government administration. One of the benefits would be that the United Nations itself would be rid of all operational tasks, with the single exception of providing aid and training in administrative techniques. This, the most delicate task of all, should be left to the office of the Secretary-General of the United Nations; and the work ought to be done by members of his own staff seconded for the purpose, not in the manner of other U.N. agencies hiring outside experts.[4]

At the centre, then, there would be an organization standing apart from, and above the U.N. agencies. In each country the Resident Representative would have full administrative responsibility for all the technical aid activities of the United Nations, and would also report back on his country's economic development and policies to the head of the combined Technical Assistance Programme and U.N. Special Fund in New York. Any request for aid by a country would have to go through him. He would be a powerful man with a unique role, half economic adviser and half ambassador.

Then there are the four regional Economic Commissions of the U.N.—in Europe, Latin America, Asia and Africa. Each of these would operate as a microcosm of the Department of Economic and Social Affairs in New York, reproducing its functions, and especially sending out members of its own staff on temporary assignments to governments which need expert help in economic planning and other matters of public policy and administration. At the moment only the Economic Commission for Latin America does this at all actively and it finds itself limited by the shortage of expert manpower.

To recapitulate: the purpose of this whole exercise is simply to create the conditions for a genuinely integrated United Nations programme of aid to the underdeveloped world, with a sense of purpose and direction imparted from the centre. The reader may feel that this is a long way round to get it, but there is no alternative short cut. Institutions, like people, have to be taken as they are; and they can only be reformed if they are first made responsive. To begin with, it is necessary to break down the present illusion of power in the U.N. headquarters in New York and start substituting the reality. The way forward is by bringing the influence of the paymasters— the U.N. Special Fund and the reformed Technical Assistance Programme—to bear on the altogether too independent U.N. agencies; if the paymasters have enough money their influence will in the long run be effective. Finally, the head of this combined programme ought to be established formally in the new role as the overlord of the economic activities of the whole United Nations family, with the Department of Economic and

Social Affairs under him and a very substantial freedom of initiative to make policy. He must be a big man, who would be able to stand by the side of the U.N. Secretary-General and not be dwarfed by him, as his senior colleagues are under the present arrangement, which is more of an *entourage* system than a cabinet system. Freedom from the day-to-day political considerations of the Secretary-General is essential, if the United Nations programme for the undeveloped countries is ever to get off the ground. Mr. David Owen the Chairman of the Technical Assistance Programme, once made a shrewd observation: "Aid from the United States must," he said, "be known to have no strings whatever attached—not even United Nations strings."

*Notes*

1. The U.N. hierarchy of office establishment is as follows, in ascending order of importance: unit—section—branch—division—bureau—department.

2. See for example Mexico, Chapter 5, p. 67.

3. Up till now UNTAO in New York has done the administrative work and looked after the finance of the technical aid programmes of the smaller agencies, but there have been some irksome problems about the distance from operational headquarters, most of which are located in Europe.

4. Mr. Hammarskjöld would also retain control of his own special scheme for filling in the administrative gaps in undeveloped countries by a special service of recruitment through the United Nations —OPEX (Operational and Executive Personnel programme). Some other social and economic work, e.g. control of narcotics and protection of human rights, would also remain at U.N. headquarters in New York. But the bulk of the work of the Bureau of Social Affairs would be transferred to the new agency in Geneva, to join up with the work already being done in this field by ILO.

As to the remaining responsibilities of TAO, the obvious solution would be to transfer two of the most important of them, transport and water (not irrigation, which is FAO's concern), to the World Bank in Washington. These are two subjects on which the Bank probably has more experience than anyone else, having disposed of over $2 billion in loans for transport and hydro-electric schemes. It also provides upwards of half a million dollars of technical assistance in various forms, and it has developed the art, which might be copied by other U.N. agencies, of using outside consultants' services wherever possible, instead of saddling itself with expensive permanent staff.

# AN OPPORTUNITY

IT might be thought, after the critique presented in the last three chapters of the way in which the United Nations conducts its affairs, that the whole thing is hardly worth bothering with. But the matter is a little like the story of the man who, during the horrors of the Lisbon earthquake in the 18th century, when arraigned before a court for selling earthquake pills, silenced his accusers thus: "What", he asked, "would you put in their place?"[1] For the truth is that we must either build up the United Nations as the main instrument of technical assistance in the underdeveloped world or do without an effective programme of technical assistance. The defects of the national programmes have not been examined in detail in this book: many of them are at least as profound as those of the United Nations—and less remediable. They range from the excessively unambitious (e.g. the Colombo Plan) to the extravagant and ineffectual (e.g. the U.S. aid programme).

Here, for instance, is a piece of self-criticism taken from the report to the U.S. President by one of his appointed committees, the Committee on World Economic Practices: "Our efforts to date have suffered from fragmentation and division of responsibility among many Departments, Agencies and Committees of the Government. ... Inefficiency, ineffectiveness and delay have resulted."[2] The latest of the investigations ordered by the U.S. President into ways of improving the American programme, by the Draper Committee, recommended that a larger proportion of U.S. technical assistance should be channelled through multilateral agencies, because there are certain subjects on which underdeveloped nations are "reluctant to become overly dependent on any individual country". The United Nations, it pointed out, is the obvious alternative instrument.

Indeed it is clear that in the mood of 1960, the United States government is looking for an opportunity to transfer the control of part of its technical assistance work to an effective United Nations body. And if the Americans did it, the smaller nations, like the Scandinavians, the Canadians and the Dutch, who have already made tentative approaches to the U.N. in this sense, would no longer have any reasons of pride impeding them. In fact it is a nuisance for a small nation to get into the pernickety business of administering a technical aid programme; and as for the big nations, their experience is that it is easy to be too big to inspire the confidence necessary to make technical aid effective.

The problem for the United Nations therefore is not just a matter of mending a machine that creaks, but of seizing a historic opportunity. This sense of occasion is indeed reflected inside the United Nations in an elaborate exercise in introspection—the so-called "Forward Appraisals" of policies and programmes submitted by each organization in 1959.[3] If the chance is to be seized it will have to be by an overt act of will: the United Nations must not only change, but be seen to be changing. One important way in which the spirit of reform could be made immediately manifest would be by undertaking a thoroughgoing revision of the talking procedures on economic and social questions. So far in this book we have considered mainly the problems of the administrative machine—the civil service of the United Nations, rather than the legislature—and that accurately reflects the realities of power, for in this instance it is the civil servants who matter. The process of consultation in the formal meetings of the national delegates to the United Nations is of small practical account. Nevertheless, these meetings could do rather more, and they certainly ought not to be allowed to waste so much time.*

It ought to be frankly admitted for a start that the Economic and Social Council has failed to fulfil a useful function and ought to be discarded. The Secretary-General has in fact been urging the need for the reform of this body, and its replacement by occasional brief, high level meetings attended by a few ministers of important countries, to deal with specific topics. At present ECOSOC, meeting twice a year, goes over the same ground as the annual meetings of the General Assembly—in its Second and Third Committees which deal with economic and

* See Chapter 7, p. 96

social affairs—only rather less usefully.[4] It is clear that the smaller countries will not give up the right to state their views directly on economic policy, which is offered by the debates in the Second Committee of the General Assembly—and why should they? It is, after all, the sense of active participation by the poor and small, as well as the rich and big countries, which gives the United Nations its special value as an instrument for economic development. Even the World Bank, which has a very independent management making decisions with the minimum of formal debate, allows all member nations the opportunity to make themselves heard at the Annual General Meeting—only the meeting is short and the speeches are usually fairly close to the point.

The eighteen nations who are represented on the Economic and Social Council do not provide a substitute for full debate, nor has the Council succeeded, by making the membership small, in creating the atmosphere of an informal company boardroom type of discussion among experts; the set speeches go on regardless. A closer approach to what is required is achieved by some of the working committees of ECOSOC, e.g. the Technical Assistance Committee (which looks after the TA Programme), where there is some genuine body of expert knowledge and some of the habitual desire of experts to get on with the job. A more developed form of this type of organization is the Governing Council of the U.N. Special Fund, and the final sophisticated version is the Executive Board of Governors of the World Bank and of the International Monetary Fund. The superiority of the last two depends partly on the quality of the officials, who are able to enter into a useful discussion with the management on points of substance and not just to make set speeches written by a man in the ministry at home, and also on the boardroom atmosphere, with its emphasis on informality and brevity, that has been firmly established. This is what the governing body of any future integrated programme of United Nations technical aid should aim at—though admittedly it may be more difficult to achieve with Soviet representatives sitting at the table.

Having got rid of the Economic and Social Council, can the general standard and usefulness of the debate in the General Assembly be improved? It is tempting to see the Second

Committee of the General Assembly as some future economic parliament of the world, forming policy by majority vote and keeping the senior U.N. officials on their toes by a series of pertinent parliamentary questions. But in practice there are a number of decisive differences between an international and a national assembly, which are likely to prevent any such dream from being realized. For one thing effective majority rule depends on the emergence of a very few parties, each with a strong sense of discipline which keeps its members voting together. There are as many parties as there are countries in the U.N., though they do sometimes form coalitions. Another important prerequisite for effective democratic rule is the recognition by the representatives of differences of degree among themselves: an effective parliament relies on a few important speakers, who utter a very large number of words, and a willingness among the great majority of members to shut up. It would require an altogether new view of the rights and proper manners of sovereign states to produce the same kind of willingness in the General Assembly in New York.

The more modest improvement suggested by Mr. Hammarskjöld—periodic U.N. meetings of a small group of senior ministers from various countries carrying some weight in the conduct of economic affairs—would however represent real progress. If the task of the United Nations were enlarged by the absorption of other programmes, and if it were conducted in such a way as to make the full weight of its influence felt on the economic policies of the undeveloped countries, the ministers would surely make themselves available. An incidental benefit would be that since these meetings would have to be kept short, it would be necessary to invent procedures which were a lot more agile and less ceremonial than at present. Anything which cuts down the length of set speeches will make the institution more respected, as well as better liked.

All this would help to enhance the authority of the United Nations on matters which go far beyond technical assistance. Its successful conduct of a difficult relationship with the governments of undeveloped countries would establish it in a new position of trust. One way or another, governments have got to get used to dealing with the United Nations as an effective supranational body, if the world is to survive the next hundred years. Success in this task of economic leadership in the under-developed countries would make a useful start in preparing the right habit of mind.

*Notes*

1. Quoted by Sir Lewis Namier, *In the Margin of History*, Macmillan.

2. Quoted in the Draper Committee's Report on "Economic Assistance Programs and Administration", Washington, 1959.

3. See "Consolidated Report on Programme Appraisals 1959/64", United Nations, 1960.

4. See "The United Nations as a Political Institution", by H. G. Nicholas, for a discussion of how the U.N. committees and ECOSOC work.

# APPENDIX I
## The Flow of Economic Aid and Long-Term Capital to Underdeveloped Countries Outside Europe (1958) [a]

|  | $m. | $m. |
|---|---|---|
| *Public Aid and Investment:* | | |
| *U.S.A.:* International Cooperation Administration, Development Loan Fund, Export-Import Bank | 1,900 | |
| Surplus food shipments under Public Law 480 [b] | 350 | |
| Total U.S.A. | | 2,250 |
| *France* [c] | | 500(?) |
| *United Kingdom* [d] | | 150 |
| *Soviet Bloc* [e] | approx. | 150/200 |
| *Reparations from Germany and Japan* [f] | | 250 |
| *World Bank* [g] | | 350 |
| *United Nations* [h] | | 100 |
| Total Public Aid and Investment | | 3,850 |
| *Private Investment* [i] | | 1,900 |
| *Total Public and Private Capital and Aid, say* | | 5,700 |
| *Less:* | | |
| Servicing of public debt [j] | 800 | |
| Servicing of private capital (dividends, profits and debt amortization payments) [k] | 800 | |
| Investment in main oil-producing countries (Middle East and Venezuela) [l] | approx. 400 | |
| U.S. economic aid to the "ward" countries (South Korea, Formosa, Viet-Nam, Laos and Cambodia) [m] | approx. 700 | |
| Total, say | 2,700 | |
| *Net capital flow to the main body of undeveloped countries* | | 3,000 |

*Sources:* IBRD., United Nations, U.S. and U.K. governments.

# APPENDIX I

## NOTES

(*a*) Comprises the whole of Latin America, Africa, except Union of South Africa, and non-communist Asia except Japan. 1958 is the latest year for which comprehensive data on the flow of aid and capital are available; however, indications of the current trends are given in the notes for individual countries.

(*b*) *Actual* agricultural shipments under Public Law 480, Title I (*not* disbursements as official grants and loans), less that part of the value of the surplus food shipments which is converted into counterpart funds by the U.S. government for its own expenditure. The shipment of food to undeveloped countries outside Europe is rising; in recent years close to half has gone to countries in Europe, excluded from this table.

(*c*) A large part—close to half—went to Algeria; it is impossible to say how much was investment expenditure incurred, for instance, for resettlement in the course of the war with the rebels. The figure excludes French direct military and administrative costs in overseas territories. There may be some double counting in this figure and in the estimated total of French private investment in the undeveloped countries. (See Note (*i*) below.)

(*d*) Excluding emergency aid to Cyprus, Malaya and Kenya. Colonies in the European area—Malta and Gibraltar—are also left out of the table. U.K. assistance, particularly in the form of loans to the Commonwealth, went up sharply in 1959–60 to nearly double the 1958 rate.

(*e*) Estimate of actual disbursements of aid by the Soviet Bloc over the two years 1957–8 is around $300m. The sums earmarked under loan agreements to be disbursed over a number of years are considerably larger; thus in the course of 1958 the Soviet Bloc countries offered about $1,000m. in aid to developing countries outside Europe.

(*f*) Germany—$180m.; Japan—$64m. No significant loans were granted by Germany to undeveloped countries before 1959.

(*g*) Disbursements.

(*h*) Technical assistance, UNICEF, UNWRA, etc.

(*i*) See "The International Flow of Private Capital, 1956–9", United Nations. The total includes some $400m. of oil company investment in Venezuela and the Middle East, $500m. of French private investment (see Note (*c*) above), and $1,000m. in the rest of the undeveloped world. The figure of $1,000m. is *net* of exports of private capital by the citizens of the countries concerned.

(*j*) Excludes main oil-producing countries.

(*k*) Excludes oil companies' share of profits in Venezuela ($600m.) and the Middle East (approximately $1,100m.).

(*l*) This is not an exact figure. The only comprehensive statistics (published by the U.S. Department of Commerce) are of the net flow of capital from the American oil companies to the Middle East and Venezuela. This amounted to $220m. in 1958. Such indications as are available suggests that this was rather more than half the total.

(*m*) Includes food shipments under Public Law 480 going to these countries.

# APPENDIX II
## UNITED NATIONS AND ITS AGENCIES

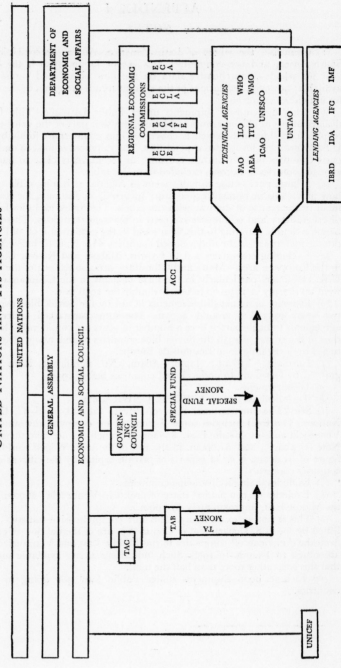

**ACC**—*Administrative Committee on Coordination*
Standing inter-agency committee, consisting of the U.N. Secretary-General, the executive heads of the specialized agencies and the Director-General of IAEA.

**ECA**—*Economic Commission for Africa.* (Addis Ababa)

**ECAFE**—*Economic Commission for Asia and the Far East.* (Bangkok)

**ECE**—*Economic Commission for Europe.* (Geneva)

**ECLA**—*Economic Commission for Latin America.* (Santiago)

**ECOSOC**—*Economic and Social Council* of the U.N., composed of representatives of eighteen member nations. Meets twice a year in New York and Geneva.

**FAO**—*Food and Agricultural Organization*

**GATT**—*General Agreement on Tariffs and Trade.*

**IAEA**—*International Atomic Energy Agency*
Jointly controlled by ECOSOC and the Security Council

**IBRD**—*International Bank for Reconstruction and Development,* or *World Bank*

**ICAO**—*International Civil Aviation Organization*

**IDA**—*International Development Association*
"Soft loans" agency, staffed by World Bank.

**IFC**—*International Finance Corporation*
"Hard loans" agency (for private enterprise) affiliate of World Bank.

**ILO**—*International Labour Organization*

**IMCO**—*Inter-Governmental Maritime Consultative Organization*

**IMF**—*International Monetary Fund.*

**ITU**—*International Telecommunication Union*

**OPEX**—Technical aid programme for supplying *operational* and *executive* personnel.

**SUNFED**—The proposed *Special United Nations Fund for Economic Development,* to distribute grant aid.

**TAB**—*Technical Assistance Board*
In charge of TA Programme of the whole U.N. family

**TAC**—*Technical Assistance Committee* of ECOSOC.

**TA Programme**—*Technical Assistance Programme,* also known as **EPTA** or **ETAP**—Expanded Programme for Technical Assistance

**UNESCO**—*United Nations Educational, Scientific and Cultural Organization*

**UNICEF**—*United Nations Children's Fund*

**UNTAO**—*United Nations Technical Assistance Office*
Dual function: part of U.N. Secretariat and also operational agency carrying out technical assistance activities on behalf of U.N. headquarters, New York.

**UPU**—*Universal Postal Union*

**WHO**—*World Health Organization*

**WMO**—*World Meteorological Organization*

# APPENDIX III

## U.N. Expenditure on Economic and Social Activities—1960
### ($ million)

| | Regular Budget[1] | Extra-budgetary funds | | | TOTAL |
| --- | --- | --- | --- | --- | --- |
| | | Technical Assistance Programme | Special Fund[2] | Other[3] | |
| U.N. Secretariat[4] .. .. .. .. | 19·2 | 2·1 | 0·7 | — | 22·0 |
| UNTAO .. .. .. .. | 2·1 | 6·7 | 3·0 | — | 11·8 |
| FAO .. .. .. .. | 9·5 | 8·0 | 3·3 | — | 20·8 |
| ILO .. .. .. .. | 9·1 | 3·2 | 1·4 | — | 13·7 |
| UNESCO .. .. .. | 13·3 | 4·5 | 2·3 | 0·25 | 20·4 |
| WHO .. .. .. .. | 16·2 | 5·1 | — | 15·2 | 36·5 |
| Other Agencies[5] .. .. | 13·1 | 2·6 | 1·6 | — | 17·3 |
| UNICEF[6] .. .. .. | 29·1 | — | — | — | 29·1 |
| Grand Total .. .. .. | 111·6 | 32·2 | 12·3 | 15·5 | 171·6 |

*Sources:* TAB and Special Fund reports, U.N. secretariat and agency budgets and forward appraisals.

# APPENDIX III

## *NOTES*

1. Working budget figures, as published by the institutions: owing to differences of accounting procedure, there are certain inconsistencies of treatment, e.g. WHO excludes its undistributed reserves, while other agencies include them.

2. By the end of 1959, nearly $32m. of Special Fund money had been allocated to forty-four projects, extending from six months to six years. The following is an estimate of how this money will be spread among the U.N. agencies:

|        |        | $ m.  |
|--------|--------|-------|
| FAO .. | ..     | 10·2  |
| ILO .. | ..     | 5·1   |
| UNESCO | ..     | 7·6   |
| UNTAO  | ..     | 5·8   |
| WMO    | ..     | 1·3   |
| IBRD .. | ..    | 1·9   |
|        |        | 31·9  |

Actual expenditure of Special Fund money will increase very sharply in the years ahead as projects already approved get under way. At the same time it is expected that the amount of money committed each year will rise as follows:

|      | Commitments | Actual Expenditure |
|------|-------------|--------------------|
|      | $ m.        | $ m.               |
| 1960 | 39·6        | 11·6               |
| 1961 | 59·4        | 23·7               |
| 1962 | 76.9        | 43·7               |
| 1963 | 100·0       | 58·6               |

3. Covers the following voluntary funds:

*UNESCO Special Account*, intended to meet urgent needs which cannot be financed from the regular budget.

*WHO Malaria Eradication Special Account* ($7·1m.); other sources of finance for malaria control are provided from the regular budget of WHO, and by PAHO and UNICEF money (see below).

*Pan American Health Office*—PAHO ($7·1m.); this is in effect WHO's regional office for Latin America, though it is not included in the agency's regular budget, because of its special relationship with the Pan American Union.

*Other Special Accounts* (research, smallpox, community water supply): some of the contributions to these Accounts are in kind (e.g. vaccines); the estimate of $1m. is therefore notional.

233

# APPENDIX III

*Funds-in-Trust:* A certain amount of work is done each year by the UN agencies for cash payment on behalf of member governments; this is known as the "funds-in-trust" system. Owing to the nature of these arrangements no estimate of expenditure under this head for 1960 can be made at the time of writing; the 1959 figure was $2m.

4. U.N. budget expenditure under the heading of Economic and Social Activities, less the amount appropriated to UNTAO. Includes expenditure of High Commissioner's Office for Refugees, but not the independent fund for Arab relief (UNWRA). The secretariat expenditure of the Technical Assistance Programme and the Special Fund is shown under their respective headings.

5. Budgets of smaller agencies, ICAO, WMO, ITU and IAEA, receiving finance from the Technical Assistance Programme and the Special Fund; also money ($1·3m.) allocated to World Bank by Special Fund for pre-investment projects. Two other agencies, UPU and IMCO, do a little technical assistance work out of their regular budgets which have not been included in this table.

6. UNICEF, financed by voluntary contributions, supplies aid in cash or kind direct to governments for health and nutrition purposes.

# SHORT BIBLIOGRAPHY

ASHER, Robert E., and associates, *The United Nations and Promotion of the General Welfare*, The Brookings Institution, Washington, 1957.

AVRAMOVIC, D., *Debt Servicing Problems of Low Income Countries*, Oxford University Press, 1960.

HIRSCHMAN, Albert O., *The Strategy of Economic Development*, Oxford University Press, 1959.

LEWIS, W. Arthur, *The Theory of Economic Growth*, George Allen & Unwin Ltd., 1955.

MYRDAL, Gunnar, *Economic Theory and Under-Developed Regions*, Duckworth, 1957.

NICHOLAS, H. G., *The United Nations as a Political Institution*. Oxford University Press, 1959.

ROSTOW, W. W., *The Stages of Economic Growth*, Cambridge University Press, 1960.

\* \* \*

*Consolidated Report on Programme Appraisals* 1959–1964, United Nations, New York, 1960.

*Economic Survey of Africa since* 1950, United Nations, New York, 1959.

*Economic Survey of Asia and the Far East*, United Nations, Bangkok. Published annually.

*Economic Survey of Latin America*, United Nations, Santiago. Published annually.

*World Economic Survey*, United Nations, New York. Published annually.

# INDEX

Action Committee for a United States of Europe, 85

Administration, public, methods of, 69, 70, 79, 141, 212–214, 219, 220

Afganistan, 11

Africa, 8, 9, 12, 23, 41, 56, 62, 71–74, 76, 79, 98, 100, 120, 123, 130, 157, 176, 184, 211, 212

Africa, Economic Commission for, (ECA) 220

Agra (India), 30, 31

Agrarian reform, 121–127, 167–171, 189, 190

Agriculture and Food, 25, 26, 27, 35, 37, 38, 55, 56, 57, 69, 70, 73, 83, 114, 116, 120–127, 166–171, 188, 189, 191, 192, 196, 207, 214, 219

Agricultural credits, 122–125

Agricultural extension, 171

Agricultural investment, 121, 122, 127

Animal husbandry, 192, 204, 205

Locust control, 22

Nutrition, 210, 214

Prices, 125, 126, 167, 168

Surplus foods (also see U.S.A.), 168, 169, 173, 174

Aid—see Economic, Technical Aid

Algeria, 11, 12, 62, 73, 149

Allesandri, President, 5

Aluminium, 72, 130

America, North, 27, 41, 46, 155

Anderson, Mr. Robert, 148

Argentina, 4, 12, 42, 47, 69, 71, 76, 141

Asia, 8, 9, 12, 15, 20, 21, 23, 27, 33, 37, 45, 54–56, 62, 77, 79, 81, 84, 85, 108, 117, 120, 123, 124, 132, 133, 157, 167, 168, 169, 176, 184, 189, 197

Asia, Economic Commission for Asia and the Far East (ECAFE), 54–56, 124, 220

Aswan Dam (Egypt), 73, 74

Australia, 114, 128, 131, 138, 184

Belgium, 155, 157

Benelux, 94, 157

Bhakra Dam (India), 15, 118

Black, Eugene, 92, 105, 108, 110, 112, 113, 130, 133–140, 144, 146, 179

Bolivia, 13, 45, 211

Brazil, 6, 13, 14, 39, 45, 47, 61–66, 69, 70, 74, 76, 77, 90

de Breuvery, Father, 193, 194

British Commonwealth—see also under Imperial Preference, 51, 54, 73, 149, 151, 184, 185

Burma, 21, 27, 37, 38, 42, 55, 217, 218

Cambodia, 9

Canada, 151, 155, 157, 185, 223

Capital, public and private (see also Economic Aid), 8, 9, 10, 12, 13, 18, 27, 28, 91, 130, 132, 152

Capital-Output Ratio, 74, 75, 76
Capital goods, 8, 14, 16, 25, 30,
    32, 35, 59, 60, 68, 115, 119,
    120, 121, 128, 132, 160,
    164, 171, 173, 174
    second-hand, 164–166, 174,
    176
Central America, 49, 50, 51,
    106
Central American Integration
    Project, 48, 50
Ceylon, 82, 185
Chile, 4, 5, 12, 45, 48, 69, 76
China, Communist, 13–17, 35,
    55, 117, 122, 171, 188,
    211
China, Taiwan, 9, 55, 153
Coale, H. A., 85
Cocoa, 41, 116
Coffee, 41, 64
Coldwell, M. J., 197
Colombia, 141, 142
Colombo Plan, 183–185, 197,
    222
    Bureau of Technical Coopera-
    tion, 184
Communist methods, 13–17, 36,
    58, 102, 117, 168, 188
Community development, 176,
    188–192, 197, 203, 214
Conan, A. R., 24
Congo, 72, 73
Consumer goods, 16, 29, 32, 59,
    115, 122, 170, 171, 174
Cooperatives, 124, 188
Copper, 41
Costa Rica, 46, 48, 49, 50
Creditworthiness, 90, 91, 113–
    115, 128, 129, 131, 141–143
Currency (including stabilisation
    convertability), 37, 44, 65,
    76, 162
Czechoslovakia, 10, 159

Depreciation of capital, 75, 76
Development Assistance Group
    (DAG), 155–157
Dillon, Mr., 155
Disarmament, 89
Dumont, Professor R., 197

Economic aid, 8–14, 18–24, 41,
    57, 71, 78, 79, 80, 89, 93,
    94, 122, 130, 131, 148, 154,
    155, 158–163, 166, 172, 173,
    179, 181
    Bilateral, 158–163, 172, 173,
    179, 181
Economic Commissions for Africa
    (ECA), Asia (ECAFE),
    Europe (ECE), Latin
    America (ECLA) — see
    under appropriate region
Economic growth, 6, 25, 57–81,
    141
Ecuador, 116, 117
Education, 3, 4, 5, 171, 188,
    190, 191, 200–204, 215
    "Fundamental education"—
    see UNESCO
    Vocational training—see ILO
Egypt, 73, 74, 191
Eisenhower, President, 148, 154
Electricity, 20, 72, 73, 136, 164,
    194, 204, 221
El Salvador, 48, 49, 206
EPTA, ETAP — see United
    Nations Technical Assis-
    tance Programme
Europe, 41, 52, 77, 81, 102, 110,
    160, 166
    Underdeveloped countries of,
    77, 81
European Common Market, 40,
    45, 51, 81, 149, 155, 157
Europe, Economic Commission
    for (ECE), 220

# INDEX

Europe, Western 8, 27, 39, 40, 44, 45, 46, 54, 72, 81, 84, 85, 113, 114, 149, 155, 158, 219, 221
Common Market—see European Common Market
Trade, 39, 44
European Investment Bank, 157
European Payments Union, 39
Exports—see Trade

Far East, 153
Fertilizers, 28, 70, 84, 120, 121, 204
Food—see Agriculture and Food
Food and Agriculture Organization (FAO), 74, 95, 99, 106, 123, 124, 191–194, 196, 199, 204–206, 208, 210, 219, 221
Administration, 196
Budgets, 192
Technical aid projects, 191, 192, 196
Water and Soil Division, 193, 194, 221
Ford Foundation Acknowledgments, 185, 190
Forestry, afforestation, 74, 210
Formosa—see China (Taiwan)
France, 11, 94, 100, 149, 153–155, 157, 161, 211
Frondizi, President, 4

Gabon, 72, 130
Gardner, Professor Richard, 12
Garner, Mr., 144
de Gaulle, General, 100
General Agreement on Tariffs and Trade (GATT), 51–53, 56
Germany, East, 31
Germany, Western, 11, 94, 136, 149, 152, 155–157, 158–160, 161, 164

Ghana, 72–74, 144
Gomulka, A., 18
Gordon, Stanley, Acknowledgments
Great Britain—see United Kingdom
Gross national product — see National Income
Guatemala, 48, 49, 206
Guinea, Republic of, 72, 100, 102, 211

Haiti, 192
Hammarskjöld, Dag, 95, 97, 102, 105, 110, 192, 209, 211–213, 219, 221, 223, 225
Handicrafts, 30–32, 191
Health—see also Malaria eradication, World Health Organization, 81, 186, 191, 214
Hoffman, Paul G., Acknowledgments, 19, 23, 79, 80, 81, 85, 94, 101, 104, 194
Honduras, 48, 49
Hongkong, 216
Hoover, E. M., 85

Imperial Preference, 51–54
Imports—see Trade
India, Introduction, 6, 11, 13, 15, 16, 20, 22, 23, 28–38, 42, 55, 58–63, 74, 76, 77, 79, 82–84, 89–92, 113, 118–122, 124, 125, 127, 131–133, 135, 137, 141, 142, 163, 165–168, 170–172, 176, 185, 189, 190, 197, 207, 208
Agriculture and food, 83, 120, 166, 171, 189
Community development, 176, 189, 190, 197

# INDEX

Exports, 28, 29, 30, 31, 32, 33, 34, 35, 38

Foreign trade, 23, 28, 29, 30, 33, 36, 37, 38, 60, 61, 62

Industries, 28, 30, 31, 33, 34, 63, 79, 83, 84

Labour, 170, 171

National Sample Survey Report, 170, 176

Plans, 2nd and 3rd Five Year, 20, 28, 29, 35, 60, 62, 63, 82, 89, 113, 132, 135, 167, 168

Population, 13, 60, 62, 82, 83

Indo-China, 9, 55, 97, 153

Indonesia, 18, 79, 124

Indus Waters Scheme, 172

Industrialization, 41, 67, 68, 81, 90, 133, 164, 168, 212, 214, 215, 219

Industrial Co-Ordination Bureau, 176

Industries, 25, 26, 28, 32, 41, 47–49, 67–69, 120, 132, 133, 144, 167, 169, 182, 210, 212, 215, 219

Industrial investment—see Investment

Inflation, 65, 76, 170, 173, 175

Interest Rates, 10, 24, 28, 67, 91, 92, 124, 139, 162

International Atomic Energy Agency, 106

International Bank for Reconstruction and Development —see World Bank

International Civil Aviation Organization, 106

International Development Association (IDA), 91, 93, 94, 140–147, 154, 155, 157, 163, 173, 180, 183

Capital of, 157

International Finance Corporation (IFC), 132, 133, 144

International Insitute of Agriculture, 199

International Labour Organization (ILO), 99, 101, 106, 186, 191, 202, 215–219, 221

Administration, 217

Productivity, 202, 215

Technical aid projects, 191

Vocational Training, 215

International Monetary Fund (IMF), 38, 39, 42–44, 53, 65, 76, 94, 105, 107, 112, 113, 127, 151, 195, 224

International Telecommunication Union, 106

International Trade Organization (ITO), 52

Investment, level of, needs for, 57–59, 63–81, 89–91, 121, 128, 130, 132, 144, 149, 157, 179, 180, 181, 182

Iraq, 9

Iron and steel, 11, 16, 42, 48, 72, 130

Irrigation—see Water, also see FAO

Israel, 11, 98, 197

Italy, 36, 114, 115, 131, 138, 155–158, 199, 206

Jacobsson, Per, 38, 42, 43, 44

Japan, 8, 11, 26, 30, 33, 36, 55, 61, 84, 85, 90, 114, 124, 125, 128, 129, 131, 136–138, 155, 158, 167, 197

Kennan, George, 203, 204

Kenya, 157

Keynes, Lord, 42, 112

Khrushchev, N., 10

Korea, South, 9, 153
Krishnamachari, Mr., 135, 136
Kuwait, 9, 151, 152

Labour, 15, 31, 117–120, 166, 170, 171, 191, 215, 218
  vs. capital, 15, 31, 117, 118, 119, 120, 166, 215
Land Reform—see under agrarian reform
Langenskjöld, Mr., 176
Laos, 9, 97, 102, 211
Lasky, Melvin, 209
Latin America—see also Central America, 4–6, 8, 9, 12, 13, 23, 26, 28, 36, 39–48, 54, 55, 61, 62, 64, 67, 74, 76, 77, 90, 108, 120, 123, 133, 134, 136, 157, 176, 191, 203, 208
Latin American Common Market, 39, 40, 44, 46, 47, 54, 55
Latin America, Economic Commission for (ECLA), 27, 28, 36, 40–42, 44, 46, 48, 54–56, 134, 203, 220
Lewis, Professor W. Arthur, Acknowledgments, 22, 36, 74, 75, 102
Liberia, 72
Libya, 73
Little, Ian M. D., Acknowledgments, 119, 127
Loans—see also World Bank, IDA, IFO, 10, 60, 90–92, 113, 115, 116, 122, 126, 128, 130, 131, 133, 145, 160–162, 171
  Impact loans, 115, 116, 122, 126
  Indebtedness, 90
  Loan service costs, 10, 60, 90, 91, 137, 139, 142, 162
  Soft loans, 91, 144, 145

Tied loans, 160, 161, 171
Locust control, 22
Luddites, 215

Malaria eradication, 74, 182, 207
Malaya, 82, 124
McCarthy, Senator, 110
Manubai Shah, 33, 34
Marshall Plan, 91, 102, 110, 113, 135, 160
Masani, Mr., 135
Mauritania, 72
Mediterranean area, 22, 73, 81
Mekong River, 12, 20
Mexico, 6, 13, 14, 23, 35, 46, 48, 61–71, 76, 77, 126, 130, 136–137, 165, 191, 206
Mexlight, 136
Monnet, Jean, 40, 85
Middle East, 9, 12, 22, 73, 156, 191
Miles, Caroline, Acknowledgments
Mineral resources—(see also aluminium, copper, iron and steel, oil), 72, 73, 130, 212, 213
Montevideo, Treaty of, 47
Myrdal, Gunnar, 56

Namier, Sir Lewis, 226
Narasimhan, C. V., Acknowledgments
National Income, 57–60, 63, 64, 66, 67, 69, 70, 75, 76, 80, 81, 155
  Gross National Product, 69
Nehru, Pandit, 141
Netherlands, 223
Nicaragua, 48–50
Nicholas, H. G., 226
Nigeria, 73

Oil, 9–11, 72, 151, 156
Operational and Executive Personal Program (OPEX), 221
Owen, David, Acknowledgments, 97, 100, 221

Pakistan, 21, 22, 55, 71, 79, 111, 122, 133, 172, 185
Paraguay, 45
PEMEX, 136
Persia, 9, 133
Peru, 4, 13, 19, 45
Petroleum, 136
Philippines, 82, 124
Planning techniques, 119, 173, 174, 220
Pliatzky, Leo, Acknowledgments
Poland, 10, 18, 31, 159
Population, 8, 9, 13, 25, 48, 57, 60, 62, 63, 69, 74, 77, 81–85, 168, 186
  Birth control, 84, 85, 186
  Statistics, 8, 9, 13, 48, 62, 63, 69, 77, 82
Portugal, 77, 155, 157
Prebisch, Raul, 40, 42, 44, 46, 47, 134
Pre-investment, 19–24, 78, 101, 102, 111, 165, 182, 183, 195, 211
Prices—see also Agriculture, 27, 28, 36, 53, 64, 69, 119, 120, 125–127, 162, 163, 167
  Shadow, 119, 120, 125, 126, 127
Private, public enterprise (and nationalization), 62, 90, 133–136, 144
Profits, 10, 24

Read, Dr. Margaret, 197

Regional Commissions — see under continents
Rhodesia, 12, 62, 151, 152
Rojas Pinilla, General, 141
Rosenstein-Rodan, Mr., 116
Rostow, W. W., 25, 36, 76, 197

Sanitation, environmental, 187
Saudi Arabia, 9
Saving, ratio, 58–60, 64, 65, 70, 75, 76, 175
Scandinavian countries, 157, 223
Social services, 72, 186, 207, 212, 214, 216–219, 221
Somoza, President, 50
South Africa, Union of, 8, 114, 130, 138
Soviet Bloc, 8, 10, 11, 17, 30, 31, 56, 64, 66, 159, 160
Soviet Union, 8, 10, 14, 17, 30, 31, 73, 74, 91, 94, 112, 113, 120, 127, 139, 140, 158, 159, 180, 201, 217
Spain, 77
Special United Nations Fund for Economic Development (SUNFED), 93, 94, 97, 105, 106, 143, 144
Sterling Area, 149, 150, 151, 153
Sudan, 73
Sweden—see also Scandinavian countries, 44, 158, 176
Switzerland, 94
Symonds, Richard, Acknowledgments

Taiwan, see China
Tata Iron and Steel Company (India), 132
Tariffs—see also Imperial Preference, 39, 40, 47, 50, 54
Taxation, role in development, 66, 67, 175

Technical Assistance—see also under U.N. Technical Assistance Board Program, U.N. Special Fund, 96–104, 111, 180, 184, 188, 195, 199, 202, 211, 218, 220, 222, 223

Technicians, availability of, 4, 5, 20, 98, 165, 180, 201, 202

Thailand, 55, 118, 124

Tinbergen, Professor, 85

Triffin, Professor, 150

Trade—see also tariffs, Imperial Preference, GATT, European Common Market, Latin American Common Market, 23–56, 60, 61, 68, 91, 116, 119, 127, 147–163, 173, 175

Balance of payments—see also U.K., U.S.A., 24, 91, 116, 147, 163, 173, 175

Deficits, 43, 61

Discrimination (bilateral and multilateral), 38, 51–56, 159, 162

Exports, 25, 26, 30, 32, 35, 56, 60, 68, 119, 127

Imports, 25, 27

Intraregional, 37, 44, 47, 49, 50, 55

Terms of Trade, 27

Trade Unions, 218, 219

Transport, 41, 126, 194, 212, 221

Turkey, 179


Undeveloped World, definition, 8

Unemployment—see Labour

United Kingdom, 3, 26, 32, 45, 46, 51, 75, 94, 105, 106, 110, 136, 149–158, 161, 164, 183, 185

Aid contribution, 152, 153, 157, 183, 184

Balance of payments problem, 149–152, 155, 158

Bank of England, 150

Export Credits Guarantee Department, 161

United Nations, Acknowledgments, 46, 52, 93–105, 107, 110, 112, 130, 141, 165, 179–181, 185–226

Administration, 205, 207, 213, 219, 221, 223

Administrative Committee on Coordination (ACC), 197

Agencies—see also under individual agency name, 52, 101, 187, 192, 193, 194, 195, 197, 202, 205, 206, 215, 217, 220, 221

Co-ordination, 191, 192, 207, 208

Economic and Social Affairs Department, 209, 213, 220, 221

"Forward Appraisals", 223, 226

General Assembly (incl. Committees), 93, 95, 96, 105, 223, 224, 225

Reform of, 194–226

Secretariat, 97, 102

Secretary-General, 95, 97, 102, 105, 110, 192, 209, 211–213, 219, 221, 223, 225

Security Council, 96

Statistical Services, 213, 219

Water Resources Centre, 193

U.N. Children's Fund (UNICEF), 195, 207

United Nations Economic and Social Council (ECOSOC), 96, 112, 223, 224

United Nations Educational, Cultural and Scientific Organization (UNESCO), 95, 107, 109, 183, 184, 191, 193, 199, 200, 201, 202, 204, 219
"Arid lands", 193
Budget, 183
Fundamental Education, 190, 191
Technical assistance projects, 183, 184, 193
United Nations Special Fund (Special Fund), 19–23, 79, 80, 94, 101–105, 111, 112, 165, 182, 183, 194, 195, 206, 212, 220, 224
Budget, 22, 23, 194, 195
Consultative Board, 112
Governing Council, 104, 105, 224
Projects, 21, 103
United Nations Technical Assistance Board (TAB), 96, 97, 99, 100, 104, 107, 194, 195, 212
Budget, 107, 194, 195
Executive Chairman, 107
United Nations Technical Assistance Committee (TAC), 224
United Nations Technical Assistance Programme, 23, 96, 97, 99, 101, 107, 194, 195, 197–198, 205–208, 220, 221, 224
Allocation system, 100
Budget, 23, 195
Resident Representative, 197, 198, 205, 206, 207, 208, 220
United Nations Technical Assistance Office (UNTAO or TAO), 99, 187, 191, 193, 212, 213, 215, 219, 221

Bureau of Social Affairs, 191, 221
United States, 4, 8–10, 19, 26, 27, 46, 51, 52, 54, 65, 67, 68, 72–74, 93, 94, 97, 105, 106, 109, 110, 114, 119–129, 130, 135, 136, 140, 147–157, 160, 161, 163, 166, 167, 169, 170, 172, 176, 179, 183, 185, 192, 204, 222, 223, 226
Agriculture, 27, 127, 169, 170, 176
Aid contribution, investment and technical, 8, 9, 10, 147, 148, 153, 154, 179–183, 222
Balance of payments problem, 147, 148, 150, 158
Committee on World Economic Practices, 222
Defence Support Programme, 10
Development Loan Fund, 154, 160
Draper Committee, 222, 226
Eisenhower Administration, 148, 154
International Cooperation Administration, 204
State Department, 155, 179
Surplus foods, 8, 62, 63, 163, 166, 167, 170, 172
Uruguay, 12
U.S.S.R.—See Soviet Russia, also Soviet Bloc

Venezuela, 9
Viet Nam, 9
Vocational Training—see Education
Volta River, 72, 74

# INDEX

Water—see also FAO, TAO, UNESCO, 20, 70, 72, 73, 83, 120, 121, 123, 193, 194, 204, 212, 221

World Bank, Acknowledgments, 6, 10, 21, 43, 65, 73, 90–94, 105, 107–123, 127–139, 140–146, 148, 157, 170, 172, 173, 179–180, 195, 196, 204, 221, 224

    Loans, 10, 137, 138

Representatives, 111

Subscriptions, 113

World Health Organization, (WHO), 99, 107, 182, 186, 191, 219

World Meteorological Organization (WMO), 107, 219

Yanhee Dam (Thailand), 118

Yugoslavia, 17, 64, 98, 122, 197, 202, 208